THE SCRIBE TRIBE

VOLUME THREE

COLLECTED SHORT STORIES
AND POEMS

THE SCRIBE TRIBE

VOLUME THREE

THE WRITERS OF
BALLA BALLA

Copyright © 2025 The Scribe Tribe Australia
All rights reserved.

No part of this book may be reproduced, stored in a retrieval system, or transmitted, in any form, or by any means (electronic, mechanical, photocopying, recording or otherwise) without the prior written permission of the author, except in cases of brief quotations embodied in reviews or articles. It may not be edited amended, lent, resold, hired out, distributed or otherwise circulated without the publisher's written permission. This book is a work of fiction. Except in the case of historical fact, names, characters, places, and incidents either are products of the author's imagination or are used fictitiously. Any resemblance to actual persons, living or dead, events, or locales is entirely coincidental.

Permission can be obtained from rcg@grigsonpublishing.com

Edited by Roderic Grigson

Published by Grigson Publishing

ISBN: 978-1-7638344-2-2

Cover design and interior formatting:
Mark Thomas / Coverness.com

DEDICATION

This anthology is dedicated to the brave immigrants who left their homeland in search of a better future. This page honours their courage in embracing a new country, learning new languages, and adapting to unfamiliar cultures. It recognizes their resilience in the face of challenges, including criticism, loneliness, and uncertainty. Their strength and determination are a testament to the human spirit and an inspiration to us all.

APPRECIATION

We extend our deepest gratitude to the writers, proofreaders, and editors, as well as the City of Casey and the Balla Balla Community Centre, for their invaluable support and commitment to bringing The Scribe Tribe Volume III to life.

A heartfelt thank-you also goes to the members of the Scribe Tribe, a group of writers who generously shared their stories and experiences, adding richness and authenticity to this collection. A special mention goes to Diane Brown, Lauren McCarthy, and Marianne Acton for their help with the publication.

It is worth noting that this anthology is inspired by the theme of multiculturalism, though its scope extends beyond this focus. Multicultural narratives are intricately woven throughout the anthology, celebrating the diversity, heritage, and shared humanity that define our community.

FOREWORD

Australia is a nation built on waves of migration. From the earliest settlers to the diverse communities that now call this country home, each generation of immigrants has left its mark, shaping Australia into the multicultural society it is today.

Migration is never easy. Whether by choice or necessity, leaving one's homeland comes with a deep sense of loss and uncertainty. Newcomers must navigate a foreign language, adapt to unfamiliar customs, and find their place in an unfamiliar land. The English language, with its contradictions and complexities, can be particularly challenging, and Australian slang can make communication even more bewildering.

Throughout history, migrants arriving in Australia have sought comfort in their own communities, forming close-knit networks where traditions, language, and culture could be preserved. These communities became lifelines, helping people find their footing while holding onto their heritage. Yet, over time, as immigrants stepped beyond their immediate circles, they forged relationships with those from different backgrounds, blending cultures and traditions in ways that enriched the broader society.

From the early European and Chinese settlers searching for gold to the waves of migration following World War II, from the Vietnamese refugees of the 1970s to more recent arrivals from Africa, the Middle East, and Asia, each new group has added to the evolving story of multicultural Australia. Today, Australia stands as a testament to the success of multiculturalism—a place where diverse cultures coexist, influence one another, and contribute to a shared national identity.

This book is a reflection of that journey. It acknowledges the struggles of those who have sought a new life in Australia, the courage it takes to embrace the unfamiliar, and the resilience that defines the migrant experience. More importantly, it celebrates the richness that cultural diversity brings to a nation—how food, language, traditions, and ideas from around the world have come together to create something uniquely Australian.

As you turn these pages, may you find inspiration in the stories of migration and multiculturalism, and may they serve as a reminder of the power of diversity in shaping the future.

Maree Cullinan
Executive Officer
Balla Balla Community Centre

INTRODUCTION

A JOURNEY THROUGH MULTICULTURALISM

STORIES OF MIGRATION AND BELONGING

In our long-established writing group known as *The Scribe Tribe*, we embarked on a creative journey to explore multiculturalism through storytelling. This anthology is the result—a collection of deeply personal narratives that capture the essence of cultural diversity and its profound impact on our lives in Melbourne and beyond.

The stories within these pages showcase the transformative power of storytelling. They bridge cultural divides, foster understanding, and celebrate their spirit. From the struggles of Chinese labourers during the Australian Gold Rush to the post-war migration of Europeans and the contemporary experiences of Vietnamese and Afghan immigrants, each narrative offers an intimate glimpse into the joys and challenges of building a new life in a foreign land.

Readers will encounter a rich tapestry of voices—stories of individuals leaving their homelands in search of opportunity, the cultural exchanges that shape their new communities, and reflections on identity and belonging. These narratives illuminate the hardships of migration—discrimination, isolation, and the loss of familiar surroundings—while celebrating the strength, ingenuity, and contributions of those who have enriched Australia's multicultural landscape.

This anthology brings together diverse cultural perspectives: Chinese labourers carving out livelihoods during the Gold Rush, Greek and Italian migrants whose traditions and cuisine have become integral to Australian life, and Afghan refugees seeking sanctuary from conflict. It also highlights European migrants who arrived after World War II, bringing skills, labour, and stories of survival and reinvention that helped shape modern Australia.

At its heart, this collection is a tribute to Melbourne, a city renowned for its dynamic multiculturalism. Its vibrant neighbourhoods—Chinatown, Springvale's Vietnamese community, Dandenong's Indian and Afghan precincts, Lygon Street's Italian eateries, Oakleigh's Greek quarter, and other post-war European enclaves—are more than just settings; they are living testaments to the city's rich cultural heritage. Some stories reflect Melbourne's historical roots, while others reveal the contemporary experiences of immigrant families navigating modern Australian society. Together, they celebrate the ongoing evolution of multiculturalism—a mosaic of cultures, traditions, and lived experiences.

Through this anthology, these fifteen writers honour the journeys of those who came before us while inspiring future generations to embrace diversity. We invite you to immerse yourself in these heartfelt stories, celebrate our shared humanity, and reflect on the richness that multiculturalism brings to our lives. May these narratives encourage you, as they have us, to see the world through the eyes of others and cherish the threads that weave us into a collective whole.

Roderic Grigson
Writer and Editor

TABLE OF CONTENTS

Dedication i

Appreciation iii

Foreword v

Introduction viii

MULTICULTURISM
    By Diane Brown 3

THE CIRCLE OF STORIES
    By Roderic Grigson 15

ALBIZIA
    By Norma Savige 22

TOKOLOSHE
    By Steph Webb 29

THE SEASONS OF MR MAE
    By Marianne Acton 36

YOU'LL NEVER KNOW
    By Zoe Skjellerup 50

AMBER
    By Hector David Sosa 63

I PROMISE
    by Robyn King 68

MEAT AND THREE VEG
    By Jane e. Wood 76

AQUA PROFONDA
    By Lauren McCarthy 83

FLAVOURS OF A CITY
    By Roderic Grigson 99

TIME TRAVELLER JOSEPH POTTS (GABRESKI)
    By Bernie Weiss 108

A COLLECTION OF POEMS
    By Maryann Grigson 132

THE GOLDEN JOURNEY
  By Roderic Grigson *137*
SEMI-DIGESTED MOMENTS
  By Hector David Sosa *146*
MOONLIGHT VISITOR
  By Norma Savige *148*
HOLIDAYS WITHOUT BORDERS
  By Corinne King *155*
MY SOLO HOLIDAY
  By Diane Brown *163*
THE FREE FRYPAN FALLOUT
  By Jane E. Wood *168*
WHEN THE FLOWERS BURN
  By Marianne Acton *173*
GRANDDAD BERT
  By Norma Savige *177*
HEALING HANDS FROM AFAR
  By Roderic Grigson *181*
A BOY CALLED TENNIS
  By Steph Webb *189*
A FICTIONAL TALE OF CHRISTMAS 2024
  By Bernie Weiss *197*
FROM DESERT SANDS TO CITY STREETS
  By Roderic Grigson *206*
A DAY WITHOUT MY MOBILE PHONE
  By Diane Brown *223*
THE CHAOTIC CLUSTER OF QUEBEC
  A surrealist poem by Hector Sosa *227*
A FORESTED LAIR
  By Steph Webb *230*
SURVIVING THE STORM
  By Jane E. Wood *238*
THE GRANDMOTHER EFFECT
  By Madisen White *243*

WHEN HEADS COLLIDE
　　By Steph Webb 247
LOVE, HATE RELATIONS
　　By Robyn King 252
GARRY
　　By Norma Savige 259
SWEET DELUSIONS AND FAMILY FOLKLORE
　　By Madisen White 264
THE COURT OF MANY COLOURS
　　By Corinne King 267
ANNABELLE AND THE OLDE LOST VILLAGE LIBRARY
　　By Bronwyn Vaughan 289
SMELSTORIUS
　　By Madisen White 298
THE FISHERMAN
　　by Steph Webb 301
ROCK BOTTOM
　　By Norma Savige 308
KALEIDOSCOPIC DREAMSCAPES
　　By Hector David Sosa 318
A COLLECTION
　　By Diane Brown 320
HERITAGE AND HEARTACHE
　　By Roderic Grigson 322

Writers' Profiles 335

Meaning of "Balla Balla" 345

THE SCRIBE TRIBE

VOLUME THREE

MULTICULTURISM

BY DIANE BROWN

Our writing group met every second Tuesday afternoon. I settled into the meeting room, expecting to spend the next few hours listening to and discussing various stories the other writing group members had written. I was surprised to hear our convenor change our afternoon discussions.

"Well, people, I have some great news," he leaned forward in his chair, his eyes glistening in anticipation as he unconsciously rubbed his bald head. "Today, we are going to embark on a new project. I have considered your request to publish an Anthology. After speaking with the Centre Management, I see that we can move full steam ahead."

The group of writers looked at each other. Some faces showed excitement, some showed concern, and a couple even negatively shook their heads.

"I can see some of you look rather startled," the convenor continued. "But if you want to become a published author, you cannot sit here each week reading out stories you have written but going no further. I have heard some promising stories read aloud during our meetings, and I believe it is time for you to move on to the next step. Contributing to an anthology is a marvellous way to enter the world of a published author, and I am hopeful that every one of you will contribute. The subject we will be writing about is Multiculturism. After our tea break, I asked the manager to come and talk to us about this subject and to give us some ideas about what you could write about."

The homemade biscuits, baked by one of the ladies for our tea break, quickly vanished before a round table discussion began. Some writing group members already had ideas of what their story would entail, others had no idea, and some even suggested the subject would be too difficult. After the tea cups were drained, the Manager arrived. She was a bubbly person and full of ideas as she chattered away, reminding us that all our ancestors would have come from another country many years ago. She spoke of the loneliness of immigrants and their fears when they left their homeland and moved to a new country. She reminded us of how difficult the English language is to learn, with words named and spelt the same but with two different meanings, and how difficult it was to understand Australian slang. She spoke of the need for immigrants from the same country to socialize together, following their homeland customs, but at the same time, learning to step outside the comfort of their own circle and start to mix and learn the ways and culture of their new country.

Arriving home after the class was dismissed, I pondered over the many areas the Manager had covered. What on earth am I going to write about? What multicultural event has happened in my life so far that I could write about?

The following week was frustrating. I spent days sitting in front of my computer, staring at the blank page on Word, starting a story, deleting a story, and searching Google to get ideas.

Perhaps I could write about the indentured or contract Chinese labourers who, after the news of the Australian Goldrush in 1853 reached

China, bravely spent several months in a cramped ship to reach Australia, leaving behind their family and friends. When they arrived at the gold fields, they kept together in groups, labouring long hours in the mines, cooking and growing vegetables, and often, in their sparse spare time, re-working claims that had been abandoned, hoping to find gold that may have been missed. They also found other opportunities to make money, working at many different jobs around the diggings, washing clothes, selling vegetables they had grown, and selling cooked food and herbal medicines.

By the late 1800s, the majority of the white population in the Australian colonies held openly racist attitudes towards people of different races. In those days, Australia saw itself as a progressive nation and wanted to attract only "desirable" immigrants. The idea was for Australia to attract a well-paid, skilled white male labour force to maintain this image. Before 1901, the Australian colonies experienced an influx of non-white migrants, especially during the gold rush. The White Australia Policy was passed in 1901, and this halted the influx of Chinese migrants.

Perhaps, I thought to myself, I could write about Greek immigration, as Greek migration to Australia also began in the 1800s. A significant number of Greek people arrived during the gold rush days, and further immigration occurred during the years between World War 1 and World War 11 when the Ottoman Empire expelled the Greek people from Turkey. But how could I write about the Greek migrants and not include the Italian migrants, who also began migrating to Australia in the 1800s during the gold rush years, seeking the better economic opportunities Australia had to offer?

Days passed, and I continued to stare at the blank page on my computer. Perhaps I should move forward from the 1800s to the 1900s and write about more modern immigration. The Chinese, Greeks, and Italians have certainly gifted Australia with a lasting legacy, weaving their own cultures, foods, and mannerisms into our society. Still, surely most Australians already realize their worth and contributions and don't particularly want to read about it over and over again.

So, what on earth could I write about?

Once again, the date of our writing group rolled around. Another round table discussion, each participant eagerly telling the class what they intended to write, some having just jotted down notes, others already completing a draft of a few hundred words. When it became my turn to talk, with downcast eyes, I managed to mumble, "I am still staring at a blank sheet of paper."

After returning home from class, I was determined to put my writing block aside and get to work. I decided I should write about something more modern than the Gold Rush, so perhaps I could write about the immigration of the Vietnamese people after the Vietnam War.

The Vietnamese War ran from 1954 until the fall of Saigon on 30th April 1975. The war began as a conflict that pitted the Communist Government of North Vietnam and its allies in South Vietnam, known as the Viet Cong, against the Government of South Vietnam and its principal ally, The United States. North Vietnam wanted to unify the entire country of Vietnam under a single communist regime, similar to the Soviet Union and China. Still, the South Vietnamese Government fought to preserve a Vietnam that was more closely aligned with the West.

By 1969, more than 500,000 U.S. military personnel had been stationed in Vietnam. On the 29th of April, 1969, Robert Menzies, the Australian Prime Minister, announced that Australian troops were to be sent to Vietnam. By the end of the Vietnam War, it was estimated that as many as 2,000,000 civilians and military personnel on both sides lost their lives.

After the Vietnam War, South Vietnam collapsed and was seized by communist forces. The country was unified as the Socialist Republic of Vietnam, with its capital in Hanoi. Saigon was renamed Ho Chi Minh City. South Vietnamese citizens now faced torture and retribution from the ruling

North Vietnamese. South Vietnamese intellectuals and other potential enemies of the resolution were rounded up and shipped off to re-education camps, which were actually forced labour camps designed to break the will of the South Vietnamese people and indoctrinate them with communist ideologies. Many residents of Saigon, the former capital of South Vietnam, were forced to move to the countryside to labour on collective farms. Desperate families packed their belongings in a single suitcase, fleeing their homes by any means available. They ended up in refugee camps, where they waited many months and even years before being permanently re-settled in more than 20 different countries.

In 1975, the White Australia Policy was lifted, and this enabled many Vietnamese people to migrate to Australia. Australia participated in "Operation Babylift", bringing many orphaned Vietnamese infants to Australia, and a surge of immigrants in Australia was the first test for multiculturalism after the White Australia Policy was lifted.

Yes, I thought to myself, I am sure I could write about the Vietnamese people.

Maybe I could write about how hard the Vietnamese people worked after arriving in Australia, many of them leaving behind employment where they were well respected for their intelligence, but only able to find work in factories and at other physically hard labouring work, often working two jobs, sharing small rental premises with other families, growing fruits and vegetables such as eggplants, limes, Vietnamese mint, basil and snake beans.

Maybe I could write about how immigration to Australia changed the lives of Vietnamese women. Strong and intelligent women who had held important positions of employment in their own country but who now took in washing and sewing, working from early morning until late into the night, all working hard for the same goal, to give their children a good education and to make a new life for themselves in their new country.

After working long hours over months and years, some Vietnamese people opened restaurants, offering new and exotic foods to the Australian diet. Soups, spring rolls, Vietnamese street foods, sizzling pancakes, and many other appetizing treats that the Australian palate had never experienced before became hugely popular.

I spent a lot of time researching Vietnamese people, hoping to write about their journey to Australia, their entry into our society, their cultures and successes, and their contribution to their new home. But as I delved further into my research, the stories I read brought me to tears. Those brave people trying to escape their war-torn country, boarding old wooden and overcrowded boats, all hoping to reach a country that would give them asylum, young men, older men, women of all ages, little children, and babies. The dangers those people faced on the water broke my heart. Many of the boat people were attacked by pirates, cruel men who robbed these fleeing refugees of the few belongings that they managed to carry. Even their clothing was stolen. Some of the women were kidnapped and raped by the pirates, who, after fulfilling their lust, threw these helpless women into the sea. Many of the "boat people", as they were labelled, arrived in Australia broken and traumatized.

As well, upon returning to Australia, our Australian troops were met with scorn and abuse when they arrived home. They were accused of fighting in a war that had nothing to do with our country.

After all, they had suffered; when arriving in Australia, many Vietnamese people were subject to abuse and distrust. They were accused of "queue jumping" and of "taking Australian jobs", and one senior politician actually voiced on the media that we were being "taken over by Asians."

I am not proud of this time in Australia's history. I admired the strong ethics and willpower of the Vietnamese people and all they introduced to Australia. After reading of their suffering and treatment during those early days of migrating, as well as the treatment our Australian troops received when returning home from the war, I decided I would not write my

Multiculturism essay on the Vietnamese people and would need to write about something else.

But what on earth am I going to write about?

Many thoughts rolled through my mind, the same thoughts, over and over again.

Close the computer and walk away. I tell myself. Give yourself the afternoon off and try again tomorrow.

Sleep was not kind to me that evening as different ideas flowed in and out of my mind. I eventually drifted into a fitful sleep, and upon awakening, I immediately realized what I would write. There was no reason why I should write about one particular race or one particular time in history. Instead, I would write about my own multicultural experiences.

I first met someone from another country when I entered boarding school in the 1950s. Among the eight girls with whom I shared a dormitory was a quiet Asian girl named Maylin. Maylin kept mainly to herself, never joining in our games, instead spending most of her time studying and writing long letters on thin paper. Her dainty hand wrote up and down the page with great speed, and occasionally, when I looked at her work, I noticed she wrote in an unusual style, the writing creating lines and little boxes instead of the letters we wrote in class. Maylin was always polite, slightly bowing to us when we said good morning or good night but never smiling or showing any emotion on her pretty oval face. Her eyes were shaped like almonds, and on the rare occasions when she looked directly at anyone, I noticed how dark brown those eyes were.

After many attempts at encouraging Maylin to join in, we all decided that she did not want to do so. Therefore, we left her to study and write letters while we moved on with our everyday lives.

I was surprised that Maylin did not go home for the Christmas holidays but remained at school in the care of the teachers who boarded. When I returned to school after the holidays, I discovered that Maylin was again sharing the same dormitory I had been allocated to. As I entered the room, she bowed and uttered a gentle good morning. I did not try to enter into conversation, as I knew she would not respond, but I often studied her when she didn't realize I was watching. Maylin seemed emotionless, never smiling, never raising her voice, and only muttering one-word answers when spoken to.

One evening during the first week of term, we were spending quiet time in the dormitory before evening prayers. Our dormitory door opened, and Maylin loudly called out as she jumped from her bed and raced to the door. Another young girl with the same features walked into the dormitory, and the two girls wrapped their arms around each other, hugging closely as tears streamed down their faces. Maylin turned toward me and said,

"This is my cousin, Lei."

I looked towards Maylin, quite surprised to hear her speak such a long sentence but even more surprised to see that she could actually cry. I had become so used to seeing Maylin expressionless that I assumed all Asian people never smiled, laughed out loud, spoke long sentences, or even cried.

I grew closer to Maylin and her cousin, Lei, during the following year. I discovered they were from China, and their parents, aunties and uncles had saved their money to enable the two girls to travel to Australia to study. There was not enough money for Maylin and her cousin to return to China during the holidays, so it had been pre-arranged that they remain at school. Both girls were very academic, understanding they had been given a rare opportunity to study in Australia. They explained that they were expected to gain good marks and move on to university to gain good employment when they eventually returned to China. As they were both only children, they realized they were expected to look after their parents financially when they became working women. They showed me their unusual Chinese writing, and they shared wonderful stories of their homeland, talking about the different foods they ate and how much they missed their parents but to me, as a young girl of 11 years of age, the thing I learned most, was that although they looked different, and although they spoke differently, inside, their emotions were just the same as mine.

Swedish neighbours moved into the house next door when I was a young mother with primary school children. On their first Christmas morning in Australia, I noticed the lady of the house sitting alone in the garden. She seemed so lonely and maybe a little homesick, so I picked a large bunch of blue hydrangeas and took them into her. She was so appreciative, and after that, we became close friends.

As Christmas grew closer again the following year, my neighbour asked what Christmas traditions we had in Australia. I detailed the list, explaining Carols by Candlelight on Christmas Eve, attending church Christmas morning if you were religious, Santa arriving on Christmas Eve, opening presents before breakfast Christmas morning, and explained the many different meals we served for Christmas lunch, from a traditional English styled roast, a seafood buffet, to a picnic at the beach. I also mentioned that Boxing Day was usually filled with sporting activities such as cricket, sailing, and beach games. Our neighbour was surprised to hear how loose our traditions seemed to her and went on to explain the Swedish traditions that her family followed. She told of how, on the 13th of December each year, their young daughter dressed in a white gown and walked through the house holding a small candle. She offered her father and brother a sweet, sticky bun called "Bulle" before leaving the candle on the windowsill. She added that in Sweden, Christmas is celebrated on Christmas Eve and that presents are never opened before dark. She asked if we would like to join them on Christmas Eve.

Christmas Eve was a wonderful opportunity to experience a different culture. We were offered a drink called "Glogg", which consisted of warm wine flavoured with fragrant spices. Their Christmas dinner, called "Julbord", was an absolute feast. In the centre of the table was a large leg of lamb, with numerous side dishes surrounding the lamb. These dishes contained hot and cold gastronomic delights such as spicy sausage, red cabbage, smoked salmon, potato gratin, and assorted cold meats and cheeses. The beer and wine flowed, and just when we thought we could eat no more, a dessert of pears in red wine and apple cake was served. It was the most unusual but one of the most enjoyable Christmas dinners we ever experienced. Fortunately, we lived next door, as we never would have been able to drive home.

Christmas was followed by an extremely hot summer, so we decided to mulch our front garden. A delivery of pine bark arrived from the local nursery. After spreading the bark over the garden beds, we rested indoors. I looked out the window, surprised to see my four neighbours standing in our driveway. When I queried why they were standing there, they replied that they were smelling the fragrance of the pine bark, as it reminded them so much of home.

Another time and again at Christmas, I waited in line at the checkout area of a supermarket. A young woman stood in front of me, holding the hand of a young boy who looked about 4 years old. She was dressed in a long, black flowing robe, her head was covered in a black scarf, and her face covered in a black veil, with only her dark eyes showing. Even her hands were covered in black gloves. Christmas music was playing through the speakers in the store, and the familiar song "Jingle Bells" boomed from the speakers. To my amazement, the little boy started to sing quite loudly to the tune, knowing all the words and jigging his little body in time to the music. I looked at the little boy and noticed the mother also looked at him before she glanced at me. Her dark eyes smiled, and I returned her smile. It felt good to share the innocence of a little child enjoying a Christmas song.

I turned on my computer. My page was no longer blank as I re-read my story. I wondered if I had written too much or not enough. Multiculturalism has changed our world in so many ways over the years. Some changes have been embraced, and some have been discarded.

When I stared again at the pages of my story, I wondered if perhaps I should have written just a statement. A statement that simply said:

As your feet touch my earth for the first time, I welcome you. I feel how apprehensive you must be to arrive after such a long journey. I am so different from your old homeland, but take your time to get to know me, for I am your new home.

Staying close to your countrymen is usual, but once you have settled, don't spend too much time staying in one place or doing only one thing. Of course, you treasure your memories and cultures, but I can also offer you so much.

Put aside any fears and embrace my offer. If possible, take your children and travel my wide and varied land. Your children are the lucky children, the children who will grow into adults knowing two cultures, the children who will become the leaders of tomorrow.

Swim in my oceans, and enjoy the warmth of the sand on your bare feet. Travel to my centre and gaze at the beauty of the red cliffs and deep gorges. Listen to the stories of the outback people and the traditional owners of my land. Travel to the towns that grew from the gold rush days, visit the museums, walk in the bush, and breathe deeply as the smell of dried grasses and eucalyptus invade your senses. Visit the vineyards, taste the wine, visit the snowfields and delight in the coldness, drink from the icy streams, visit the tropics, enjoy the rainforests, and eat the fruits you may never have tasted before.

Open your eyes and your mind with kindness and interest. Meet my people, the people from all walks of life. Meet the shopkeepers, the bus drivers, and the office workers. Meet the surf lifesavers, the farmers, the winemakers, and the vineyard workers. Encourage your children to listen to their stories and ask about their heritage and their culture. Share with these people your own stories. Stories become memories, and memories last a lifetime. It is in the listening and the telling that friendships are born.

I am Australia, and this is my offer to you.

THE CIRCLE OF STORIES

BY RODERIC GRIGSON

In a quiet, sun-dappled corner of Australia, where the vast land stretches to the horizon and the red earth holds the secrets of the past, Ngarra, an old Aboriginal woman, sat beneath the shade of a towering gum tree. Her wrinkled skin seemed to glow like the ancient rocks around her, and her dark eyes, deep as the earth itself, reflected the wisdom of generations. The land was alive with the songs of the wind rustling through the leaves, the calls of the birds, and the quiet hum of the earth beneath her.

Ngarra had lived on this land her whole life. She had witnessed many changes—decades of transformation that seemed both rapid and slow, like the shifting tides. But through it all, her people's stories remained steady, anchored in the land like the roots of the trees. These stories were not just told with words; they were written in the stars above, in the rivers winding through the land, in the songs sung around the fire. They were the Dreamtime, the timeless stories that spoke of creation, of the animals, the spirits, and the deep connection between her people and the land.

One afternoon, Ngarra received an invitation from the town's multicultural festival—a celebration that was now an annual event, bringing together people from across the world. The organizers had asked her to speak, knowing that her wisdom would bring a unique perspective to the gathering. Ngarra was intrigued. She had heard stories of the immigrants who had arrived in Australia, bringing their own histories, their languages, and their customs. While her people's stories were ancient, she also understood that all stories were part of the same cycle, woven into the same land.

On the day of the festival, Ngarra stood before a crowd in a bustling hall. The walls were adorned with colourful tapestries and flags from all over the world—red and gold banners from China, the green, white, and red of Italy, and the deep blue of Greece. The air was thick with the sound of multiple languages, each voice a unique note in a song of diversity. People from different corners of the world had gathered—Sudanese elders and families from Vietnam, the Pacific Islands, Torres Straits, Sri Lanka, a group of young Koreans, and local Australians—their faces all lit with curiosity and excitement about the festival. The smell of food filled the air—spices from Sri Lanka, roasted lamb from Lebanon, sweet pastries from Greece—mingling together in a fragrant celebration of culture.

Ngarra stood at the front of the room, her presence commanding yet peaceful. She wore a simple dress of earth tones, with intricate patterns of ochre painted on her skin—a mark of her connection to the land and to her ancestors. Her long silver hair was tied in a loose braid, and her hands, weathered and strong, rested on a walking stick carved with symbols of her people's stories. She took a deep breath, feeling the weight of the land beneath her feet, the heartbeat of Australia. The room quieted as she began to speak, her voice a soothing rhythm that seemed to blend with the natural world outside.

"I come from a land that speaks in whispers," she began, her voice calm yet rich with the depth of time. "The land speaks to those who listen carefully.

It tells stories of the animals, the trees, the sky, and the stars. It tells of my people, the first people, who have walked this land for tens of thousands of years. Our stories are woven into the earth, and they are told not just by words but by the wind, the river, and the fire."

As Ngarra spoke, the audience listened intently, some nodding along, others gazing at her with wide eyes. She could see the curiosity in their expressions—the desire to understand, to connect. She paused for a moment, allowing her words to settle in the air like the dust after a storm.

"When we first met those who came from distant lands," she continued, her gaze sweeping across the room, "we did not see strangers. We saw travellers—like the birds who travel across the seas, like the rain that comes from faraway places. We understood that we were all part of the same land, though our ways were different. Your ancestors, like mine, have stories to tell. And now, our stories will meet, like two rivers coming together, each bringing its own gifts."

As Ngarra spoke of the Dreamtime—the sacred stories of creation—she could feel the connection between herself and the people in the room. It was a connection not bound by time or borders but by the land that held them all. She spoke of how the land was a circle, how it had always been a place where many stories converged, a place where different peoples had once walked together in harmony and could do so again.

"The land is a circle," she said softly. "It does not begin or end in one place. We all share this land, and in sharing it, we create a larger circle—a circle of stories, of experiences, and of understanding. We must learn to listen to each other to honour each other's journey, for we are all part of this same story. We are all the keepers of the land's secrets, and it is through the coming together of all our voices that we will find true strength."

The room was silent for a long moment as if the land itself had paused to listen. Then, one by one, people began to speak. A young Lebanese woman with dark, soulful eyes stood and spoke in her native tongue. A translator stepped forward, and in English, she spoke of her family's journey from the war-torn streets of Beirut to the peaceful shores of Australia. She spoke of the pain of leaving her homeland, of the difficulty of adapting to a new culture, but also of the beauty in finding a new home. Her story was raw, filled with hope and hardship, and it resonated with the people in the room.

A tall Filipino man with a broad smile followed. He spoke of his childhood in the Philippines, of growing up in a small village where everyone knew each other, and how his journey to Australia was a leap into the unknown. He spoke of learning the language, of working multiple jobs to support his family, and how, over time, he had found his place in the Australian community—how his children were now proud to call Australia home while never forgetting their roots.

One by one, others stood to share their stories—stories of courage, loss, and love. A Sudanese woman told of her escape from violence and her journey to safety in Australia. An elderly Italian woman shared tales of her childhood in Sicily and the traditions that had been passed down through generations. The room filled with voices, each one a thread in the larger fabric of the land's story.

Then, a soft voice emerged from the back of the room. A woman wearing a colourful hijab and a soft smile rose to her feet. Her name was Laila, and her eyes reflected the strength of someone who had endured more than most would ever know.

Laila was an Afghan refugee, and her story began in a land that had known much turmoil. She took a deep breath, her voice steady despite the memories that stirred within her.

"I came from a land where the mountains spoke of wars and the winds carried the scent of sorrow," Laila began, her accent rich with the sounds of her native Pashto. "I was born in Kabul, a city that once thrived with the laughter of children and the voices of families. But as the years passed, it became a place where fear settled in the streets, where mothers wept for sons who never returned. The world I knew shattered in an instant. We fled, walking for days, with nothing but hope and the clothes on our backs."

The room was silent as Laila's words lingered in the air. She spoke of her journey across borders, of living in crowded, unsanitary refugee camps, of the terrifying uncertainty while waiting for their application to the UN asylum program to be processed, and the pain of being forced to leave behind everything she had ever known. She spoke of families that had been broken apart by being offered settlement in different countries and continents. Yet, even in the face of adversity, Laila's words carried a sense of resilience.

"When we arrived in Australia," she continued, "we were extremely grateful and considered ourselves lucky, but I felt like a stranger in a strange land. The language was different, the customs unfamiliar, and the faces I saw were not like my own. But I found something here that I had not expected—people who welcomed me, who listened to my story and shared theirs with me. I found kindness in places I never thought to look. Slowly, I learned to navigate this new world, and as I did, I realized that our stories, no matter where we come from, are not so different. We are all looking for peace, for love, for a home where we can build a future for our children."

Laila's eyes shone with quiet strength as she spoke of the joy she had found in Australia—the opportunities to learn, to work, to contribute. She spoke of the dreams she had for her children, dreams that had once seemed impossible but now seemed within reach.

"We all come from different places," she said, her voice filled with emotion, "but we are all connected by this land, by the stories we carry, and by the hope we share for a better tomorrow. My journey is just one of many, but it is a journey I am proud to walk. And it is only through the sharing of our stories, through the coming together of our voices, that we can truly heal and build something strong."

The room erupted in applause, not for the strength of her words alone but for the courage and vulnerability she had shown. Ngarra, standing quietly at the front, felt a warmth in her chest. This was what she had spoken of—the circle of stories expanding, the coming together of different histories and experiences, all woven into the tapestry of the land they shared.

Then, Ngarra smiled and began to share her own story—one that had been told many times around the campfire, passed from elder to elder, a story written in the very bones of the land.

"My ancestors have walked these lands since the beginning of time," she began, her voice lowering as she remembered the stories her grandmother had told her and her grandmother's grandmother before that. "We are the keepers of the earth, the sky, and the water. When I was a child, I would run barefoot across the red earth, feeling the pulse of the land beneath my feet. The stars above would guide us, and the elders would speak of the animals—kangaroo, emu, and the eagle—each carrying lessons of strength, wisdom, and patience."

Ngarra's eyes softened as she remembered her youth—the land as a vast, living entity and the sense of belonging that came with it. "When the first settlers came, they spoke of owning the land," she continued, her tone steady. "But we knew that the land could not be owned. It could only be cared for like a mother cares for her children. We shared the land, we shared the fire, we shared the stories."

Her voice grew even softer as she spoke of the darker times when her people were pushed aside, their voices silenced, and their ways misunderstood. But Ngarra spoke not of bitterness but of strength, of the quiet strength of survival and of the deep knowledge that the stories of her people would never fade.

"The land remembers," she whispered, "and so do we. The stories of my people are not gone. They live in the song of the wind, in the rustle of the trees, and in the hearts of those who listen."

As Ngarra finished, she looked around the room, seeing faces that had been touched by her words. The circle of stories had expanded, encompassing not just her people's ancient tales but the stories of all who called Australia home.

And as she walked away from the gathering, Ngarra felt a deep peace in her heart. The stories of the land were not just her people's to tell; they were for all who cared to listen. The circle was growing, its voice stronger, its reach broader. And she knew, as she had always known, that the land would carry these stories forward, for the land itself was the greatest storyteller of all.

ALBIZIA

BY NORMA SAVIGE

'They're back!' The door slammed as Jason walked into the kitchen with a basket full of plums.

'Hmm?' His mother concentrated on carefully pouring warm strawberry jam into hot jars of various shapes and sizes.

'The Muzzies are back, Mum. Two cars this time; they're multiplying.' He dumped the plums in the sink and began washing them. 'I wish they'd nick off.'

'Hmm?' Mary was now putting lids on the jars and wiping any spilt jam from them. She began running water into the preserving pan in the other sink beside her son. 'Watch out. This pan's still hot.' She looked up at Jason and gave him a gentle shove.

He looked down at her. 'Are you even listening to me, Mum? I said they're back.'

Mary looked up as she crossed the floor to gather up the neatly written jam labels from the table. She smiled as she saw the plump, smiling strawberries with green flat caps her daughter had drawn in the corners of each one. 'These labels are gorgeous,' she turned to face Jason, showing him the top one. 'Your sister is very talented, don't you think?'

He shrugged. 'What do you reckon they're up to?'

'Who?'

He groaned. 'I knew you weren't listening to me.' He turned to watch her as she returned to the jars. 'The Muzzies are back on the footpath. There are more of them this time.'

'Please don't use that word. I don't know if it's OK, so I'd rather you not say it.'

Really, sometimes, his mother seemed as if she were on another planet.

Mary grabbed the empty basket and walked out towards the fruit trees. As she turned the corner of the house, she looked up to see a small group of people gathered quietly on the footpath in front of the side garden.

A middle-aged man and woman supported an elderly woman dressed in black from head to toe. Circled around them were a couple about thirty years old, with a toddler, a bigger child, and a baby. To the side was a teenage boy.

They looked up as they heard Mary's fly screen door slam. She waved to them and called hello before walking away to begin gathering wind-fall plums. When she returned, she noticed they were still standing quietly in almost the same formation around the older woman, who seemed to be wilting a little.

'What are they doing?' Jason greeted her as she entered the hot kitchen. 'What do they want?'

'I don't know. They seem to be there for the old lady, but she looks like she's getting tired. I don't think they'll be there much longer. Why don't you go out and offer them some cold lemonade? It's getting pretty hot out there.'

'You're joking. We don't know what they're up to. I don't want to encourage them.' He stormed out, leaving her shaking her head in the middle of the room. *What is wrong with that boy? I didn't bring him up to be like that. He needs to change that attitude. Fingers crossed, he'll grow out of it – and soon.*

Mary emptied her basket and filled it with some plastic glasses and two bottles of lemonade from the fridge. *That old woman looked like she was fading fast. She might be thirsty.*

She walked out the front door and onto the footpath, then strolled towards the group of people standing there. As she approached, every one of them turned to her. Some looked curious, but some seemed very wary.

She held up her basket. 'Good morning. It's very hot out here today. Would you like some cold lemonade? I made it yesterday. It's nice and cold.' She started handing out the glasses and poured the first one for the old woman who had been watching her nervously. After a sip of lemonade, she recovered her composure, smiled, and nodded. 'Thanks.'

The older woman spoke quietly, and one of the others translated for her, 'She says it tastes like heaven. Thank you. My name is Amir, and this is my mother Soraya and the rest of my family.' He waved his arm to indicate the rest of the group proudly. 'I apologise if we are bothering you. We try to be quiet, but sometimes children struggle with that for too long.' He smiled indulgently at the young ones. 'We will leave now. Thank you for the delicious drink.'

'You are not bothering me at all, but I admit I am curious. This is the third year that I think you have come here. Would it be rude to ask why?'

'No, that is not rude. This is the fifth time we have been here. We come each year for my mother, who is getting very old and missing her old country and family memories.'

Mary gazed curiously around her. 'What is it that brings you here?'

Amir pointed into Mary's side garden. 'It is your beautiful tree. We come when it is in full flower. My mother looks forward to seeing it every year.'

'You mean my Persian Silk Tree?' She smiled. 'I love it. I planted it fifteen years ago, and it has flourished.'

'Excuse me, please.' He turned to speak to his mother and looked back at Mary. 'My mother speaks Persian, the language of her birth country. She tries to learn English, but it is very hard for her. She told me she remembered a huge tree similar to that in her family's compound. When she was a child, it was her task to sweep up the fallen flowers from the tiled courtyard every morning.'

Soraya mimed a sweeping movement and smiled at Mary. She pointed to the tree in Mary's garden, nodded and in broken English said, 'Beautiful. I love. My mother grow.'

She folded her hands over her heart, looked back at the tree and sighed.

The tree's canopy stretched over several metres, and its crown was covered in bright pink blooms that looked like dainty pom-poms. The fern-like leaves provided filtered shade over the grass below.

'Sleeping Tree,' smiled Soraya.

Amir explained, 'We know the tree is called an Albizia, but we have always called it the sleeping tree as the leaves close up overnight.'

Soraya stood a little straighter and took a deep breath. She reached out and held Mary's hand. 'You cook strawberry?'

'Yes. I'm making jam.'

She nodded and looked over at the house. 'I cook strawberry, too. When I young woman with little baby.'

Mary held her hand above her head, 'My baby is this tall.'

'Mine also,' she pointed at Amir.

Both women laughed. Mary was struck by how easily women can find something in common whether they speak the same language or not.

The baby started fussing, and Amir took him in his arms. He pointed to a young woman, 'This is my daughter, Sara, and this is Frankie, my grandson. I think he needs changing, so we will leave you in peace. Thank you for the drinks. You are very kind.' He pressed his hands together in a sign of gratitude and turned to gather his family together. 'We always have a picnic in your lovely town when we come here, and I think everyone is getting hot and hungry.'

'Do you think your mother might like to have a picnic under my tree? I would be very happy to share it with her.'

As he repeated Mary's offer, Soraya's face lit up. She looked askance at Mary. 'Is OK?'

'Yes, it is OK.'

'We always buy our food in the town to support the local traders. Are you sure we can bring it back here?'

'You are welcome. Come back soon.'

She turned and hurried to the house. 'Jason, Jason, quick! Come and help me. I need some stuff taken out to the side garden.' She began rushing around collecting up serviettes and other bits and pieces.

'I see you got rid of them at last. What were they after?' He was cleaning the preserving pan and spoon and wiping the benches ready for her to begin the plum and raspberry jam. 'Are you going to put any port in this jam? I loved it last year.'

'Don't worry about that. Would you please wash these glasses and make a couple more bottles of lemonade for the fridge? I think we need some mint leaves, too.'

'OK. You didn't tell me what they were up to out there. What did they want?'

'I have no time for chit-chat. I have work to do. Come on. We're hosting a picnic.'

'Yay. Who's coming?'

'Lots of lovely people. Let's move it.'

When the visiting family returned, they were surprised to see a picnic table and folding chairs under the Albizia tree. Picnic blankets were spread out with cushions, and an ice bucket held two bottles of lemonade. The group stood on the footpath but did not enter the garden.

'Come in. Come in,' called Mary. 'We will help with your food.'

She helped to settle Soraya comfortably under the tree in a padded folding chair and then called Jason. 'Our guests are here. Come and help them carry their things.'

'On my way.' Jason called and smiled as he walked outside, but as he walked around the corner, he stopped and stared. The whole family of strangers was there; some were already seated under the pink tree.

'There you are. Would you help bring the food over? No, wait! You can carry the baby in its carrier. Be gentle; he is asleep.'

Nonplussed, he reached over to take the carrier and walked slowly over the grass. He looked down just as the baby opened his huge brown eyes and stared up at Jason. Jason stared back, and the baby slowly smiled. Jason found himself smiling back.

'Thanks, Man. I usually cop that job,' said a youth a little older than Jason as he walked ahead with a soccer ball at his feet, carrying a nappy bag. 'He is cute, though, aren't you Frankie?' He reached back and tickled the baby under the chin to be rewarded with a bigger smile.

Mary looked around the group when the family was settled beneath the tree. 'Is there anything else I can do for you?'

'No, you have been very kind. We won't stay long. Thank you very much. You have made my mother very happy – and, therefore, you have made us all very happy.'

'Stay as long as you like. You are very welcome. Please come to the house if you need the toilet or something else.'

When she reached the house, Mary turned back and saw Soraya gazing up through the tree leaves at the silky flowers, and the rest of the family was watching her contentedly. She smiled as she watched. *What a wonderful family, being prepared to spend this whole day to make their matriarch happy.*

Later, Jason walked along the driveway between the house and the side garden and noticed the teenager sitting a little apart from the others, absorbed in his phone. Jason's curiosity got the better of him as the boy jiggled his feet and ducked his head, unaware he was being watched. *Weirdo.* 'What are you watching?' Jason asked.

The boy looked up and showed him. 'They won't let me juggle the ball here, so I'm just watching the Aussies in the World Cup.'

'You can have a kick down the back behind the fruit trees if you like.' Jason suggested shyly. 'Can you show me how to juggle the ball?'

'You play? Great. Let's go. I'm Darius, but everyone calls me Dazza. I'll just let Dad know where I'm going.'

'I'm Jason, but everyone calls me Jay,' he turned and strolled towards the small orchard.

Dazza put on an amazing display of what a talented person can do with a soccer ball, ending with a balancing act on the back of his neck. Jason was in awe. 'Can I try that?'

Within twenty minutes, he overcame his embarrassment and managed to juggle the ball from his instep to his knee and neck without using his hands. Mary had been watching quietly from the house but forgot herself and clapped loudly, 'Yay, Jay.' He dropped the ball and blushed.

'This is Dazza. He's going to send me a link with demos of other tricks he trains with. I'm going to have a go and show him what I can do when they come back next year.'

Mary nodded her thanks to Dazza, then turned towards the house, managing to hide her satisfied grin from her son.

TOKOLOSHE

BY STEPH WEBB

The wooden engraved box on the shelf of the Op shop caught Nandi's eye as she walked past it. The skeletal arms on the squat and the rounded body shape of the African figure carved into the Lebombo ironwood drew her closer. It played with her emotions as she puzzled over long-forgotten memories from her childhood. She couldn't quite recall what this little figure represented or its connection to her. Nevertheless, it intrigued her. The highly polished wood was a deep reddish-brown, with a distinctive grain pattern and spiralling curling and twisting knots. Picking it up she discovered it was weighty for a small wooden box. Something rattled from inside the box. Nandi looked for a clasp but couldn't find one. However, there was a little 'made in South Africa' sticker under the box. It was just what she was looking for. She was sure her mum would love to see that there were some reminders of her birth culture here in her new country. She missed the familiar arts and crafts from home, colourful fabrics, beadwork, and quirky décor that were so popular in Africa. A tremble played across her lips and tugged at the corners of her mouth. Glistening, unshed tears filled her lower eyelids, threatening to spill over her dark eyelashes and tumble down her high, rounded cheeks.

The African box was a perfect gift for her mother, who was arriving in Australia from South Africa at the end of the week. She was so looking forward to seeing her mother face-to-face again instead of FaceTiming her a few times a week like she usually did. Nandi quickly paid for the little box and took it home. She put it away on a high shelf in the linen cupboard, intending to wrap it in a colourful cloth scarf later to give to her mother. She felt a lot better after a strong cup of coffee. Her face began to brighten up, thinking of how thrilling it would be to see her mother again. It had been nearly five years since she and Tom had returned 'home' for their wedding in the Drakensberg mountains before settling down in Australia, Tom's homeland. Oh, she missed the high, rugged peaks of the Drakensberg mountains with their big, rolling, treeless green hills and high, squared, jagged pinnacles. She began to reminisce about many a holiday spent in 'The Berg' as it is known to locals. Her mother's family originated from those majestic hills. Aching memories tugged at her heart as an invisible cord was trying to pull her back to the land of her birth. But she loved Tom, having met him in London and spending some time working and travelling around Europe together until it was time for them to think about settling down and hopefully starting a family together. Australia was appealing to both of them for work prospects and lifestyle, so here they were.

Later that night, while they were sleeping, Nandi woke up as loud scratching sounds tore through her dreams, waking her and jarred from somewhere further away in the house. 'Darn! We must have rats in the ceiling again,' she muttered as she attempted to cover her head with her pillow. The insistent scratching and dragging sounds intensified.

'Tom, Tom! Wake up! I can hear a rat in the roof again!' she huffed with frustration. Tom dragged back the bedding and stumbled out of bed. He went to investigate, but the scratching quickly stopped. 'Typical', she grumbled as

Tom came back to tell her that he couldn't hear a rat inside the roof.

The next day, Nandi bought a sonic device to put into the roof to drive the pesky vermin out of the house. Night after night, the insistent scratching or dragging sounds woke Nandi up, and she would stumble out of bed, trying to find the rat. Nandi resorted to buying rat poison to throw in the ceiling cavity. She looked for a more environmentally friendly one to use just to feel better about what she was planning to do to the rat. Nothing seemed to be working.

On Friday, a sleep-deprived Nandi arrived at the airport to pick up her mum at Melbourne International. She dragged her body out of the car and all but stumbled through the terminal to where her mother was already waiting, big red bags of luggage at her side, her arms flung wide and flashing her beautiful toothy smile. Her face alight with pleasure at seeing Nandi.

'Eish Nandi! You look so tired. Were you travelling with me on my long flight?' laughed her concerned mother. Nandi sighed deeply, and with a light, forced laugh, she agreed that she had been awake thinking of her mother on the long twenty-two-hour journey, which included connecting flights. If only! Nandi wasn't going to tell her mother that they had rats in the ceiling, and she was so sleep-deprived due to their scuttling around. Her mother would be repulsed to sleep in a rat-infested home.

That night, there was no hiding the fact that something was scratching in the house, as it woke her mother up, too. The next day, her mother insisted that the house was cleaned from top to bottom, not that it was dirty, not that it hadn't already been scrubbed, fumigated, vacuumed, and dusted repeatedly in readiness for her mother's arrival. A few days before, a pest control company had been called in to investigate, but no rat had been found. It was so puzzling for the frustrated and exhausted Nandi and Tom.

On the fifth evening after her mum arrived, Nandi was again woken by a strange sound. It was more of a rustling sound. She groggily opened her eyes and noticed a dark shape at the foot of her bed. She sat up to get a better look. The shape moved. She opened her mouth to scream, but no sound came out. The dwarfed silhouette of a person stood there, covered with long dark hair and piercing inky black eyes, glinting as the streetlight reflected in them. A long, bony hand with sharp, tapered fingernails stretched out from the hairy  creature and gripped Nandi by the ankle. The power in that hand was like a vice as the skeletal hand pressured against her skin, pressing down to dig into the bones of her ankle. Suddenly, she found her voice, and a shrill screech vibrated through the room. She felt its nails raking her ankle painfully. The thing gripped her ankle again. Tom suddenly sat bolt upright in bed as her screams shattered the night's silence. His eyes stretched and strained as he tried to focus, looking for answers that were not there.

At that moment, with blood-curdling screams and Tom's 'What! What! What!' the door was yanked open and hit the wall with a resounding whomp; there stood her mother, hair standing on end, the whites of her eyes like headlights. She flicked the light switch on, blinding everyone with the light bulb's sudden brilliance.

'What on earth is going on here?' boomed her mother through the muddle of screams and confusion.

With that, Nandi burst into tears and grabbed at her ankle, which felt like flames of fire were running around where the scratches were. The creature was gone. As Nandi gulped through the tears, she blurted out that she had just had a horrible dream. She couldn't process what she had or had not seen. That was when her mum noticed the scratches. With a glare at Tom, she pursed her lips and wagged her finger at him.

'I have eyes in my head. I can see what is going on here! I am watching you!' she thundered with anger, glaring at Tom in accusation, before heading out of the room to get Nandi a cool, damp face washer. Tom, in the meantime, put his arms around Nandi as they sat on the edge of the bed. He held her, talking calmly to help her relax.

'Mom, I had a bad dream. That's all!' Nandi spluttered through deep sobbing sighs as she tried to stop the tears and steady her breathing. Her mother didn't look convinced as she stayed for a bit longer and held onto her daughter's hand. Eventually, everyone was able to return to their beds, but sleep was rather illusive.

After breakfast the next day, with the sun shining brightly through the house, her mother began to question her about the dream.

'Dreams are important in Zulu culture, Nandi. You know this. We need to find out what the dream means. Tell me what you saw in your dream, Nandi?'

Nandi hesitated at first, 'I am not sure if it was a dream or not. I saw something next to my bed. It seemed too real. A person. Short, hairy. No, I don't know. But I am not sure what to think anymore. It was a dream. A nightmare! I am so tired from lack of sleep. That rat has been waking me up, scratching every night. We have been trying to get rid of it for weeks.'

'Mmmmmm....' Muttered her mother, cupping her chin with one hand and staring at the wall. Frown lines deepened into furrowing ridges across her forehead. Her mother's face ashened as something seemed to click within her mind, and realisation flicked across her troubled face. Her coal-dark eyes fixed stonily onto Nandi's.

'That rat! Tell me, how long has the scratching been going on, Nandi? When did this start?'

Nandi thought for a while and then said, 'Actually, it was the same night that I brought the African box from the Op shop.'

'What African box?' her mother hissed through clenched teeth.

'I bought it as a present for you and forgot all about it,' Nandi apologized.

She took her mum to the laundry cupboard, and there sat the little wooden box on the shelf, behind some blankets, where she had placed it two weeks ago. She picked it up and handed it to her mother. Her mother stepped backwards, fearfully staring at the engraved figure on the box. She flung her hands up as if in defence and refused to touch it.

'We must take it to the lake Nandi.'

'Why'

'It is wanting to go back to the water where it belongs'.

'It's a box mama!'

'Nandi, I think the Tokoloshe lives in this box. How did it get to this far-off land? Maybe someone brought it in this box for muti (medicine). We must free it into the lake so it will stop tormenting you like this.' Her mother's words tumbled out as the thoughts raced through her mind, trying to fix the family's dilemma.

'Mum, I don't believe this stuff. You know that.'

'Nandi, after what you have heard and seen, you still do not believe?'

'Muuum!' wailed Nandi in frustration with her mother's stubborn insistence on believing in a mythical creature used to scare children and gullible adults.

Nandi was too tired to argue any further. She was ready to try anything to just get a good night's sleep. Her mother wouldn't let this thing rest now, that much she knew. You can't argue with deeply ingrained beliefs. At this moment, she was far too exhausted to do anything else but go along with her mother's reasoning.

So, Nandi and her mum took a long walk to the lake. Nandi carried the box in a shopping bag, and her mum walked a few steps behind her, muttering Zulu, talking to her ancestors, and enlisting their help to keep them safe. When they got to the lake, Nandi took the box out and put it into the water. It dropped like a stone down to the bottom of the lake. Bubbles floated to the surface of the water, and then the lake began to ripple. As Nandi and her mother watched, a wake formed as if something was moving through the water. Their frightened eyes watched. In the middle of the lake, the movement stopped when it encountered a large clump of reeds. The wild ducks and water hens fossicking in amongst the reeds let out piercing shrieks and squawks as they flapped their wings and kicked at the water to flee. There was a rustling through the reeds, and the long bullrushes swayed as if something was moving them, then it stopped, too.

'Come, quickly, Nandi, we must go now!' her mother insisted, and she took her by the arm and pulled her away. As they passed the park garbage bin, Nandi's mother insisted that the shopping bag must be tossed in there before they reached home.

Nandi's mother found bricks from which Nandi had no idea and then placed them under the base of the bed to raise it higher from the ground, as is African custom.

'It's to prevent the Tokoloshe from reaching you and harming you or stealing your souls when you are asleep', her mother instructed her. Tom shook his head when he saw the bricks, but he was not going to argue with Nandi's mother. Nandi, on the other hand, was rather confused about what to believe after her unforgettable experience with the humanoid creature and what she had witnessed at the lake.

That night and every night since then, Nandi slept deeply and soundly. When her mother was safely on her flight back home, Nandi and Tom returned home and removed the bricks under their bed.

As for the Tokoloshe, he still lives in the lake and wanders about at night, steering clear of Nandi's home as her mum, unknown to Nandi, had sprinkled protection muti around its perimeter.

THE SEASONS OF MR MAE

BY MARIANNE ACTON

HOLI

A seed crossed the salted seas in the pocket of a man. On new land, he knelt and toiled the earth with his weathered hands. Once a practice planted out of survival, it now bloomed under a different sun. He watered the dirt and patted down the soil. Standing, he took in his yard. In a blink, a garden flourished before him.

*

Arms laden with groceries, the old man hobbled up the driveway to his flat. He heaved himself up the stairs, a newspaper tucked under his arm. In his pocket, he retrieved a set of keys, the metal jingled in tune with wind chimes. Bent down, he slipped his hand into the plastic handle of the bag, straightening up the weight snapped out from his fingers. The newspaper flapped to the concrete ground.

'Hell's bells,' he sighed.

The paper fluttered against the dropped bag of oranges. He stretched to reach for it, the wind faster, the gust kited the front page down toward the hedges of his front garden. Caught in the branches, he watched a small hand snatch it from the dense shrubbery.

Tottering back to the mailbox, he heard a faint chorus of giggles that shook with the leaves.

'Rohan, Sanya. Quit pulling up Mr Mae's plants.'

A woman hurried up to his mailbox. A stern expression pulled her face as she looked down. A boy stepped out from behind the brush. In his hand, the front page, the edges frayed from its escape.

'Rohan, what do we say?'

'Sorry, Mr Mae.'

Mr Mae chuckled, taking back the page. 'Not a worry, I should be thanking you. Saving an old man from his creaky knees,' he said, hovering his leg, and the sound of a rusty hinge whinged from the side of his mouth.

Rohan beamed up at Mr Mae with a toothless grin before turning to his sister in a fit of laughter. Chasing after each other, they ran up and down the length of the street.

Their mother sighed, 'Stay on the footpath, you two. Good afternoon, Mr. Mae.'

'And to you, Mrs Arora.'

'I apologise for the bother. Kids can only stay still for so long. Can I help you with your things?'

Mr Mae waved Mrs Arora along, 'Not a bother at all. However, I must insist you stay for tea.'

Calling for her kids, the pair bolted up the driveway. Mr Mae and Mrs Arora in tow.

*

On the front porch, sitting on wrought iron chairs, a saucer of biscuits between them, Mr. Mae and Mrs. Arora shared a pot of tea. The newspaper was laid out on the table. The kids lay underneath the tree, pointing out the differently-shaped clouds through the bare branches.

He flipped the page; the bright colours on muted newsprint caught Mrs Arora's attention. 'Holi,' she told him, was a festival that celebrated the triumph of good over evil. She went on to describe the festival, how fistfuls of colour were thrown at one another. Skin, hair and clothes were dyed in a vibrant kaleidoscope of colour, all while laughter and song rang in the air. Mrs Arora's smile wavered before turning her face away from Mr. Mae.

'This will be the first year I will celebrate Holi with my mother here at home,' her voice creaked.

Mr Mae handed her a sleeve of tissues. She nodded her thanks and pulled one free, patting it under her eyes.

'To celebrate love with loved ones is a blessing.'

Mrs Arora sniffed, her smile returning. 'That it is, Mr Mae.'

*

Amongst his garden, watering can in hand, Mr Mae gave the hedges a drink. Leaves of green bounced under the sprinkle. He patted his hands dry on the pants of his trousers, streaks of pink and yellow smeared across the fabric. He squinted and rubbed his fingers together, the colours mixed into that of a pale sunset, now stained across his palm.

Sprung up from the other side of the bush, Rohan and Sanya caused Mr. Mae to hop back, both of their faces tinted bright. He clutched his chest, and realisation dawned on him.

Mr. Mae held up his arms, the pelt of powder dusted across his front. Wielding his watering can, he held it high. The kids shrieked with delight, fleeing from the downpour.

'Happy Holi, Mr Mae,' Mrs Arora called out to him from up the road, an elderly woman's arm threaded with her own.

'Happy Holi, Mrs Arora,' Mr Mae waved a smile spread across his hue-patched face.

SUMMER SOLSTICE

Beaded down his temples, the sweat spilt onto his cheeks. Mr. Mae took off his hat and fanned a cool breeze over his face. Flies dodged the flap of his hand. Underneath the foliage of the tree, he inspected the trunk. Parched bark cracked with the heat, and pests buzzed around the weeping wound.

Stood on shaky feet, Mr Mae held onto the tree, his breath laboured. Hat secured on his head, he walked up the driveway and stopped at the garage door. He clutched the handle and recoiled back to his side. The heat of the metal singed his fingertips.

'Darn door,' He jutted out his elbow and pressed it down on the door handle, using his foot to push it open.

'Is that you, Mr Mae's?'

Mr. Mae retrieved a spray bottle from inside the door. 'It is. How are you fairing this summer's day, Elin?'

A woman poked her head over the fence. Mr Mae made his way over, seeing into Elin's yard. Pots of hanging plants hung from her veranda, and lazy vines dangled from over the rail. She held a bright red drink in her hand, and ice cubes rattled against the glass.

'The summer solstice is certainly living up to its name, but there are no complaints from me.' Elin lifted her glass in a cheerful toast.

'I'd return the gesture, but I doubt insecticide would be to your taste.'

'Are pests troubling you too?' Elin cringed, swatting a bug on her arm.

'Unfortunately, perhaps your garden could use a dose?' Mr. Mae held out the spray bottle to Elin, who exchanged her drink with him. Her head dipped out of view. Mr Mae heard the pump of the bottle, and the smell of floral vinegar wafted back to him.

Elin reappeared, her grin brighter than the sunlight they stood under. 'Would you be interested in an exchange?' She pointed to the drink in his hand before he could nod. 'Lingonberry cordial, have a sip. I have a bottle to spare.'

The ice had melted into shards, the condensation slick on the outside of the glass.

Mr Mae lifted it to his lips, a sweet tartness spread across his taste buds. 'That is delightful.'

She asked him to wait. Mr. Mae heard the rock of her path crunch under her shoes. Under the sun he baked, tempted for another drink, Elin clamoured back her weight and made the rails of the fence screech as she leaned over.

Mr. Mae handed Elin back the glass. In return, she gave him his spray bottle, a bright red bottle of cordial, and a bouquet of baby blue flowers.

'What a stunning bloom. What are they called?'

'In Swedish it's called, "äkta förgätmigej", but I believe they are "forgot-me-nots" in English…' They spent the rest of the afternoon swapping gardening tips when Elin eventually tracked over to help him spray down his tree. Exchanging his pesticide recipe for her Lingonberry drink mix, they finally parted ways when the afternoon sun burned out to the night.

*

Mr. Mae settled into his chair for the evening. A drink was mixed, and by his side, he flipped through the channels on the TV. He skipped past programs with titles like, 'Celebrity Cage Fight,' 'Puppet Master,' and 'Questioning Questions.' Instead, he settled on the documentary channel.

He turned up the volume, and the narrator spoke with a slight British accent. 'The Summer Solace. Marks the longest day of the year with a festival celebrated throughout Europe. Here in Sweden,' The narrator said, 'It is more commonly known as "Midsommar." Footage of Maypoles, flower crowns and bonfires flitted across the screen. 'A time spent with family and friends,

Midsommar allows loved ones to share morish foods and delectable drinks. Truly a festival for the young and old.'

Mr Mae took a swig of his drink. Held high, he returned Elin's toast. 'Skål, Elin.'

DIA DE LOS MUERTOS

Mr Mae stood at the window. He shivered with the windy chill that batted the withered leaves off the branches. Comforted by the cup of tea between his hands, the brew balmed the aches of his body till the last dredges.

He placed the sole mug in the sink and walked to the front door. In the entrance hall, he side-stepped a picnic basket, slipped his arms into his coat and zipped it up. Mr Mae fitted a knit cap over his head, the cable stitch pulled taut behind his ears.

*

Outside, Mr Mae heaved a rattled breath. Through the cloud of condensation, he pried the garage door open, the gust persistent in keeping the handle of his rake from reach.

By the morning's end, Mr Mae was spent losing the war to the wind. He leaned against his weapon- a rake with a broken tine- and watched the neat hills of fallen fronds flattened in a single burst of breeze. It wasn't until he rolled out his compost bin that Mr. Mae finally conquered the leaves.

Elbows deep in rotted foliage, Mr Mae hauled armfuls into the open mouth of the bin.

The rumble of an engine parked in the driveway. In the time it took to peel a soggy leaf from his arm, two pairs (not of his own) had wrapped themselves around his legs.

'Granddad!' a little girl with his eyes squealed up at him. 'Guess what.'

'What's what?' Mr Mae asked.

With a crooked smile, she held up her hand. On her palm sat a wind-up frog. 'I got a prize at school 'cause I spelt the best.'

Mr. Mae bent as low as his knees allowed, returning her hug. 'Well done, Mara, you should be very proud of yourself,' he said, a grin spread across his face. 'How about you, Oscar? How is school?'

Oscar's arms dropped to his side, his head bowed, and he stepped back.

'Oscar goes to a special class now,' Mara chimed; the frog now hopped across the lip of the bin.

'Shut up, Mara,' In a swift snatch, Oscar grabbed the frog and launched it across the garden. He ran from Mara's cries and up the sidewalkway of the house.

'Oscar,' a woman called out from the driver's seat of the van. She swung her legs out under the steering wheel as Mara tottered toward her. Tears streaked down her face, her arms thrown around her mother's bulging belly.

'Mara, honey, not so tight. Starting the day off strong, huh, Dad?'

Mr Mae picked up the frog, dusted off the dirt and handed it back to a quivering Mara.

'Remind's me of when you were a kid, Evada. I'll check on Oscar, will I?'

*

Mr Mae poked his head around the corner. Oscar rested his forehead on his knees, his arms squeezed around his legs. Soft sobs racked through his body, accompanied by the drip of the nearby tap.

He heaved a heavy sigh, upending a bucket. Mr. Mae sat beside his grandson.

'She didn't mean it the way she said it, Oscar.'

Oscar lifted his head, eyes puffy and nose running; he sniffed, 'Yes, she did. She always does.'

Mr. Mae let the leaky facet fill the silence. 'Did you not want to tell me?'

His lashes damp, Oscar scrunched up his sleeve to wipe them dry. 'Maybe, I dunno,'

From his pocket, Mr. Mae handed Oscar a handkerchief. 'Everyone needs a little help sometimes.'

'Not Mara.'

'Even Mara needs help; there is no shame in asking for it. Who was the one to teach her to tie her shoes?'

Oscar stared up at him.

'Who showed her how to fold a paper plane?'

A smile twitched at the corners of Oscar's mouth. 'I did,' he croaked before his face fell again. 'That's only two things, though.'

'It's two things she didn't know before, that is, until you taught her.'

Oscar picked his head up, 'Dad was making dinner and couldn't help Mara with her homework; that's how she got the frog,' Oscar held out his hand and counted on his fingers. 'Di-no-saur, Mrs B says when you say the word out loud, you can count the parts into sounds to make it easier to spell.'

'See that,' Mr Mae said.

'See what?'

'You just taught me something new, Oscar. Imagine what else you can teach us all in that new class of yours.'

Oscar's eyes crinkled his smile, the biggest his grandfather had seen him wear in a while.

*

Mr Mae and Oscar walked through the front door into the sickly, sweet scent thick in the air. Mara sat in front of the television, and Oscar left his grandfather's side to join her.

In the kitchen, Evada held the bowl on her belly, looking down at her phone.

'Evada, what are you doing?'

His daughter looked up from her phone and then to the television, where her children laughed at the cartoon antics on screen.

'Everything OK?' Evada nodded toward Oscar.

'He is alright now,' Mr Mae said, rounding the kitchen bench. 'You, however, should be sitting down.' He took the bowl from Evada's grasp and stirred her toward the dining room chair he pulled out.

'Dad, I'm pregnant, not helpless.' Evada huffed before a groan of relief left her as she took her seat.

'I never said you were helpless, but you can be helpful and read out the recipe,' Mr Mae handed Evada her phone, taking up the bowl and spatula.

*

In the oven, a loaf rose, and on the stove, a sugar glaze cooled. Infused with orange, the citrus perfumed the kitchen. Mr Mae and Evada stepped into the backyard and took in the garden. The overcast sky split into clouds, letting the afternoon sun feed the swaying flowers.

Along the porch railing, a garland of marigolds had been left to dry. A miss-match of sunset oranges and yolky yellows made the puffed petals appear full and soft to the touch.

'Dad, should I call the kids out to help?' Evada asked, her nose buried in the buds. A peppery, earthy scent bloomed from the blossom.

'I'll be alright. Everything else is in the basket by the door. Just have to fetch her photo.'

Smiling at Evada, Mr Mae heard the screen door clatter, his daughter's voice rallying up her kids.

*

Underneath the bare-branched tree, an ofrenda had been set. Encircled by the garland, a woman looked from the photo, her arms wrapped around a girl, and they both shared the same smile. A crop of oranges, green bananas, and apples were placed around the frame. Sugar skulls of different designs were sat in a bowl, with a plate of pan de mureto half gone between Mr Mae and Evada.

'Haven't seen this blanket before,' Evada ran her hand over the knit. A bouquet flourished in yarn underneath them.

'Took an age to finish. I'm not as fast as your mother was,' Mr Mae nodded toward the picture of his wife.

Off her belly, Evada brushed crumbs from her dress. 'You learned to knit?' Evada asked, her eyebrow hitched in bemusement.

'Is that doubt I hear?'

'Absolutely.'

Mr. Mae leaned over the blanket and pointed to the stem of a blushed pink orchid. 'See how the pattern goes from smooth to not so smooth.'

Evada chuckled, 'I take it you're "not so smooth?"'

'Your mother thought differently.'

A twitch of disgust crossed his daughter's face, and her cheeks ballooned up to feign sickness. 'Ew. Please stop.'

Mr. Mae hid his chuckle in a mouthful of bread. Oscar crept around the van, and Mara hopped, intimating her prized frog. In a pounce, Oscar declared his kill.

'I ate you, Mara. You can't move anymore.'

'Lions don't eat frogs. Mum, tell Oscar lions don't eat frogs,' Mara yelled across the lawn.

'You were a poisonous frog, so you both died. Play another game,' Evada, a piece of the bread, and place it back on the plate. Mara chased after her brother, fingers sticking from her mouth. She screamed. Her transformation into a vampire frog needs fresh blood.

'Stay in the yard, you guys,' Evada yelled after them. 'Wish she could have met them,' she said, looking at her mother. 'Could you imagine the trouble Mum and the kids would have gotten themselves into?'

Mr Mae bumped his daughter's shoulder with his own. 'All either of them would have to do is bat their eyes at her, and she would be putty in their hands.'

'She would have loved them,' Evada said, wiping her eyes.

'More than anything,' Mr. Mae said. 'More than anything.'

CHRISTMAS

Alone at his dining room table, Mr Mae waved. From the tips of his fingers, ribbons of tape flailed with his hand. Adhesive caught lengths of wrapping paper in its glue trap.

A grunt bristled past his moustache. Mr Mae laid his hand flat against the table. He pinned his elbow to the tape and, with a yank, ripped his hand away. Lint-tufted pieces were then rolled up into a ball and tossed across the room. Mr Mae grabbed the roll. With his thumbnail, he caught the edge and tore a fresh strip off.

'Victory,' he snickered. Tongue between his teeth and brow furrowed, a knock jolted his jaw shut. Mr Mae groaned, rubbing a knuckle into the side of his cheek. Another rap buckled the wood of his door. 'In a moment,' Mr. Mae called through a bitten mouthful.

Mr Mae pushed himself out from under the table. The wooden legs scraped against the oiled planks of his floor.

He gazed through the peephole. A man stood, his eyes darting behind square-framed glasses. In his hands, he held a foil-tented dish. Mr. Mae unlocked the door. Before he could greet his visitor, they pushed past him and into the house.

Mr Mae followed him to the kitchen, where he crouched before the oven, twisted the dials, and opened the door. He placed the dish on the middle rack, shutting it in the oven.

'Andrew, everything alright?'

By the bench, Mr Mae stood, Andrews's face pulled into a frown. 'Mr Mae, I am so sorry for intruding on you like this,' he took his glasses from his face and, in rhythmic circles, cleaned the lenses with his shirt. 'My oven decided today of all days to stop working,' Andrew said, replacing his specks. 'Today, I'm meeting my partner's family, and without this,' Andrew jabbed a thumb behind him. 'I'll have nothing to feed them,' Andrew reached for his forehead and kneaded out the scrunched muscle.

'Take a seat, Andrew, I'll put on some tea.'

*

Mr Mae pushed crinkled wrapping paper to the other side of the table and placed a cup before Andrew.

Andrew thanked Mr Mae, and he flicked his wristwatch over to peer down at the screen. Mr Mae passed him a napkin and dropped a cube of sugar into his tea, watching Andrew fidget over the rim of his mug.

'Thank you again, Mr Mae. I'm sorry to impose, especially on Christmas,' Andrew hovered his hand above his tea, steam curled up and around his fingers.

'Not an imposition at all. Besides, it's nice to have some company,' Mr Mae looked back to the kitchen. 'And whatever you're cooking smells delightful.'

'Rosemary and thyme make anything smell delicious. Mr. Mae,' Andrew cleared his throat,' I hope you don't mind me asking, but don't you usually spend Christmas with your daughter?'

'I do. However, she had just given birth, and I didn't want to burden her with a visit or to visit. Evada did call this morning. Baby number three has a pair of lungs on her,' Mr Mae smiled.

'Congratulations, you must be very proud,' Andrew said, folding down the corners of his napkin.

'Very proud indeed. Though I must admit this time apart has allowed me ample time to practise my abysmal gift-wrapping skills,' Mr Mae gestured to the pile heaped at the end of the table before he bowed his head. 'I do apologise for the state of things.'

Andrew sipped his tea with a smile. 'No need to apologise. If you'll allow me, I'd like to return the favour.'

Mr. Mae's eyebrow quirked in question.

'I don't mean to brag, but I am a fantastic gift wrapper.'

*

'If you crease the paper beforehand, it should slot against the box more easily,' Andrew pleated the wrapping paper around a box with an illustration of a jumping frog. A speech bubble stretched from its mouth that proclaimed it could jump 'up to 1 metre high.'

Mr Mae nodded along, tape dispenser in hand.

'I'll hold down the edges, and Mr Mae, can you tape down along the seam?'

Mr Mae serrated a small snippet of tape ('It's easier to use smaller pieces of tape instead of a long strip,' Andrew had informed him) and dotted it to stick the overlapped pieces of paper together.

Both stood back and admired their teamwork when a beeping erupted from Andrew's watch. He raced into the kitchen, grabbed the tea towel and opened the oven. The aroma of herbs and sizzling fat perfumed the house. Andrew took off the foil and tucked underneath the lamb roast, which contained crispy potato and roasted julienne carrots.

'My, if your in-laws aren't impressed by that, nothing will.'

Andrew gave him a bashful smile before replacing the foil. His pocket buzzed. He took out his phone, and his face fell, skimming the message.

'Andrew?'

'Yes, sorry,' he said, shoving his phone back away. 'My partner just told me their family will be here in half an hour.'

Mr. Mae clapped Andrew on the back. 'I understand you're nervous, but just be yourself. If they can't handle that, just be glad you'll only have to see them once a year.'

Andrew let out a long exhale, rolled his shoulders to straighten up and pushed his glasses back up his nose. 'Could I ask another favour, Mr Mae?' Andrew inclined his head to the towel.

'By all means. May it serve you luck.'

Mr. Mae walked Andrew to the front door, where they exchanged thanks for each other's help. Andrew descended the stairs with cautious steps. He hurried down the driveway before stopping and threw over his shoulder a, 'Merry Christmas, Mr. Mae.'

'And to you too, Andrew.'

EPILOGUE

Rain had pelted his roof for a week. He stood most mornings by his window and watched his tree suffocate under the flooded lawn.

When the sun finally broke through the clouds, it shone on the damage that had already been done. Mr Mae consulted every book about plants he could get his hands on. When those in his possession were exhausted, he turned to the library. Yet, he knew it was all delaying the inevitable.

Eventually, he knew what had to be done. Evada's partner helped him dig up the roots. The trunk was soaked and soft, crippled under its own weight. It was his daughter who suggested keeping a branch, which now hung above his front door.

After it was uprooted, Mrs Arora came to his doorstep. She offered a Thermos of chai and a sympathetic ear. Elin would spend afternoons discussing new species to plant in its place. She had suggested spruce, though Mr Mae had a feeling she was biased. Andrew, encouraged by his hit of a Christmas dinner, continued cooking and ventured into baking. Both he and his partner expressed their condolences with a plate of sapling-shaped biscuits.

Instead, Mr. Mae embraced the loss. With the tree's life withered and his own nearing its end, the memories it brought would always remain. The soil where he had planted the seed so many years ago would nurture another with new memories to call its own.

YOU'LL NEVER KNOW

BY ZOE SKJELLERUP

"I'm looking for a decent bunch of talkative randoms to add to my collection," my brother Liam reads as I fill out my dating profile.

A confused expression lies perfectly on his face. "What is that supposed to mean? Talkative randoms?"

I look up from my phone screen. "In other words, I'm just looking for a friendly/relaxed conversation and everyone's welcome to join me."

Liam stands there in a pondering pose. "Hmm! That is an interesting choice of words. You got it, Zoe. But don't you think it's a little bit rude?"

My mouth gapes open wide. "Excuse me! Rude!? Oh no! Of course, I don't mean it that way. What if I just wanted a sense of humour?"

"You can use whatever words you want, Zoe. But what if you hurt their feelings? You can't just go around calling strangers 'random.'"

"Well, that's what they are, aren't they?" I reply. "Firstly. You receive a random number of friend requests- some people will be talkative, and some will not be. Secondly, you haven't met the strangers in person, so in that case, they're a talkative random-"

"It's like calling them weird." His fianceè Madi chimes in. "You don't want a whole bunch of weirdos, do you?"

We stand in the open lounge room. "Well, I'm definitely not looking for a decent bunch of talkative weirdos, am I?"

"That's exactly how it sounds!" Madi says.

"Can't you just say something like you're looking for someone nice to talk to? There! A much nicer way to put it." Liam adds as he scans over my bio once again.

"Should I change it then?" I ask. "Gosh! It's my dating profile. Why don't you like my choice of words?"

"I honestly wouldn't like to be called a random!"

I burst into laughter, "Liam. You're not random. You're my brother! It's different, okay?"

*

I grew up in Australia with a multiple complex disability called CDG syndrome type 1a (also known as PMM2). This causes me to use crutches for support, and I've been diagnosed as legally blind.

Yes, I've experienced interactions with all sorts of different cultures myself! Australia is seen to have a multicultural society as a whole. Still, individuals have both positive and negative experiences in life over here.

Today, I'm going to share with you my story. It all happened back in 2022.

Of course, I had completed my dating profile, uploaded a picture of myself and waited around for a few notifications.

Within a brief second, I receive a whole bunch of friend requests. Many strangers- either across the globe or in my own country wanted to talk.

Wait, did I say talk?

I learnt pretty quickly that they didn't really want to have a friendly conversation with me. These dating apps were full of weirdos instead. Most of them just wanted to message on another social media platform and send inappropriate photos to each other. Sometimes, this could end up being a type of scam, where they would try to exchange sexy pictures in order to blackmail you for money.

I must have looked horrified as I received an unpleasant photo. "Eww! That's just disgusting. I don't want to see that!"

Sure, I didn't want to get involved with any of this! It was probably best that I stayed away from those dating apps. They didn't want friends. It felt like everyone was looking for the same thing- to trick people into sending photos. And who knows where they end up!

Liam glances at my phone screen. He sees the disgusting picture. He gasps. "Zoe! What exactly have you been signing up to?"

"I didn't sign up for this! I signed up for dating. I want to get to know people. I had no idea people would be like this..."

I heave a deep sigh of disappointment. "I was only hoping that this would be a real messaging platform. But no! They all have to be weirdos wanting nudes and making us puke!"

"Zoe, I don't think you should be using online dating to make friends!"

"Yeah," Liam adds. "If you're looking for someone nice to talk to, how about you try Facebook or Instagram? Now that's a real messaging platform, and you probably don't receive any of that crap!"

He continues. "Those sick weirdos just seem to only care about one thing and then disappear without a word. As your older brother, I'm just trying to watch out for you, that's all."

Sure, my brother was right! Many of them do seem to come and go whenever they want. It's almost like they pick a pretty target, and if they receive the picture, they get what they came for, and they head straight out the door feeling pleased with themselves. And if they don't find what they want, they move on and find someone else who will.

I have been through something similar in 2020. It was on my online

Scrabble game. They called themselves romance scammers! And they also wanted to message me on another social media platform.

Yes, it was to trick someone into a fake relationship to get money - a similar reason there. And yes, I've gotten myself into plenty of arguments with them to waste their time, too!

So, I seemed to know what to expect while using online dating. To me, It is nothing new. Because all they ever wanted was to scam! I decided not to play by their stupid rules, and I kept refusing to message on other sites.

Along with the scammers, some people talk about spooning and feeling horny in the very first sentence...

What the...? What is this? I wonder. People shouldn't be acting up like this. If this is a chat app, why don't people just want to chat?

It almost feels like a whole new language I don't speak!

Madi looks over a creepy message and gasps. "Oh my... well, I guess you've got yourself a weirdo there. Is this what you mean by talkative randoms?"

"This is exactly what she's been trying to say to you all along! There are plenty of weirdos out there!" Liam adds.

"I understand. I have a whole bunch of weirdos right now, and I must fix it somehow." I reply. "Any idea how I would do this?"

"I guess you could take down that profile picture! It's a lovely photo, but I feel like this might grab their attention!"

After removing the profile picture, I discover that the whole bunch of weirdos have suddenly disappeared. Not everyone on the dating apps is like this - sending inappropriate photos and talking about spooning. I hoped to have fixed it!

I started having positive experiences, too, and decent connections with only a couple strangers. However, the good people who wanted a friendly/relaxed conversation were difficult to find online. It's like sorting through a stack of unwanted files and hoping that you would find something good out of it.

And, of course, you instantly doubt that you will ever find what you're looking for! A great conversation. Someone like-minded. It took a long time for me to come across genuine connections.

But I eventually got there at the end. All was well until...

I looked up from my phone screen. My eyes widen with horror. "Oh, crap! Liam! I think I've accidentally unmatched someone I enjoy talking to, and they won't appear on my feed again. How would I get him back?"

Madi chuckles ruefully. "Oh no. Zoe, you can't!"

"Well, that's a bit crap, isn't it? I liked talking to that person.-"

"I'm so confused," Liam interrupts, "how can you even accidentally unmatch someone anyway?"

"I find it easy to bump buttons as apps have different layout structures, and I'm partly blind. Can't I just swipe until I find him again?"

"Zoe. I'd hate to break the news to you. But I don't think a dating app is supposed to work that way! You can never find them again."

My jaw hits the floor, "It doesn't work that way?! Don't tell me I lost him."

After quite some time swiping through the photos, I accepted that I still couldn't find him again on this account.

"Maybe I could create a new account to find my decent conversation! Maybe if I could just respawn with a second account, "I reasoned, "he should be there again!"

Liam smacks his forehead in frustration. "No. No. No. You don't understand how online dating works! Don't you realise? This isn't right! Someone might think you're pretending to be someone else."

Sure enough, my brother was right about this as well! I didn't fully understand how online dating worked.

"Firstly, the app is full of horny guys. Secondly, I don't like receiving those inappropriate photos and people asking for other social media. Thirdly, I'm freaking out, and I don't feel relaxed about any of this. But unmatching this guy is definitely an accident."

So, I changed dating apps. This is when online dating seemed to change for the better! Sure, I've come across many horny creeps, scammers and inappropriate conversations since the start. It has been a trial by fire, but I was determined to get to know new people and find out more information about them.

*

Now I can hear you wondering, what does any of this have to do with multiculturalism?

Shortly after I changed dating apps, I found myself speaking online with people from different cultural backgrounds. Some people lived overseas. Some had moved to Australia from their home country. Some wanted to explore different parts of the world. Meet new people. Have new experiences in life. Try different foods that aren't available in their country and learn more about others.

I've spoken to many people - those who arrived from New Zealand, people from African countries, people from Asian countries, and people from India, who mainly stayed in their own country. I even spoke to Queenslanders, too. Yeah, I seem to get around on my apps!

By chatting online, I learned more about how people aren't very inclusive towards others. They isolate them all because of a visible difference.

For example, I've matched with plenty of people from India during my time using dating sites, but I had mixed experiences with them. Many were very eager for a relationship, too enthusiastic for me. They were kind but overwhelmed me with their love hearts, flower emojis ⚘ and flirtation. Many spoke about wanting to have children together in the first few days of messaging! It was all a bit full-on.

From my past experience with romance scammers, I worried that the people I met from India may end up trying to trick me. But one Indian man wanted a friendly/relaxed chat with someone worldwide - someone like me. He approached many new people, trying to start chatting with them. He was sweet and introverted like me - an engineer who was using the app to gain the confidence to go out in the real world. Every day, I would spend many hours just talking with him online. We shared our favourite music, recipes, stories about our families and our experiences with COVID restrictions and lockdowns in different countries. People had very different experiences in their own countries and between states.

However, through my conversation with him, I found out most people wouldn't give him a chance. Many people he came across on dating apps wouldn't even interact with him.

But why? All because he had an Indian name. Something that stands out to people! It was almost like nobody ever cared enough to chat with him. He felt alone, and he just wanted someone to talk to.

Many people in his home country isolated him, too. My new friend told me that he had a frightening experience with racism walking home from the pub, where he was assaulted.

So, I decided to continue the chat with him and actually be there for him. I feel like that's the right thing to do! We both gave each other the confidence and companionship we needed.

Until one day, he told me that he was going to leave the app. He said that I'd achieve what I needed to in life and thanked me for staying on the app and talking to him. He was one of the first people I had a genuine connection with. He proved to me there are good people out amongst the bad eggs, after all!

I was happy that I did what I did during that time. I gave him what he was hoping to achieve. A friendly chat.

I learned how important it was not to judge someone by their name or where they come from. You'll never know until you get to know a person. Are they kind, or do they need someone? What difference does it make if they have an unusual name?

They're still people with feelings! People who need company. People who need love and kindness in their lives. People who need someone to talk to.

You should never treat others unfairly based on their differences. It just doesn't make sense. It won't hurt anyone to just say hello. Suppose you don't take an interest in people who are different from you. In that case, you're basically just shutting relationships and opportunities out for no good reason.

I've already been through something similar out in the real world myself! For me, I tend to get stared at by people all the time on the streets, at the shops, and almost everywhere in public, especially by younger children. This happens to me more than just once in a while - it has occurred pretty much all my life.

But for what reason? I'll tell you, it's because I am visibly different compared to others.

It's because I'm living with a condition where I need the support of crutches. It's really just the crutches that cause attention. They can be loud as they clip, clop and clatter on the ground. They're something obvious! Something that stands out to people. Something that others don't often need.

The awkward staring makes you feel uncomfortable.

It makes you feel different and excluded.

The staring says, '*Who are you?*'

'*What happened to you?*'

'*I don't relate to you!*'

I call this 'the random stare'.

I understand the curiosity. But some people think that it's rude to randomly stare at others. They don't say hello or ask questions. They try to mind their own business and get on with their life. It almost feels as if I don't exist in the world - like I'm invisible even though I stand out.

As I grew up, I realised that it's good to be different and good to stand out. The awkward staring, the people who don't say hello - they can just do what they do. It doesn't bother me as much anymore.

And it's sad for them, really! Almost as if people just stare right through my soul, not knowing what to say or how to interact with a disabled person. It's almost like they haven't seen anyone with crutches before.

*

Time went on, and I met another man online. He was from New Zealand, just like my family. He told me about his past in a video call and that he had once fallen deeply in love with an Indian woman.

He was making plans to move overseas to live with her permanently. She had come to visit him in Australia, and he likewise travelled overseas to spend time with her in India.

Of course, he had people in India just stop and stare at him for being different, too. Naturally, he didn't like the random stare either! Who would?

Could it be because of a lighter skin colour? A different language? A different nationality coming into another country? He didn't feel included either - all because of something different about him.

But what happened to his relationship? During the conversation, I found out she had already been married to an Indian man. They went their separate ways.

My new friend was an aged care worker. He understood the struggles of disability, as he, too, lives with an eye condition as well as dyslexia. He was using the app to find a serious relationship and was determined to find someone.

Not all disabilities are obvious. Some can be invisible. So it's clear that the staring he had experienced wasn't because of this.

When speaking to him, I also found out that he moved with his family to Australia for a better life and better opportunities a couple of years ago- something that they never had back in New Zealand.

At first, he wasn't sure about moving and wanted to stay behind with his father, but he gradually changed his mind and settled into the country. He traded dangerous earthquakes for venomous snakes. He found life to be positive over here, with more jobs to choose from, and he took up more responsibility on his shoulders. The transition from New Zealand to Australia was easier for him than for others. He had less visible differences, and the cultures were quite similar. Still, he missed his friends back in New Zealand.

We laughed together about our shared culture and our memories of nostalgic foods. My dad arrived from New Zealand years ago with his family, and ever since, I've grown up with mashed potato and Marmite on toast, just like my friend did. I would share a peanut butter and cheese sandwich with Dad, too. Crunch on some celery with cheese and Marmite. In New Zealand, people eat yoghurt with peanuts as well.

It seemed like we had so much in common, and we came from very similar backgrounds. I wondered whether this could be the start of a deeper relationship we both wanted. But as I got to know him more, I discovered that he wasn't as nice as I thought. I could tell by his actions and words and how he made me feel about myself. Despite our similarities, we went our separate ways in the end, too.

*

Time flew by, and I met another man online. He was from Asia and wanted to explore more parts of the world. He travelled overseas to Queensland for a working holiday and eventually moved to Melbourne to study.

During his time over here, he had many Australians isolate him and knock him around. Sexism and racism were all a part of his experience - more so when he was living in Queensland. For similar reasons, my new friend was excluded because of a slightly darker skin colour, for being a man from a foreign country who didn't speak English confidently yet.

He was also looking for new relationships and using the app to practice speaking English. He was sweet when I talked to him and was looking into disability support as a job while he was studying. He understood sign language and liked helping others.

Through our conversation, I found out most people wouldn't give him a chance on the apps either. Again, because of a different nationality! But he just wanted to connect and get better with his English. How rude is this?

So I got to know him better. Patience and support are all we need. That's what people should do, isn't it? No matter their differences.

We should be there for someone who's having a tough time and do something good for them. Because nobody likes to be left out!

One time, during the conversation online, he told me that he went to a church in Queensland and spotted one of the group members isolated from others. Someone with Cerebral palsy. He came over, sat with her and chatted. Others wouldn't sit with her. But he did something good.

Both people here had a negative, isolating experience living in Australia. But again, there's something that stands out about both of them. You can see it's because of his nationality and her visible condition that people seem to avoid them and mind their own business instead. It doesn't hurt to reach out and connect - instead, it started a new friendship.

So what? Just because he came from a different country and is not the same race as you, and she's living with a visible condition, doesn't make it right to overlook them.

The Asian man. The Indian guy. The New Zealander and I. We all stand out to people in our own individual ways.

Many people who are different in skin colour or have a disability get treated unequally by others! It's important to include them and respect them for who they are.

These three stories above all seem to combine into one tale with a common theme - isolation!

Even though we've experienced being left out in a completely different way, I can still understand how they're feeling deep inside.

And let me tell you something... It doesn't feel too good to leave someone out! I know this from my own personal experience, and I never liked how people stopped and stared without getting to know me.

All because of a pair of crutches! But that's just life for me. It's just a part of who I am. I don't know anything different. And neither do they! Maybe they never had anyone to challenge or educate them, to give them a new perspective. Or perhaps they did, but they just didn't care.

Sometimes, spotting a clear difference in a person is all it takes for people to isolate others and keep to themselves. Why do this to them anyway? Different people have so much to share and teach you so many interesting stories about them. If you choose to leave them out, you'll never know how interesting life can be.

The people who shut others out simply because they are different are the people who obviously don't care and don't wanna know. I wouldn't like to be the type of person who would leave others out. Because I've been dealing with a whole lot in my own life, I want to be inclusive as much as possible. I want to learn and grow as much as possible.

To me, it didn't really matter who I came across on those dating apps. I just wanted to have a good conversation with someone, just like what all of my new friends were looking for.

So, you've basically got yourself a bunch of randoms. A circle of people who seem to understand each other in many ways here, even though they're different. We're all individuals.

Maybe you can change your name, but you can't experience a life you've never lived before or choose where you originated from before you were born. You are just you! You're born as who you are, and you go through life as who you are. That's all you get.

Include others, or don't. Help someone out, or keep to yourself. It's your choice! But please do the right thing and make the best decisions you can in the life you have. I will always try to show kindness and thoughtfulness to people no matter their differences because I know what a hard day is - extremely isolating.

And by the way, do you remember the person I accidentally unmatched earlier? Well, I did end up finding and matching with him again. And now, we're happily in a relationship.

AMBER

BY HECTOR DAVID SOSA

Walking purposely through the various convenient retail outlets of the vociferous Casey Central Shopping Centre, I casually came upon an Asian variety store. My initial intention was to head to the car and return home, but since I had efficiently finished undertaking the dull task of buying the essential groceries for the coming week, I had gathered some time to spare, so I impulsively decided to have a look at the miscellaneous items that this shop had to offer.

I began to carefully scan the assorted products for sale in case I found a bargain on something neat. I must admit, I had no plans of purchasing anything, but if I was to find something useful or special, I thought that I would get it, so long as it was marked at the right price.

"They have multi-coloured gel pens!" I excitedly thought to myself, looking at the small stationary section they had there, which had brought out my nerdy side.

As I slowly approached the furthest corner from the checkout, I started smelling strong citrus incense in the air, but I could not detect smoke anywhere. Immediately after this sensation, I instinctively felt an overwhelming presence around me, as if I was being watched by someone powerful or something dangerous.

I tried to shake this feeling off. I briefly turned away for a moment when a set of androgynous whispers directed me towards an antique, highly decorated wooden box. Intuitively, I "knew" that it was the source of the unique scent I was smelling despite the lack of fumes coming out of it.

I examined the mysterious box, and I realised that it was unlocked, so I opened it, expecting to see a bar of soap or something similar that would explain the exquisite fragrance.

I found nothing but a small rectangular mirror.

As I briefly saw my own reflection, an intense light flashed before my eyes, and instantly, I was transported away from…the universe!

I found myself in a pitch-black environment. It was so dark that I could not see my hands as I raised them in front of me.

What had happened?

Where was I?

How was I to get out of there?

As my heartbeat increased from my frightened state, I heard distant thunder behind me. The roar then travelled closer and nearer until – bang! A huge ring of fire manifested ahead where I stood.

Before I could process what was occurring, a lion's head materialised at the centre of the radiant ring.

"Welcome." announced the face in a deep, commanding voice.

"Who…who are you?" I nervously managed to ask.

The lion paused for a moment before speaking these familiar words:

In the euphoric era of yesterday,

During the vigorous youthful years,

I crossed paths with diverse souls of all species,

And varied races of all kinds,
From fiendish enforcers of fear,
To the graceful keepers of the honest heart,
Divided between brief friendships,
And harsh but valuable lessons,
All necessary to what has inevitably passed.

The lion's words hinted at something I knew, which had a calming effect on me, and I began to relax.

He continued.

Eternal brothers disguised as distinct classmates,
Feeling at home with fellow Salvadoreans,
Engaging in art appreciation with a Polish pal,
Growing up with an Italian ally,
Agreeing with a Croatian comrade,
Joking around with a Maltese associate,
Having a beer with a Sri Lankan buddy,
And learning about logic and loyalty with Australian colleagues;
All essential for the building of character,
And the formation of the idea of companionship.

Having heard such specific things made me nostalgic, recalling my thrilling time in high school, as the lion had somehow described in detail, not only the activities that I undertook with my former friends but also their different nationalities.

The big cat proceeded.

Immortal lovers met as apparent strangers,
From that innocuous crush on that Scottish lass,
My clever Hungarian sweetheart of the past,
To having been captivated by my elegant Irish lady friend,
And fancying that charming Russian maiden,
All as a chaotic course of spiritual development;

An authentic depiction of my sense of beauty.

At such a stage, I realised that this was no coincidence. This beast also knew the various girls that had crossed my life. As I anticipated the next words, I wondered, "What else does he know?"

As ethereal music emanates in the overcast sky,

While sadness echoes in the confused streets,

My vivacious spirit shall rise high,

For I have known the richness of engaging play,

I have felt the unmistakable madness of infatuation,

And I have tasted the bitter fruit of the lower realms of the psyche.

Before me, the soil remains fertile for new plantations,

And what is to be sowed must be carefully cultivated.

Such metaphors had hit me with a wave of astonishment. This creature had stated my perception, my emotions, and inner experience like no other living thing had done before.

The cold autumn and freezing winter may come forth,

But so will the warmth of spring and the heat of summer.

Let the sensational flowers emit wonderful colours to the receptive eyes of their admiring observers,

For what's alluring inspires hope,

And hope is the luminous light that decorates the daring darkness.

Who am I?

I believe you have your answer.

And as the lion spoke his final words, the light of the ring of fire increased in brightness so rapidly that in a couple of seconds, pure white brilliance blazed everywhere. I returned to the physical universe, back to the here and the now.

As I composed myself of what had just happened, I carefully closed the box, put it back where I had found it, and exited the store in shock but also in total amazement.

I had casually walked into a random Asian shop, purely by chance, only to have faced the fateful reflection of what I had understood was my own unearthly fiery soul.

I PROMISE

BY ROBYN KING

Nell was sitting on the park bench eating a pork roll from the local Vietnamese shop. She pulled her dress a little lower as she felt it was a little too short, and it made her feel uncomfortable. The lady that serves in that shop was taken to hospital the night before with chest pains. Nell had never met the young man who served her today. He introduced himself as her son.

He said she woke in the middle of the night with severe chest pains. She tried to hide it, but the household heard her scream.

Nell felt sad for the lady, as she was not very old. Nell thought that the lady did not look well the last time she saw her. But she worked very hard in that shop. The son introduced himself as Harry, like Prince Harry. I laughed because that name did not suit him. He looked more like a William. Nell thought.

As Nell was sipping her coke, she saw Harry talking to a girl on the other side of the playground. He was trying to talk to her, and she was pushing him off and saying something like go away. We are finished. He kept saying sorry.

Nell tried to analyse the situation, and she came to the conclusion that he had done something wrong. It must have hurt the girl. Maybe he was unfaithful. Or perhaps he neglected her in some way. Whatever happened, she didn't want to have anything to do with him.

Harry stood there and just stared at her. Called her stupid, and she slapped him.

The girl threw her hands to her face and started to cry. This time, she was sorry. He wrapped his arms around her and cuddled her. They were going to be okay. Thought Nell. Lover's tiffs can be hard, but this one, Nell was sure, was going to end up with make-up sex. The best kind. Thought Nell.

Nell looked at her smartwatch. "Shit, 12.30. Nell was late to return to the office.

She picked up her handbag and the paper wrapping, and while scurrying back to work, she went through her rubbish in the bin and continued to head towards her building.

"Nell!" Someone was yelling her name.

Nell turned around. It was Harry.

"Hi Harry, What do you want? I am in a hurry. I have to get back to work.

"I need to talk to you. I think you can help me?"

Nell could feel her thighs chaffing as she walked. Her legs were in a bad state. Ever since she and Brett split a year ago, the COVID lockdowns were in, she put on a hefty 32 kilos. Netflix got a hammering, and online shopping became a dream. Nell ordered all her favourite foods. The ones she refused to eat while working in the office, as the other girls would look at her from all directions. Nell knew they were thinking she should not be eating all those carbs. Now, the consequences of that lack of discipline, she stacked it on. She felt ugly, and she had rashes to prove it. The doctor says she has diabetes, and her blood pressure is high.

"Harry, I can't talk now, but I will meet after work."

"I can meet you at the gym. I will be there from 3 p.m. You can have a workout with me." Harry responded without looking at her big body to try not to make her feel embarrassed.

Nell smirked. God knows I should go back to the gym." Nell Replied.

"I will see you then, yes,"

"Okay, Harry. But I don't know how I can help you."

"I will explain everything. I will see you at the café in the gym."

"I'll be there about 5.10. When I finish work.

"Nell, It's Monday," Harry said with a giggle while rubbing her arm.

Harry ran off, saying. "Thank you, Nell. I know you can help me."

Nell returned to work, sat at her station and answered a ringing phone. She looked over, and Samantha in the next cube looked at Nell and then her watch.

Nell chose to ignore her, but she felt intimidated nonetheless.

Samantha and Nancy were at the water fountain when Nell returned from the toilets. They were giggling and smirking and stopped just when Nell walked past.

Nell could feel their eyes following her all the way back to her seat.

Samantha returned to her cube, and the phones stopped ringing. So Nell stood up and reached over to Samantha. When she sat down, she said, "If you have something to say, say it to my face. I can explain myself if I only knew what the question was, Samantha, you turncoat." Nell said with anger but had control.

"Nancy and I were wondering if your love life has improved. I mean, you know, it's been, what 3 years? I don't care, really, but you have stacked on the weight and the fellas I've dated all say they hate fat girls."

Nell was astounded but didn't want to let on that she was upset.

"As a matter of fact, I'm dating a fella," Nell lied.

Samantha looked interested.

"Really, what's his name?"

Nell didn't want to get into details because she didn't have any.

"None of your business," Nell replied, her head facing the other way.

Nell wondered if Samantha could tell she was lying.

"You're lying, Nell Browne. You don't have a boyfriend. You would have said something."

"No, I wouldn't. I won't tell you anything. Because you would use it against me because that's what you do. You and Nancy are mean. And the boys you go out with don't like you really. They know they can have some fun. But my fella likes me for me." Nell smirked as she wished that were true.

"Well, I don't believe you, Nell Browne."

"Stop saying that."

"What's his name?"

"Harry, There I said it. His name is Harry." Nell felt proud and cheeky even though it was a lie.

"I am meeting him today, and he is going to show me some exercises to help me lose weight."

Nell bit her lip. Too much information. "Shit, shit, shit," she whispered to herself.

"Stop talking, Nell." She told herself.

Both phones started to ring. Nell was pleased with the distraction.

The afternoon ran smoothly after the girl's interaction. Nell couldn't wait to get out of the building.

She headed down to Pump's Gym. The big, wide doors opened automatically, and she entered the foyer. She looked up at the signs when a beautiful redhead with the most amazing thin but muscular body asked Nell if she could help her.

"Yes, I'm looking for the café. Could you point me in the right direction?"

Nell's thighs were rubbing, and her ankles hurt.

The redhead pointed down the corridor, "and turn left."

Nell took a toilet stop first and felt relief when she pulled her cotton trousers down, sat on the toilet, and separated her thighs. She looked at her rash. The ointment she bought wasn't working. Nell thought she'd have to buy the expensive one again.

When she exited the toilets, she spotted Harry talking to the redhead.

They eyed each other, and Nell walked over and ordered a coke.

Harry walked up behind her and touched her on the shoulder. Today, you will drink water.

"But I don't drink water."

"Today, you will have water. Coke has seven teaspoons of sugar in it, and sugar turns to fat if you don't exercise it off."

"Okay. I will drink water."

They sat at the closest table to the passageway and smiled at each other.

"What did you want to talk to me about?"

"Let me tell you about myself, Nell. I was born in Vietnam, and I came to Australia with the intention of marrying an Australian and staying in the country. I will be honest. I will come straight out with it. No strings attached. I was hoping you could marry me, and I will do whatever you want. Within reason, of course. I won't do anything dangerous." Laughed Harry.

I have to live with you for a year, and I will apply for an extended visa. I will worry about the paperwork. I will not put you in any discomfort. I will do anything you ask me to. Even if I don't like it. I have the money, but I just need a woman to marry."

"You can shut your mouth now, Nell."

All sorts of pictures were going through Nell's mind.

I showed Samantha that I really do have a boyfriend.

> My lonely days are over.

> Having a man to help with the bills.

> He is very handsome. He has strong arms. Nell noticed the minute he handed her the pork roll.

> And company, Lord knows I needed company.

They sat there just looking at each other and saying nothing for some time.

"I'll do it!"

Harry's eyes widened. He couldn't believe his luck. "Really, Don't you want to think about it?"

"Well, yes, I'll think about it all the time. It's what I dreamed of."

"We will be married, but that's it. After the required time, I will move out, and we'll get a divorce. I will pay for that also."

Nell was hopeful they would make a loving couple.

Harry was hopeful Nell wouldn't go back on her word.

Nell dreamed of him making love to her, and they both having a cigarette afterwards, even though they both didn't smoke.

Harry thought of Julie, the lady in the park. She can get lost now. She couldn't be trusted. Too demanding and too emotional.

Nell looked forward to telling Samantha she was getting married.

Harry thought about his ambition of running his own gym. He would extend his working visa. The government likes that as he would be employing people and paying taxes.

Nell thought about how she would tell her mother. She didn't care. He was everything she dreamed of.

Harry was hoping Nell wouldn't expect him to be home every night as some girls would like his company. But it's Harry's secret, and he doesn't want to upset his citizenship prospects.

Nell thought they could even have some children. She smiled. She turned 30 last month. Better get a wriggle on.

Harry wanted to see Julie but would lay low for a while. Get things in order first.

While they were both busy thinking, two more glasses of water were put on the table.

Nell drank the water without noticing it wasn't coke.

"Nell, tell me you haven't been married before, have you?"

"Noooo. That wasn't even on my radar." She laughed.

"Good, I mean, you know that would be an issue. Now, Nell, what would you like me to do? You name it, and we will make it happen."

Nell happened to look over towards the doorway where she entered, and there was Samantha. Walking towards Nell's direction, holding a towel and a water bottle. Heading towards the pool.

"I want two things," Nell said, turning to Harry.

"Two?

"Yes"

The first one is to kiss me, not just any kiss, but passionate. One that will sweep me off my feet, and with it, I want you to hold me and put your hands through my hair like you really mean it.

Samantha stopped to look at the swimwear on a rack, and she had her back to Nell.

It gave her time to finish explaining to Harry what she wanted.

"Then I want you to look at me, then give me a second kiss. Just a peck, like a thank you peck, on the lips."

Harry looked around. Nell thought he did that because he didn't want anyone to see this happening. He spotted Samantha, but she had her back to him. So she wasn't a threat.

Harry stood up and said he would. Nell stood as Samantha turned. Harry had his back to her and, with the palm of his hand, grabbed Nell's hair, pulled her towards him, and kissed her forever. He pressed hard against her, and the kiss went on for a little longer. Then they unjoined, and he kissed her on the lips. Just a peck, and it was exactly what she wanted.

Samantha was gone. Nell didn't see where she went to the pool or back out the door. Nell wanted her to see. "Did she see anything?"

They sat back down again.

Harry put Nell's number in his phone and texted her. I will keep in touch.

"I will, too. We have to do this properly. The government will knock me back if they have any suspicion that we planned this. There will be interviews, papers signed, and a whole lot more. But I will appreciate you so much if you do this."

Harry attempted to get up and go.

"Sit down, Harry. I said two things I wanted."

Harry felt uneasy.

"Yeh, what's the other?"

Nell hesitated but knew exactly what she wanted. More than anything. More than oxygen.

I want you and me to have a baby. Starting from now. I want one now. And I promise you I will marry you. If we don't try to have a baby, the deal is off.

The deal will not go ahead unless I get this wish. I mean it, Harry. It is your ticket to live in Australia.

MEAT AND THREE VEG

BY JANE E. WOOD

One Saturday lunchtime, two young women stood on the forecourt of the western tower of the Princes Gate precinct in Flinders Street. They scanned the full height of its fifteen floors, taking in the details of the façade as it was the first time either of them had been that close to it, even though it had been built ten years previously in 1967. Ten of its floors were occupied by the Gas and Fuel Corporation, their destination.

"Not the most attractive building, is it?" Susie volunteered, an opinion many shared.

"I quite like it," her friend and work colleague, Louise, disagreed. "Anyhow, let's get in there. I'm really looking forward to these classes."

Louise and Susie had enrolled in a series of French 'cordon bleu' cooking classes to be conducted in the kitchens on the ground floor of the Gas and Fuel offices. Louise, who was married, wanted to extend her repertoire of cooking skills. Susie, who lived with her parents, wanted to find out if there was a world of food beyond meat and three veg., which was, by far, the most common meal served in her family home.

Her father liked his meat grilled, fried or roasted, his potatoes deep fried, roasted or boiled and his greens of peas or beans boiled. There was no 'medium rare' in his house; it was only 'well done,' and that applied to vegetables as well. Her mother liked to serve offal, too, such as tripe and Lamb's Fry, which her father only just tolerated.

Louise and Susie made their way into the building and easily located the demonstration kitchen. Chairs were arranged around a large bench, cooktop, oven, and appliances that were all gas-fueled, of course. Their instructor introduced herself and began the lesson.

Three hours later, Susie and Louise were back on the forecourt, bubbling with the excitement of what they'd just been introduced to; French cuisine!

"I can't wait to make it myself!" Louise enthused, confident her husband would welcome new recipes.

"I'm going to make it too." But Susie didn't sound quite as confident as Louise; she knew her father would be less than enthusiastic about a variation on his usual fare.

Back at home, Susie shared her day's experiences with her mother and asked if she could make the dishes. Delighted that Susie was keen to replicate the recipes, her mother agreed to buy the ingredients the next time she was at the shops.

Several days later, Susie had the chance to dazzle with her new knowledge. She made every dish introduced to her on the previous Saturday, beginning with the soup. Susie carefully placed a bowl of Orange Spinach soup in front of her father.

"There you go, Dad. First course."

He looked at Susie, looked at the bowl, glared at Susie, and grimaced. "What is that? It's GREEN!"

"Just try it, Dad. It's just a vegetable soup."

"Doesn't look like your mother's vegetable soup," he grumbled.

"Please, Dad." Susie didn't want to beg, but …

He took a deep breath, lowered his spoon into the bowl and lifted the green concoction to his mouth.

"I can smell orange. How can it smell of orange and be green at the same time?" he growled.

"Come on, please, Dad."

With his nose wrinkled, he took a small sip and then another mouthful, which Susie saw as a positive sign. Until he put his spoon down and huffed, "It's too green. That's enough for me. What's next?"

Next was Supreme De Volaille Farce (stuffed chicken breast) accompanied by Orange Stuffed Potatoes (stuffed potatoes, who knew?) and Tomatoes Clamart. Now, full of trepidation after her father's reaction to the soup, Susie gingerly placed the plate of food in front of her father.

"Hmm. What's this?"

Susie told him.

"Orange again! In the potatoes? Why?" He was astounded.

"It's the recipe, Dad. Please have some."

Her father tasted a small portion of each item, trying one at a time, and his facial expression was a clear indication of his opinion. He surprised himself by enjoying the chicken but wasn't keen on the rest. Still, Susie felt she'd had a small victory. Her mother loved it all (especially the fact that she hadn't done any of the cooking).

Over the next month, Susie presented Galantine of Duck, Seafood Lasagne and Filet de Boeuf Clamart accompanied by a variety of vegetables, all of which seemed to be stuffed or served with sauces or both.

He tolerated tasting them all stoically, some he even thought acceptable. By far, his greatest (and possibly only real) enjoyment of Susie's new knowledge was the exceptional desserts that were presented to end each meal, Passionfruit Soufflé and Crepe En Surpris being his favourite.

She was so pleased with the progress she perceived in her father's acceptance of French cuisine that when her friend, Louise, suggested they enrol at a Chinese cooking school for a four-week course, Susie was all for it. A famous Chinese chef and restauranteur was taking the classes, and the location was quite near where the two women lived.

Excited, Susie couldn't wait to tell her mother, who was again supportive and pleased with her daughter's newfound interest in cooking.

"But you know this really might be a stretch too far for your father. I can't see him eating it. I know he tried everything that you cooked for him on the 'cordon bleu' menus, but that doesn't mean he liked it." she warned.

Not deterred, Susie sat down next to her father at the dinner table that night.

"Dad, I've enrolled in another cooking class.," she bubbled. Her father's face grew pale, but Susie failed to notice. "A Chinese cooking class. It's for four weeks, so I'll be cooking for you once a week again. Isn't that great?"

Her father's skin was no longer pale; it was sheet white. "You're going to cook Chinese for us for four weeks.?" he managed to splutter.

"Oh, Dad, you managed the French cuisine, you'll be fine." She hugged him and headed for her bedroom.

In the first week of lessons, Susie learned how to steam rice, which she was careful to serve along with the stir-fried chicken and vegetables when she tried the new recipes at home. She felt she'd done very well for her first effort with Chinese cuisine and was proud of what she placed in front of her father at dinner time.

"What is it?" her father asked, pushing the contents on his plate around with a fork.

"Stir-fried chicken, vegetables and rice. It's just meat and three veg Dad, only all mixed in together, and with seven veg if you count the ginger and garlic," she enthused.

"Ginger!" he looked at Susie, alarmed. "Your aunt makes cakes with ginger. It doesn't look anything like her Ginger Fluff sponge."

He turned back to the meal.

"What are they?" her father asked, full of suspicion.

"Those are bamboo shoots, and those are water chestnuts."

He speared the previously unheard-of vegetables and took a nibble.

"They're crunchy!" And a moment later. "And quite tasty, but you've given me too much rice."

"Just give it a try, Dad. It can't taste worse than tripe," Susie encouraged her father.

He pushed his fork into a piece of chicken, hesitated a moment and then popped it into his mouth. He savoured it and passed judgement.

"Oh! I quite like that." And he went back for more. "But I'm not eating that rice."

That was week one.

In the following lesson, Susie was taught three main courses, so she cooked dinner three nights that week.

All three meals contained Chinese dried mushrooms, amongst other new ingredients, so her father would sample new foods each night. He tasted black beans, barbecued roast pork (Chinese style), bean shoots and oyster sauce, amongst other new flavours, textures and smells. As the weeks went on, he stopped questioning the contents, but the rice, when served, was still ignored.

At the end of the four classes, Susie was delighted to discover that there was a more advanced course she could undertake. She enrolled and couldn't wait to tell her mother and father.

Her mother was again delighted; she enjoyed the different cuisine that was now being served in the house, and she was thrilled with her daughter's skill development.

"So what do you think, Dad? Are you up for some new recipes?" Susie waited for her father's response.

"I guess so," he said but looked a little nervous.

The objective of the new Chinese cooking classes was to teach the students how to create a banquet of five or six courses, all recipes being more complicated and complex than those from the first series. More sauces and more flavours were introduced, and Susie was delighted to produce the dishes for her family. After the first week's lesson, when she placed five different courses on the dinner table, her father asked her to name them. He helped himself to a little of each and, satisfied with what he tasted, shortly afterwards went back for more.

"What do you think, Dad?" Susie hoped her father's second helping indicated a favourable opinion.

"Mmm, I like this one. Is this the Szechuan Chicken? This is very tasty. But I'm not eating the rice." And he didn't.

Impressed that her father had remembered the name of the dish, Susie confirmed he was indeed correct. She was relieved that he'd actually liked the dish and hoped there'd be other dishes in the coming weeks that he'd approve of.

When Susie's father sat down at the dinner table for the second week's banquet, he rubbed his hands together in gleeful anticipation. He asked, "What's on the menu then? Is there any more of that delicious Szechuan Chicken that we had last week?"

Her cheeks glowing from the compliment, Susie said, "No, Dad, but I can certainly make that for you again. I think you'll really enjoy tonight's satay prawns, though."

"Sounds good. Let's get started then." He tucked into his bowl of Velvet Chicken and Sweetcorn soup and then couldn't make up his mind which to try next; the Pork Spare Ribs or Satay Prawns. He compromised by taking some of each.

"Delicious!" was his judgement when the meal was over.

Susie exchanged a look with her mother, who could only smile at the change in attitude.

Her father greeted the next three banquets with genuine enthusiasm. He didn't enjoy everything; the Mandarin Duck he didn't rate. Perhaps its orange flavouring reminded him too much of the Spinach Orange soup served months previously.

And that was it. Chinese and French cuisine was officially on the menu at Susie's family home. Over the next seven years, while Susie continued to live in her family home, she cooked at least once a week. Meat and three veg were not banished, but her mother also became more adventurous. Chow Mein, Spaghetti Bolognaise, Curried sausages and Apricot Chicken found their way onto the table, amongst other dishes.

Ironically, the last meal Susie was to share with her father before his death, some thirty years later, was a takeaway from his favourite Thai restaurant.

But he still didn't eat the rice.

AQUA PROFONDA

BY LAUREN MCCARTHY

"Let go of the wall and lean back," said Elise. "If you know how to float on your back, they will put you in the middle class when we have swimming lessons at school this year. I am right behind you, and I can catch you."

"I'm scared. What if I sink?" Adriana's teeth chattered, and it was not just from the cold water.

"You won't sink. I will hold you, but you can also just put your feet down if you get too scared. We can stand here easily, so don't be scared. Elise reassured her friend. "We will get you out of that baby class. You can do it, Adriana."

Elise had attempted the Aussie Crawl the year before during their school swimming lessons held at the Fitzroy Baths during the first term. Elise looked longingly towards the deep end of the pool, where there was a diving board. All the big kids left their towels on the back brick wall where the huge painted sign DANGER DEEP WATER and, directly underneath it, those strange words - AQUA PROFUNDA.

"One day, I'll get there." she thought, envious of the kids in the deep end.

Adriana and Elise were nearly eight years old and had been next-door neighbours since they were three. Before starting school, the two of them had started talking through a knot hole in their shared backyard fence. It was the 1970's and kids played in their streets. Adriana and Elise lived on a small side street of thirty-plus houses in North Fitzroy, a working-class area with tiny houses with postage-stamp-sized backyards. Their houses faced the backyards of homes on the other side of the street, and there were only two or three residents with cars living there. Few cars and no traffic turned their street into a kid's playground during the day. Their backyard friendship blossomed, and soon, Adriana and Elise were playing outside in the street; Adriana was closely supervised by her mother and brothers, and Elise was loosely supervised by her older sister, who had her own friends who congregated in their tiny street. Soon, they had other little Italian girls, Gina and Mirella, who were being minded by their Nonna on the corner of their street, join Adriana and Elise when they played outside.

"I'm holding you, Adriana, and you are so light in the water. It's like holding a feather." Elise enthused with a huge grin. "C'mon, Adriana, isn't this better than being stuck at home when it's so hot?"

Adriana was fearing for her life, shivering with her teeth chattering, "B-b-but w-w-what if I s-sink?" Adriana started to regret insisting she should be allowed to go to the Baths with her brothers, but Elise promised she would teach her to swim so she could advance in school swimming classes in Grade Three. Her brothers were free to roam, play, and explore while she was stuck at home, and she was only able to play three to four houses on each side of her house under the watchful eyes of her Mum.

Adriana and Elise got out of the pool and grabbed their towels off the burning hot concrete, splashing water on their feet so there was a cool spot to stand.

"Adriana, look, the baby pool's almost empty. We should go in there.

That's where my sister taught me to float!"

Adriana was so relieved; the water to her waist was deeper than she liked, but she didn't want to disappoint Elise, who was determined to help her get into the middle swim class at school this year. Adriana was grateful that her friend had offered to help her.

The girls were really looking forward to Grade Three. They would move to the new building, maybe in an upstairs classroom; the first term meant swimming classes twice a week for a couple of weeks.

Elise was disappointed that she and Adriana weren't sharing a classroom this year. She was a bit miffed that her school best friend, Jane, would be in the same class as Adriana and Mirella. Elise would be on her own, but she consoled herself by thinking about recess and being able to play with Adriana and Mirella after school. Elise was puzzled when Adriana told her she hated school swimming lessons.

"All we do is hold our noses and put our heads under the water, but I still can't swim. The water is freezing, and I don't want to go. The teacher keeps putting me on the same level, so I don't learn anything new."

Adriana was amazed that she was allowed to go with her brothers and Elise. She was thankful that her older brothers argued with their parents on her behalf and that she was allowed to go. She was the only girl and youngest child in her family, and her mother was very protective of her. Her Mum and Dad moved to Australia from Italy when her older brother was born. Her Dad knew some English, but her Mum wanted only to talk to other Italian ladies. She would get upset when her brothers tried to teach her common English words.

It was a real adventure for Adriana; the first time, apart from school, she was able to be with her friend without her Mum close by. Her big brothers were allowed to play at the park in the Edinburgh Gardens, but she was only ever allowed to play with Elise and the other little girls on their street.

The walk to the Fitzroy Baths was familiar once they got to the park. It was the same way they walked from school for swimming lessons. On their way, they stopped at the playground, and Elise and Adriana braved the big slide, encouraging each other to climb the ladder to the top. The metal slide was hot, and the girls decided one slide was enough, proud that they had gone down it on their own but rubbing the backs of their thighs that felt raw after a hot slide down.

Adriana's brothers were ready to head to the Baths, so they walked through the shady Oak trees, past the Rotunda before following the wide path that ran behind the old Fitzroy Footy Ground and between the disused railroad tracks. Elise shuddered as they neared the Pink Bridge that crossed the rail tracks, a shortcut to Clifton Hill. She looked up at those steep stairs with dread, noting the missing planks on every second or third step and was thankful they didn't have to cross it today.

Adriana's brothers walked the two girls to the traffic lights on the busy corner of Alexandra Parade and Brunswick Street to cross over to the Fitzroy Baths. This was the same way they walked from school. Elise was very relieved because her older sister wouldn't walk the extra distance to the lights. When she took Elise to the pool, they just ran across Alexandra Parade dodging cars.

The girls put their towels on the bench seat in the baby pool area. Elise ran to the deeper part and jumped in, and Adriana called out, "Don't run; you could get chucked out!"

Adriana used the steps at the shallow end and was pleased that the water wasn't as icy as the big pool. Elise was like a fish and splashed her way to Adriana.

"I know, let's pretend we can swim! I'll show you; it's easy!" said Elise, lying on her tummy in water so shallow that only half of her body was in water. She used her arms like she was doing the Aussie Crawl, and as her arms went underwater, she grabbed the bottom of the pool with her hands to propel herself forward.

"Now you try." she squealed. Adriana was amazed that she could do this and that she was able to keep up with her friend 'pretend swimming', only Adriana stopped halfway, daunted by the deeper water. She saw Elise continue to the end of the pool with her head craning out of the water. The girls splashed and played for a while.

"Well?" asked Adriana.

"Oh yeah! I forgot I was having so much fun." laughed Elise. "Let's go down the other end where it's a little deeper."

Elise wondered how she was going to teach Adriana to float. The little girls were kneeling at the bottom of the pool, and the water came just below their chests.

"Adriana, you can hold me in the water like we did in the big pool."

Adriana's disbelieving look said it all.

Elise laughed, knowing Adriana thought she was too heavy to carry in the water.

"You're not heavy! This is easy, like you're a bambina." chuckled Adriana, surprised by Elise's buoyant weight in the water.

"Now look at what I'm doing," instructed Elise as she straightened her body, lifting her hips slightly. "Take your arms away now," Elise ordered her friend. Elise floated in the water while Adriana stared on in admiration.

"Now you can be my Bambi…..what was that word you said?" asked Elise.

"Bambina, you nearly got it", giggled Adriana.

Elise, determined to impress her friend who was teaching her some Italian, barked, "Vieni qua bambina!" She hoped she got it right.

"Molto Bene Elise. Come here, baby." Adriana translated as she waded over to Elise, who was kneeling in the water with her arms out.

Elise scooped her up, cooing over her and giggling as if she were indeed a little baby. She then told Adriana to lie flat while supporting her.

"Keep laying straight and try to lift your bum a little," murmured Elise, keeping her voice low. She then loosened her arm under Adriana's legs.

"You're gonna get this Adriana. Your legs are staying up on their own. Make sure you keep your chest lifted," Elise said while loosening her arms from under her friend's back but not quite letting go. "Adriana, you can't sink. This water is too shallow." She removed one arm slowly and then the other, holding her breath, hoping this would work.

Elise let out her breath with a huge grin on her face. Adriana was floating, with her eyes squeezed tightly shut and a determined purse in her mouth. Adriana's eyes opened to a loud whistle, and clapping, startled, she splashed onto her knees in the water.

"Well done sis! I didn't learn that until I was in Grade Four," shouted Tony.

Adriana glowed under the praise of her brother; he was two years older, and he generally ignored her. He wandered off to the big pool to shadow their older brother Fab, who was doing bombs from the middle of the pool near the five-foot marker and ladder. The girls continued practising Adriana's new skill in the baby pool until Adriana could float on her back without Elise having to hold her first.

They got out of the pool, grabbed their towels and went to sit on the concrete spectator stand steps to watch Fab and Tony do bombs before the lifeguard yelled at them to stop. Tony was closer to the three-foot depth marker and ladder, not being as tall as twelve-year-old Fab. For two thin boys, they sure made a huge splash, leaping into the water with their knees up, trying to bomb water on the little girls watching from the bottom step.

"Ouch! The concrete is burning my legs and bum." squealed Adriana, leaping to her feet.

Elise laughed, not bothered because her towel was underneath her legs.

"Let's go back to the baby pool. It's still empty, and we can pretend we're rich and own it," suggested Adriana. They started to skip but quickly changed to a fast walk after spying on the lifeguard, making his way towards the boys doing bombs.

Adriana perfected floating on her back in the little pool in water so shallow that Elise kept ordering, "It's cheating if you let your bum touch the bottom of the pool."

Elise was amazed at her friend's chattiness and confidence today. Adriana was often timid and quiet and sometimes relied on Elise to speak up for her in class. She played quietly with Elise when her Mum was close by and was a little louder when Gina and Mirella visited their Nonna and came to play with them or when her Mum went indoors to check something in her kitchen. Elise realised that Adriana preferred to float on her back in water knee-deep and decided to continue their lesson at that depth. They splashed around, and Elise showed Adriana how to hold her breath and puff her face instead of holding her nose when bobbing her head underwater.

They stayed in the shallows, and the sun and water glistened on their tanned skin. The girls played a new game that Elise ghoulishly called "dead man drowning", showing Adriana how to float on her front with her head in the water.

"Hold your breath the way I showed you, lay on top of the water, and hold your arms and legs straight with your face in the water. You can put your knees down to the bottom of the pool if you get scared or need to breathe." coaxed Elise. They played and practised until Adriana was no longer afraid; she didn't float for very long, but she mastered the technique.

Both girls were very tired after the long walk home after their fun afternoon at the baths. Normally a picky eater, Adriana devoured her dinner when she got home. She excitedly told her Mum that she learned to swim.

Tony, talking rapidly in Italian to their Mum, said to her that Adriana had only learned to float. He may have also taken credit for teaching her. Adriana let it pass but told her Mum that she hoped to advance in swimming lessons when they started at school while she was getting into her pyjamas. Her mother was amazed; her little girl ate all her dinner, and she was going to bed without the normal fuss.

Nonna and some of the Signora's with children stood around in groups on the footpath in Nicholson Street after Mass at St Brigid's. Their boys and girls were in the special Sunday school classes to prepare them for their upcoming Holy Communions after Easter. Nonna had been making suggestions to her daughter-in-law about Mirella's communion dress – she wanted her granddaughter to be the most *bella raggaza* receiving her Holy Communion at St. Brigid's that year. Perhaps Mirella should forgo swimming lessons this year so the extra money could be used for her bridal dress, shoes and veil, Nonna suggested to Mirella's Mum.

St. Brigid's was a community hub for local Catholics, regardless of their cultural backgrounds. Eight years earlier, during the late 1960s, the Scalabrinian Fathers were introduced into the parish, making it a multicultural community with an Italian Parish priest. The Scalabrinian mission was to maintain the Catholic faith and practice among Italian emigrants in their new countries. The Australian Catholics, many of whom came from Irish backgrounds, were accepting of this change and felt privileged to have an Italian parish priest because, to them, he was a link to the Vatican in Rome.

The Italian men had already left after chatting about the best Saturday to hold *Passata Day*; some grew their own tomatoes, and they were eager to commence as their tomato harvest was abundant. The families that didn't have a vegetable garden ordered crates of fresh tomatoes from the Nicholson Street Green Grocer – he understood the importance of keeping this tradition alive, coming from an Italian background as well.

The families would get together during a hot weekend in February. A day was spent stewing tomatoes, squeezing them and bottling them for the year to come to ensure a ready supply of passata to make sugo or pasta sauce. It was a festive tradition they brought with them to Australia, and those with extended families came together each year and enjoyed the hot, sweaty work – sometimes with music from home. The Signoras would prepare antipasto and a signature pasta dish, and the men would enjoy a glass of Foster's, laughing about starting their bottle collections for next year's Passata Day.

The children didn't appreciate that they were being shown traditions from their parents' experience growing up in Italy, listening to songs from their youth captured in scratchy vinyl and played on portable turntables. They remembered the festive air, music, and food. Some of the signoras, after only one glass of *Vino*, would dance to the music, remembering their youth in Italian villages and cities. They would become raucous, singing along to Tintarella de Luna; in unison, they would turn in time to the music, all pointing to their tanned children chanting the line "*tintarella color latte*", giggling in the waning evening sunlight.

The Australian Catholic mums also briefly chatted about Holy Communion outfits for their children but would generally have to rush back home to attend their traditional Sunday Roast dinners, which usually consisted of a leg of lamb, a tasty and affordable cut of meat. Some of the younger Aussie mums were starting to serve salads with their Sunday Roasts during summer. They used leftover meat for sandwich lunches during the week. Their own mothers were horrified, as only roast vegetables would do, and leftover meat was only ever used in Shepherd's Pie, which was usually served for Monday or Tuesday evening meals.

The Aussie Catholic men also stood in groups but would move closer to Alexandra Parade to give the Italian Signoras space to chat freely. Their discussions centred on the upcoming footy season; most were Fitzroy supporters. However, some were starting to follow Collingwood, Richmond and Carlton since the Fitzroy VFL team stopped playing games at the Brunswick Street oval. They chose teams whose grounds were close enough to either walk to or catch a train or tram to.

Others discussed the impending State Election, and although many of them were traditional Labour Party voters – they thought Rupert Hamer's experience was preferred to Clyde Holding, who was perceived as a social radical. Some of the men would pop in to have a pot of beer during the morning session at one of the many local pubs before heading home for a big Sunday lunch.

*

Adriana was thrilled – she was no longer in the bubs swimming group. The wide grin on her face said it all as she lined up with a yellow kickboard at the shallow end of the big pool. She made eye contact with Elise, who was about to get into the water near the five-foot marker and ladder. Elise's grin matched Adriana's, and both girls pumped their fists into the air.

"Miss, I already know how to put my head in the water," explained Adriana to Miss Gibson, who was teaching Adriana's group. They had spent the previous lesson holding onto the edge of the pool while kicking their legs.

Adriana daringly put her face in the water, holding her breath and puffing her face. Looking around, she noticed she was the only one in her group doing this. During the middle of today's lesson, they were all given yellow kickboards and were instructed to hold them with their arms out straight, chins lifted out of the water, and start kicking. Some of the more adventurous kids were making great progress in the water, enjoying the splashes as they made their way to the other side of the pool.

Miss Gibson spent time with some of the more timid members of the group, trying to build their confidence. Towards the end of the lesson, she explained that they would be putting their faces in the water with their kickboards during their next lesson the following day. Miss Gibson was shocked to hear the confidence in Adriana's voice, as she was considered to be one of the very shy Italian girls in Grade Three.

"Why don't you show us." encouraged Miss Gibson.

Adriana, with a determined look on her face, grabbed her board, put her face in the water and started kicking furiously, making powerful splashes for such a small girl. She didn't think she'd gone very far before taking her face out of the water for a breath, but when Adriana looked behind, she saw that she had made it a third of the way across the pool.

The kids in Adriana's group started clapping, and she heard Elise shout, "Go, Adriana!!" from the middle of the pool.

The two next-door neighbour girls walked back to school with their arms interlinked, happily chatting and giggling, both proud of Adriana's achievement during swimming lessons. Mirella was missing from their little trio because her parents had decided against her attending swim classes.

*

One Sunday after Easter, Elise sat on her front doorstep observing Adriana's family, dressed for Mass, waiting for Mirella's family to join them for the short walk to St. Brigids. Elise was amazed and a little jealous when she saw the beautiful white dresses and veils that Adriana and Mirella were wearing. They looked like beautiful little brides about to be married. Elise jumped up from the step and approached Adriana.

"Wow, Adriana! You look so beautiful in your dress," exclaimed Elise.

Adriana blushed at this compliment from her friend. "I wish you could come to Mass with us, Elise. I am going on a picnic with Mirella's family after church. I will tell you all about it when we get home." Adriana promised.

In her Nonna's eyes, Mirella was indeed the most beautiful girl to receive her first Holy Communion that day. From her shiny, curly brown hair under her veil, the beautifully embroidered white dress, and her immaculate brand-new white shoes, she was a picture of perfection.

After the ceremonial proceedings, the first Holy Communion kids stood in groups in the church courtyard for photos taken with popular Kodak Instamatic cameras. The sun was shining, so there was no need for a flash to be added to this warm, bright April day. There was an organic mingling of Italian and Australian families, with all the women smiling, pointing and admiring the little girls in their beautiful white dresses.

Adriana was feeling a little shy about going on a celebration picnic with

Mirella's family to celebrate their first Holy Communion. Their families were friends, but Adriana's family wouldn't be attending as they were going to Edwardes Park in Reservoir, and Mirella's family station wagon would only fit so many people. The girls were allowed to stay in their pretty dresses and squished into the back seat with Gina and Roberto, Mirella's older sister and younger brother. Mirella's parents and Auntie Luisa were in the middle of the front bench seat. Jajimo, only two years old, was on his mother's lap.

After a delicious lunch comprising of crusty Vienna bread brushed with olive oil and passata and an assortment of fresh and pickled vegetables, the children rushed to the playground, racing to be the first ones to get to the swings. Adriana, not as quick as the others, sat up high on the climbing equipment with her legs swinging. She was the only person who saw Jajimo, alone on the small jetty that jutted into the weir named Edwardes Lake. Adriana climbed down the play equipment and started running towards the grownups to tell them, but she quickly changed course and headed towards the lake when she heard the splash of Jajimo falling in.

Adriana instinctively raced into the water, forgetting about her beautiful white dress. Although it was only waist deep, she had to wade through the reeds. She only just reached Jajimo as he started flailing his arms, sinking into the water, which was too deep for a little toddler to stand. Adriana stretched and grabbed him by the starched collar of his shirt, yanking him towards her and then cradling him in her arms. His screams and crying roused the grownups and children who were at the edge of the lake as she waded out of the water with Mirella's baby brother.

Mirella's mother was crying tears of relief, guilt, and fear of what might have happened if Adriana had not seen Jajimo when she did. There was a change of clothes for Jajimo, but poor Adriana had to make do with the picnic blanket wrapped around her dripping and no longer purely white dress. Six-year-old Roberto was in fits of laughter, pointing to Adriana's mud-splashed Communion dress and shoes and her dirty mud-splashed face. The grownups and girls were all subdued by their horror of Jajimo falling into the water.

Adriana was in tears as they piled back into the car. Roberto was relegated to the front seat, and Auntie Luisa sat next to Adriana in the back seat, trying to comfort her.

"You were very brave today, Adriana and you should be proud of yourself. Not only were you observant, but you bravely went into the water to save my little nephew. Thank you." she stated in her calm school-teacher voice.

"But my mum will kill me when she sees my dress!" wailed Adriana. "She was saving all year so that I could have a beautiful dress for my Holy Communion."

"Don't worry, Adriana, I will explain to your Mama how heroic you were today." declared Luisa. "Now, please tell me how you became so brave around water."

Adriana explained that they had just finished swim classes at school last week and that she had lost her fear of being around water when Elise taught her to "pretend" swim and float at the Fitzroy Baths during the Summer Holidays.

Luisa frowned and started talking rapidly in Italian to her brother and sister-in-law. The adults were talking very fast, but the girls knew the grownups were discussing swimming lessons and that Luisa was upset, but they were too tired to listen closely.

Adriana was feeling a little better about her dress. She was amazed that she did not hesitate to try to save Jajimo when she heard him fall into the lake.

Elise, reading an Enid Blyton *Famous Five* book on her sunny front doorstep, saw the station wagon pull up in front of Adriana's house. All of them spilt out of the car as Adriana's mother opened their front door and shrieked loudly in Italian when she saw the state of Adriana's dress.

Luisa, a modern young Italian woman who was training as a teacher, spoke calmly to Adriana's Mum and explained that Adriana had saved Jajimo from drowning. She suggested that they meet at her mother's house on the corner of the street once Adriana had been bathed and changed into fresh clothes.

Afterwards, Adriana and Elise sat on the footpath between their houses, where Adriana told Elise all about her adventurous day. She quickly skimmed over the details of receiving her first Holy Communion as she realised Elise had no idea about Adriana's new commitment to Jesus, their lord and Saviour.

"What!!! You just ran into the water with your bride's dress?" Elise asked in disbelief.

"I didn't think. I just did it," explained Adriana. "You should have seen Luisa yelling at her mother for making Mirella's mum stop her nieces and nephew from doing swim classes this year!" laughed Adriana. "Mirella's mum was crying and hugging me and my mum."

Elise's eyes were wide, listening to Adriana's adventures.

"Luisa is going to take us all on a picnic to the Baths once they open again in November, and I told her that you have to come too because you showed me how to swim." gushed Adriana. "My mum is not angry with me about my dress and told me she was proud of me when we walked home."

Elise couldn't quite believe that anybody would dare to yell at Mirella's Nonna. Mirella's grandmother was feared by the kids who played in their street, always dressed in widow's black with a fierce and angry air about her. "I am proud of you too, Adriana." declared Elise, putting her arm around her friend's shoulder.

*

Towards the end of Grade Three in late November, both Adriana and Elise were invited by her Auntie Luisa to Mirella's family picnic at the Baths. They had a fun afternoon splashing and playing in the baby pool.

Luisa asked Elise how she taught Adriana to float last summer. They all played, carrying each other in the buoyant water. Gina was brave enough to try floating on her back, and all of the kids gained water confidence through play. Luisa supervised Elise and Adriana at the shallow end of the big pool when they wanted to show off their skills in the water.

"I wish the Baths stayed open all year." lamented Elise. She was becoming a confident swimmer and hoped to be able to compete in next year's House Swimming competition held during the first term.

"Elise, the pool will be freezing cold in winter," explained Luisa.

"I don't care; I'd just swim until I warmed up." Elise boasted. "If I practice enough, I will be able to swim up the deep end." Elise read the sign DANGER DEEP WATER but stumbled, trying to pronounce the words underneath.

Luisa laughed as she pronounced Aqua Profonda perfectly. "You don't know what it means, Elise? It is a mixture of Latin and Italian words, but essentially, it translates to Deep Water," explained Luisa.

*

The iconic Fitzroy Baths – On the heritage listed sign at the deep end of the main pool, the words' DANGER DEEP WATER' and underneath 'AQUA PROFONDA' are painted in black on the white painted brick wall which runs along Young Street.

First opened in 1908, the Fitzroy Pool was saved from closure in the 1990s following a spirited community campaign. The pool, or Baths as they were affectionately known before the 1990s, became the focus of a community campaign when it was threatened with closure in 1994 by the Commissioners of the City of Yarra. The vocal "Save Our Pool!" group were successful in staging spectacular protests in the drained pool with huge media coverage that honed in on the diverse backgrounds of the protesters. The Commissioners reversed their decision. This outdoor pool services Fitzroy and surrounding communities, which include high-rise Housing Commission Flats in Fitzroy and Carlton, giving all, including the ever-changing migrant and low-income kids, the opportunity to learn to swim.

At the deep end of the big pool, the words' DANGER DEEP WATER' and underneath 'AQUA PROFONDA' are painted black on the white perimeter wall. This sign was painted in the early 1950s at the initiative of the pool manager, who was constantly rescuing migrant children from the deep end of the pool. He asked an Italian friend what the words for "deep water" were in Italian and had them painted at the deep end. The sign clearly demonstrates a rare testament and tangible example that the European migrants were becoming accepted members of their local communities. It is also an acknowledgement of the cultural impact of the mass migration program in post-World War II Australia.

The sign is still a symbolic reminder that the pool is a place where the diverse population of inner Melbourne can gather together on equal terms.

FLAVOURS OF A CITY

BY RODERIC GRIGSON

The aroma of sizzling lamb skewers mingling with the smoky scent of spices wafted through the air as Sophie strolled down the narrow lane in Melbourne's CBD. She had come to the city years ago to study architecture but had stayed for the food. Melbourne, she often joked with her friends, wasn't just a city—it was a feast. Each street and neighbourhood told a story, not just of migration and settlement but of adaptation, innovation, and celebration.

Sophie, whose parents had migrated from Ceylon decades ago, grew up in a home where food was a constant presence. Her mother's fish curry, fragrant with tamarind and curry leaves, and her father's love for eating string hoppers for Sunday breakfast were staples of her childhood. And then there was tea—always tea. Ceylon tea had been an unwavering presence in her home, brewed strong and aromatic, served with milk and sugar, or spiced with ginger for special occasions. Sophie had inherited her parents' love for tea, and no meal felt complete without a steaming cup.

Sophie decided to set herself a mission for the week: to eat her way across the city, discovering the cultural origins behind the dishes that defined Melbourne's rich culinary landscape. She mapped out her journey, starting in Chinatown on Monday, heading to Lygon Street on Tuesday, and visiting the multicultural heart of Footscray on Wednesday. For the rest of the week, she planned to explore the newer culinary hubs in Tarneit, Epping, Springvale, Clyde, and the vibrant Greek enclave of Oakleigh.

As she embarked on her week-long food journey, Sophie couldn't help but compare the dishes she tried to the rich culinary heritage she had grown up with. Sophie's first stop was Chinatown, a bustling hub of red lanterns and fragrant eateries that had stood the test of time. Established during the 1850s gold rush, Chinatown was one of the oldest in the world. She slipped into a tiny restaurant that had been serving Cantonese food since the 1970s. The owner, Mrs. Lin, greeted her with a warm smile.

"You must try the xiao long bao," Mrs. Lin suggested, pointing to the menu. "And don't forget the Peking duck. These recipes have been in my family for generations."

"How do you make the broth so flavourful?" Sophie asked, intrigued.

Mrs. Lin chuckled. "Ah, that's a secret! But I will tell you this—patience and good ingredients. The soup dumplings are a labour of love."

Sophie savoured the delicate soup dumplings, marvelling at how the thin wrapper held the rich, savoury broth within. She thought about the Chinese labourers who had arrived during the gold rush, bringing with them their culinary traditions. Over time, these dishes have become Melbourne staples, their flavours subtly evolving to incorporate local ingredients.

As Sophie ate, Mrs Lin shared stories of her family's migration. "My grandparents came here with little more than hope," she said. "They worked hard, but food was always a way to feel connected to home. Now, we see people from all cultures enjoying our dishes. That's the beauty of Melbourne."

Sophie nodded, thinking of her own mother's stories of bringing spices to Australia and how her parents had adapted their meals to include local produce like sweet potatoes and zucchinis. When she got home that evening, she brewed herself a strong cup of Ceylon tea, its familiar aroma filling the room, and reflected on how food and drink were universal comforts.

On Tuesday, Sophie made her way to Lygon Street in Carlton, the epicentre of Melbourne's Italian community. The street buzzed with life, its cafés spilling onto the pavement, where patrons sipped espressos and indulged in decadent gelato. Italian migrants had settled here in the mid-20th century, bringing with them their love of food and family.

Sophie stepped into a trattoria renowned for its wood-fired pizzas. Enzo, the chef and owner, was a second-generation Italian-Australian. "The pizza margherita is our pride," he said, sliding a bubbling pie from the oven. "But you must also try the gnocchi. My nonna's recipe."

"Nonna must have been an amazing cook," Sophie said as she spooned the gnocchi onto her plate.

"She was," Enzo replied with a smile. "She always said, 'You don't just cook with your hands, you cook with your heart.' That's why every dish is special."

The gnocchi melted in Sophie's mouth, its pillowy texture paired with a rich, slow-cooked tomato sauce. As she ate, Enzo explained how Italian migrants had transformed Melbourne's food culture. "Before my grandparents arrived, pasta wasn't common here," he said. "Now, you'll find it on almost every menu. And coffee? Italians gave Melbourne its obsession with good coffee."

As she sipped her espresso, Sophie thought about how her father had introduced her to Sri Lankan black coffee, brewed strong and sweet, often served alongside spicy short eats like patties and cutlets. Yet even as she enjoyed the espresso, she longed for the comfort of a cup of tea—its strength balanced by the creamy sweetness she loved. She promised herself she'd make some as soon as she got home.

As the sun rose on Wednesday, Sophie set out for Footscray, one of Melbourne's most diverse neighbourhoods. Here, Ethiopian, Sudanese, Middle Eastern, and Southeast Asian communities thrived side by side, their culinary traditions blending into a vibrant mosaic.

Sophie wandered through the market, where stalls offered everything from Ethiopian injera to Somali samosas. She stopped at a small Ethiopian café, where the owner, Amina, welcomed her warmly. A platter of injera arrived, accompanied by spiced lentils, slow-cooked stews, and sautéed greens.

"In Ethiopia, food is meant to be shared," Amina said, tearing a piece of injera and scooping up a bit of stew. Sophie followed suit, savouring the tangy flatbread and the complex spices.

"This is incredible," Sophie said. "Do you make everything yourself?"

Amina nodded. "Of course. My mother taught me how to cook. She said food is not just for the stomach; it's for the soul."

Sophie's final stop was a Middle Eastern bakery, where she indulged in baklava and sipped strong Turkish coffee. The owner, Yusef, spoke of his family's migration from Lebanon. "Food is memory," he said. "Every bite takes me back to the hills of my childhood."

As Sophie bit into the honey-soaked baklava, she thought about the Ceylonese, now Sri Lankan, sweets her mother would make for New Year celebrations—kokis, semolina-based cakes, and syrup-soaked oil cakes. Each dessert carried the warmth of home. That evening, as a final ritual to her day, she brewed a cup of tea, its earthy aroma a reminder of her roots and her family's traditions.

On Thursday, Sophie ventured further afield to Tarneit and Epping, suburbs that had blossomed into vibrant multicultural hubs.

In Tarneit, she began her exploration at a South Indian restaurant famous for its dosas. The thin, crispy crepes arrived filled with spiced potato masala, accompanied by a trio of chutneys and steaming sambar. "You must try it with the coconut chutney," the waiter suggested, and Sophie gladly took his advice. The creamy, slightly sweet chutney balanced the spices perfectly.

Next, she wandered into a local Indian sweet shop where rows of brightly coloured treats glistened under the lights. She picked up a box of gulab jamuns and kaju katlis. "These are my childhood favourites," said the shop owner, Meera, handing Sophie a warm gulab jamun to try. "In India, sweets are a symbol of celebration, and we make them the same way our ancestors did."

Sophie couldn't help but think of the festive meals her family would prepare for Sinhala and Tamil New Year, with tables laden with sweetmeats, milk rice, and pickles.

From Tarneit, Sophie made her way to Epping, a suburb known for its strong Middle Eastern and Mediterranean influences. Her first stop was a bustling Turkish kebab house where the owner, Hasan, greeted her warmly. "Our lamb kofta is the best," he said confidently, serving her a plate with fresh tabbouleh, hummus, and warm, pillowy flatbread.

As she ate, Hasan shared stories of his family's journey to Australia. "My father taught me how to make kebabs back in Turkey. Here, we use the same spices and techniques, but we've also learned to adapt to local tastes. That's the beauty of cooking in a place like Melbourne."

Sophie's next stop was a Lebanese grocer, where shelves were stocked with olives, jars of pickled vegetables, and tubs of creamy labneh. The owner, Amal, offered her a taste of freshly baked manakish topped with za'atar. "Food is about sharing," Amal said. "When we moved here, we brought our traditions with us. Now, it's wonderful to see people from all cultures enjoying them."

As the day came to an end, Sophie reflected on how these suburban culinary enclaves told stories of migration and adaptation. In both Tarneit and Epping, food wasn't just sustenance—it was a bridge between worlds, a way to preserve heritage while embracing new beginnings. That evening,

Sophie indulged herself with a fresh pot of Ceylon tea, letting its familiar aroma and warmth wrap around her like a hug from home.

Springvale, known for its strong Southeast Asian presence, was Sophie's destination on Friday. The area was a feast for the senses, with vibrant colours, bustling crowds, and the unmistakable aroma of sizzling meats and fresh herbs wafting through the air. The streets were lined with Vietnamese, Cambodian, Malaysian, and Thai restaurants, interspersed with grocery stores displaying exotic fruits like durian, mangosteen, and dragon fruit.

Sophie began her exploration at a small Vietnamese café known for its banh mi. The crusty baguette was perfectly balanced with savoury pork, tangy pickled vegetables, fresh coriander, and a touch of chilli. "This is the best banh mi I've ever had," Sophie said to the owner, Anh.

Anh smiled proudly. "It's my grandmother's recipe. She used to bake the bread herself back in Vietnam. Here, we use a local bakery, but the fillings are just like how she made them."

Next, Sophie visited a bustling Thai street food stall where she tried pad kra pao, a spicy stir-fried basil dish. The vendor, Somchai, handed her the plate with a grin. "Be careful," he warned. "It's hot, but that's how it's meant to be." The fiery heat was tempered by the fragrant jasmine rice, and Sophie found herself savouring every bite.

One of the highlights of her visit was a Malaysian mamak stall, where the smell of sizzling satay and rich curries filled the air. Sophie decided to try teh tarik, Malaysia's famous pulled tea, prepared by an energetic vendor named Azlan. With a theatrical flair, Azlan poured the tea back and forth between two metal cups, creating frothy, creamy perfection.

"This looks amazing," Sophie said as Azlan handed her a steaming glass.

"It's not just a drink," Azlan said with a laugh. "Teh tarik is a tradition. It's about taking your time and enjoying the moment. And, of course, it has to be sweet!"

Sophie took a sip and immediately understood the appeal. The tea was smooth and rich, with just the right balance of sweetness and creaminess. She closed her eyes, savouring the taste. "This is incredible. It reminds me of the tea my parents make, but so much frothier."

Azlan beamed. "That's the magic of the pull. It cools the tea and gives it that texture. You should try it with some kaya toast next time."

Sophie ended her day with a dessert stop at a traditional Vietnamese che stand. She marvelled at the colourful layers of mung beans, jelly, and coconut milk in her glass. The vendor, Mai, explained, "Che is not just a dessert; it's a celebration. We eat it at festivals and family gatherings. It's meant to bring happiness."

As Sophie walked back to her car, her bag filled with treats from the local market, she couldn't help but feel grateful for the warmth and stories shared by the community. Springvale wasn't just a place to eat; it was a place to connect with the heart of Southeast Asia in Melbourne.

Saturday took Sophie to Clyde and Oakleigh, two neighbourhoods that exemplified Melbourne's growing culinary diversity.

In Clyde, Sophie began her day at a local farmers' market, where the air was filled with the aroma of sizzling spices and freshly baked bread. At one stall, she tasted homemade Afghan bolani, flatbread stuffed with potato, herbs, and spices. "This bolani is amazing," Sophie said to the Afghan vendor, Nadia.

"Thank you," Nadia replied, her eyes lighting up. "My mother and I make them together. It reminds us of home. In Afghanistan, food isn't just about eating; it's about community. We're happy to share it here."

Sophie moved on to a Sri Lankan stall, where she tried string hoppers with a fragrant coconut sambol. The vendor, Sunil, explained, "In Sri Lanka, breakfast is often a feast. We believe food is a way to bring people together, whether it's family or strangers." Sophie laughed, thinking of her father's elaborate weekend string hopper feasts, where every bite seemed like a piece of art.

Her final stop in Clyde was at a Filipino food stall, where halo-halo was being prepared with precision and care. The colourful layers of shaved ice, sweet beans, fruit, and leche flan were both a treat for the eyes and the palate. The vendor, Maria, laughed as Sophie marvelled at the dessert. "Halo-halo means 'mix-mix' in Filipino," Maria said. "It's a little bit of everything, just like our culture."

Later that day, Sophie made her way to Oakleigh, Melbourne's vibrant Greek precinct. The streets buzzed with energy, the sounds of bouzouki music mingling with the scent of charcoal-grilled souvlaki.

She entered a bustling taverna, where the owner, Nikos, welcomed her with a wide smile. "Welcome, welcome! Let me bring you something special," he said, disappearing into the kitchen.

Nikos returned with a platter of mezze—tzatziki, dolmades, grilled octopus, and perfectly fried calamari. Sophie dug in, savouring the bold flavours. "This is incredible," she said.

"Good food is meant to be shared," Nikos said. "In Greece, the table is where life happens—celebrations, conversations, even arguments! We bring that spirit here to Oakleigh."

As Sophie finished her meal, Nikos insisted on bringing out loukoumades—golden, honey-soaked doughnuts sprinkled with cinnamon and walnuts. "You can't leave without something sweet," he said with a grin.

The sense of community in Oakleigh was palpable. Families and friends filled the tavernas, their laughter echoing in the warm evening air. For Sophie, the food was more than delicious; it was a celebration of heritage, togetherness, and joy.

As Sunday arrived, Sophie sat at her desk to reflect on her week. Melbourne's food scene wasn't just about flavours; it was about stories. Each dish she had tasted carried with it the hopes, dreams, and the essence of those who had brought their traditions to this city. Sophie had enjoyed the week so much that she promised herself she would do it again. She still had to explore the hip and throbbing Fitzroy and Brunswick Streets with their Spanish and Latin American flavours, and there was Box Hill, Caulfield and Glen Huntly.

In Melbourne, food is a universal language. It speaks of migration and adaptation, of preserving heritage while embracing change. It tells the stories of communities finding their place and making their mark. And it reminded Sophie of the beauty of diversity—how it nourished not just the body but the soul.

Sophie brewed herself a final cup of Ceylon tea for the week, the amber liquid swirling in her favourite porcelain mug. As the familiar aroma filled the room, she felt deeply connected to her roots. Tea, like food, was her way of grounding herself and celebrating the rich tapestry of cultures that made Melbourne her home. She decided she would write about her journey, capturing the voices and flavours that had shaped her city. Because in Melbourne, every meal was a story waiting to be told.

TIME TRAVELLER JOSEPH POTTS (GABRESKI)

BY BERNIE WEISS

OCTOBER 1955.

It was a warm, balmy summer day as Joseph assumed his position at the crease of the Melbourne University Cricket Club. Standing six-foot-two in his socks, the eighteen-year-old youth was clad in the traditional cricket flannels with a long-sleeved white shirt to protect his freckled forearms from the sting of the midday sun. The umpire had held his cream-coloured cable-knit V-necked jumper since he'd scored ten runs. His rich auburn hair crept out from under his baggy cricket cap, protecting his eyes from the sharp sun's rays.

Silence fell as the determined bowler began his run to pitch the ball. Joseph failed to strike at the hard, leather-bound ball before it hit his shin pad. "OUT!! Leg Before Wicket!" cried the umpire. Angrily, Joe marched towards the man wearing a knee-length white coat over black trousers, yelling, "Why don't you go back to your own bloody country! You know nothing about cricket! I was not caught leg-before-wicket! You bloody dago!"

Matt Zammit was a head shorter than his antagonist. Like so many migrants from the Mediterranean, he was short, with a stocky build and an olive complexion. "Italians are dago's, you idiot. I'm from Malta, a British colony since 1814. Cricket is our national pastime. Your Irish convict heritage makes you too dumb to know you were clean-bowled, LBW."

Joseph's nostrils flared, and his face contorted with rage. "How dare you! You don't know me or anything about my heritage!"

"True," retorted Matteo, yet you commented on my heritage! Suck it up, Paddy and get off my pitch!"

Speechless and red-faced, Joe walked away, muttering, "I'm an Australian!"

*

Joe's mood had not improved as he left the number 6 tram on High Street, Prahran, early that afternoon. Laboriously hitching his kit bag onto his shoulder, he stomped around the corner into Chomley Street. The two-story, high-pitched-gable roof with its red terracotta roof tiles of the Federation-style house was a welcome sight. He lived here with his parents, William and Dianne Potts, and his older siblings, Simon and Thomas.

The sweeping terraced gravel path and steps led to the well-appointed veranda with the two large bay windows in white trim on either side of the highly polished and carved oak door. Entering the house, he leapt up the winding staircase, two stairs at a time. Taking his cricket flannels from the kit bag, he tossed them into the laundry chute before heading to the kitchen to raid the fridge. His father, a chubby man with a greying moustache that seemed to grow around his balding head, sat at the large mahogany table smoking a cigar as he read the Herald that lay before him.

William looked at his youngest son, "How was the game?"

"LBW!" the disgruntled man/child answered angrily. His father, who was used to these monosyllable retorts, waited patiently. Sitting down with a glass of milk and three teddy bear biscuits, Joe breathed deeply. "Dad, how can I find out if there were convicts in our heritage? I'm sure you told us our Australian heritage dates to the 1800s. Matt, the umpire, reckons I have stupid Irish/convict blood in me!"

William sat back, massaging his ample paunch while stubbing out his cigar. "I'm not sure how any blood, Irish or not, can be deemed 'dumb, or stupid' as you put it."

Joe smirked, "Yeah. No. You know what I mean."

"I'm not sure I do. You were born at the Royal Children's in Melbourne; your mother's a Victorian, and I am from country New South Wales. Remember the adage, "Sticks and stones will break my bones, but words can never hurt me?"

"Dad! Be serious! That's playground stuff kids say to bullies. The boys counted on me to bring the score to around the half-century; at twenty-eight runs, the Ump called LBW and said I was the Irish scum of a convict."

"His words, or yours?"

"Mine. I'm saying how it made me feel."

"So, was the challenge about your heritage fanned by your shame of letting the team down, not by a genuine interest in your forebears?"

"Well, yes, and no. The insult made me think about my final year's dissertation topic. It has to be about personal issues that link me to my heritage. That's two years away, so I have ample time to investigate my heritage and the possibility of finding a convict ancestor."

William looked at his wristwatch as Maud, the cook, entered the room. "I will be off then," she said. I've left club sandwiches in the larder for you. Mrs Potts has given me the rest of the day off, as you will be dining out this evening."

"Yes, that's right. You go home and enjoy your evening, Maud," he said, smiling at the robust woman who treated his family as her own. Pushing his chair back, he said,

"Joe, keep thinking about it. Write down what you want to know and plan to investigate your heritage. We will talk again in, say, six to eight weeks. If I can help you, I will. However, it would be best if you established the direction and parameters of your research. Your dissertation must reflect your research, assumptions, and conclusions, not on any oral history as I or anyone else tells it."

Joe watched his father head upstairs. Why did parents hear what you say and twist it around? Do we have a convict, vagabond, or other undesirable in the hereditary line? After grabbing a couple of club sandwiches and the newspaper, Joe entered the lounge and threw himself into the brown tweed armchair, hanging one leg over the armrest to read the sports pages.

*

Returning from a dinner with friends, William and Dianne lay curled up in the warm afterglow of their lovemaking. William stifled a laugh as he nibbled at his wife's ear. "What's so funny?"

"Nothing. I was thinking about your father."

She turned around in his arms, "What? You rarely agreed on anything. Dad comes to mind as I lay in your arms?"

William leaned against their double bed's crimson faux leather headboard.

With her head on his chest, she said, "Go on, tell me what made you laugh."

"The night I asked for your hand in marriage. Your dad looked down his nose at me, asking if I were Jewish or Catholic. That was unexpected but easy,

"Neither. I'm Methodist by birth," I'd answered.

"Are you a Communist or trade unionist?"

"No, Sir"

"Have you or anyone in your direct family had any mental issues or been in jail?"

"No, Sir!"

"Why do you limp and have a scar on your face?"

"Many years ago, in country New South Wales, my horse kicked me into a barbed wire fence."

"Do you love my daughter?"

"Yes, Sir!"

"Do you drink Victorian Bitter?"

"Yes, Sir!"

"Right, then, let's get stuck into it. Welcome to the family. Son."

"You've never told me all this before. Why now?" Dianne asked, giggling.

"Well, if your dad had phrased the questions differently, I'd have told him what Joseph is bound to discover if he follows through with his plans for his dissertation."

Intrigued, Dianne sat up next to her husband. "Go on."

"Well, one of my forebears was a disgruntled Jewish-Polish soldier who absconded after the siege of Warsaw in 1794. He arrived in England in 1800. He soon married an Irish-Catholic woman, Catharine Mc Donald, who also worked in a Lancaster mill. Two years later, they were dirt-poor when they were fired. Jozef turns to stealing to support his wife and son. The English court system deemed him a resident felon and transported him to New South Wales for seven years."

"You're kidding!" was all his flummoxed wife could utter.

"No! It's true! Your father assumed I was of British stock. I couldn't exactly tell him my name was Zdobywa in Polish, translated to Wilhelm in German, and Anglicized to William by Deed Poll. And my surname Gabreski was replaced by Potts. That came as "a bolt out of the blue."

"But I've only ever known you as William Potts! Are we legally married? Are our babies……

William chuckled. "Whoa, Dianne! Trust me, we are legally married, and our sons are legally Potts. We met and married in June 1932. Sam and

I came to live lived in Melbourne in 1930."

"But why was the subterfuge?"

Enclosing her cheek in his right hand, he kissed her repeatedly until she stopped trying to pull away. "I was a teenager living in Sydney after the Great War. It was a problematic time, particularly around the Rocks in Sydney, where I lived. It became a sport to point fingers and harass anyone who was 'different'. With a Kraut name like Wilhelm Gabreski, I was picked on and bashed up quite a few times. The last time I'd been left for dead. Minutes or hours later, I don't know, I was carted off the hospital with a broken jaw, minus eight teeth, a dislocated left shoulder, a crushed left ankle, a scar from my left eye to my chin, and a severe concussion. I was deemed well enough to go onto the wards four weeks later. That's when I met Simon Cohen, known to you as Sam, in the bed adjacent to mine."

"You weren't brothers?" Dianne asked.

"Shush. Let me finish. Simon was handsome, as you will recall, looking younger than his twenty years when you first met him. Garden clippers were used to cut his medium-length hair along with his traditional Jewish side curls by street thugs. He had black eyes, bruises galore, and three broken ribs. His father, Max, a practising Jew, was a lawyer. His thick, greying beard and side curls were rarely trimmed. After Simon was discharged, Max continued visiting me twice weekly. Upon my eventual discharge, I moved in with Max, Simon, Mrs Cohen, and their daughter Rebecca. I stayed with them for a year, and Simon and I became brothers in all but blood. Eventually, Max proposed that we change our names by Deed Poll and leave Sydney for Melbourne to start new lives. That's what happened. I became William Potts, and Simon became my brother, Samuel."

Dianne looked at the man she loved for twenty-three years. She'd never known of his pain and suffering caused by misguided louts, afraid of anything beyond their narrow-mindedness. They'd married in 1932, with Sam as their best man. Together, the three had moved into the grand house on Chomley

Street. Both men were successful white-collar workers. Willaim became a co-founder of Potts and Stacks Emporium on Bourke Street. Sam never married. He treated his nephews as sons. Through tears, she asked, "Why haven't you ever mentioned it? Why didn't Sam? What did your parents do?"

"My parents? Mum was on the sherry at 10 am, and Dad never came home until after the pubs shut at 6 pm. Neither visited me in the hospital. Does it matter to you, one way or the other?' I am who I am now. I started a new life and have never looked back. As for telling you and the boys? I was waiting for a suitable time. Your father lived until June this year at the ripe old age of ninety-nine. Imagine his conniption if I'd explained all this before he'd passed away?"

Hearing their three sons noisily return home from their evening out, they switched off the bedside lights. As the house quietened, they whispered until they fell asleep wrapped in each other's arms.

*

FEBRUARY 1956.

The family sat around the dinner table. It was Thursday and Thomas's birthday. William and Dianne sat at either end of the long, walnut Queen Anne table. Their high-backed chairs were cushioned and covered with a durable floral 'Sunbrella' fabric. The table was set with a Royal Damask tablecloth with matching napkins. Twenty-year-old Simon sat to her right. Joseph, whom Dianne still called the baby, sat to her left and opposite the oldest, Thomas, who was now twenty-two.

Tapping his glass for silence, William proposed a toast, congratulating Thomas on his birthday and his acceptance as a trainee doctor at the Royal Melbourne Hospital in his final year of undergraduate studies in medicine. Looking expectantly at her husband, Dianne winked and nodded to William. In the unspoken language of family tradition, the three young men sitting at the table did not miss this hint that there was more to come.

William cleared his throat. "Harrumph. The time has come to tell you something of my past," he said, looking at Joseph, "and to tell you why you can't find much about me under the name William Potts."

Throwing down his linen napkin, Simon said, "I knew it! Joe has been secretive for months. I've seen him leave the State Library numerous times, but he won't say what he is researching! Spit it out, man!"

"Harrumph, I do not intend to spit anything out," his father said, glaring at Simon. I will explain why I changed my name from Wilhelm Gabreski to Willaim Potts." Stunned, the boys listened as the tale unfolded over the next half-hour.

The tearful Dianne hedged any attempts to interrupt. "Listen! Your father needs to tell his story. You can ask questions later."

William ended his confession on a lighter note by mentioning his then-future father-in-law's interrogation. Throughout the tale, William focuses on Dianne, his wife, or above her head, and now his gaze is turned to each of his boys.

Thomas rose first. Stepping towards his father, he said, "Grandpa would be rolling in his grave! Dad, you built a bloody good life for Mum and us boys. I love you so much." With that, he fell into his father's bear hug, which ended with them all in a huddle of shared grief, pride, and love.

*

OCTOBER 1956.

As in previous semester breaks, Joe spent many hours in the La Trobe reading room at the State Library in Swanson Street. The chief librarian, Esmay, was short of stature, somewhat plump, bespeckled, and of indiscernible age. Joe often badgered her with requests for old newspapers and records. Initially, she dreaded his appearance at her highly polished counter. His request frequently meant consulting other state libraries, museums, or the National War Memorial in Canberra to meet his needs.

Nevertheless, she became intrigued by the student and his journey through the musty records relating to the past, particularly about his uncle Sam. As a Uni student, much of what Joe cobbled together reinforced his earlier education. He knew the First Australian Imperial Force (1st AIF) relied on volunteers as two referendums had defeated conscription. When WWII engulfed the world, universal conscription was passed into law, and every man knew he would be deployed overseas. However, those in the Citizens Military Forces (CMF) or 'home guard' were limited to serving in Australia only. That changed after the Pearl Harbour bombings; the legislation changed to allow the CMF to be posted to the South Pacific Islands to protect Australia.

Joe realised that lads his age had enlisted or been conscripted to fight for the king and country. Would he ever be called to make such a sacrifice?

*

"Eureka!" Joe shouted as he jumped, sending his chair tumbling across the polished floor. Racing towards Esmay, he took her in his arms, shouting. "Thank you," he cried as he leaned down to kiss her cheek.

"I have found Uncle Sam! His squadron records provide the dates and places he served once he was conscripted into the Air Force." As pleased as Esmay was about the breakthrough, she silenced him and made him return to his desk. Joe poured over the documents she'd scrounged for him. In January 1943, Uncle Sam had been stationed in Milne Bay on the extreme eastern tip of New Guinea.

*

As a law clerk, Simon wore a three-piece blue Serge business suit, crisp white shirt, and dark blue tie. He heard a shout as he leapt from the Prahran tram's front steps that evening.

"Hey! Simon, wait up!" Sam recognised his brother, wearing the unofficial student uniform of faded Levi jeans and a jacket over a blue skivvy (a long-sleeved t-shirt with a rolled-up neck). Sam cuffed his little brother over the head as he fell into step beside him.

Approaching Chomley Street, Joe asked. "Did you know that Uncle Sam, who lived with us, was killed in action in January 1943?"

"No! But it makes sense. I was around ten, Tom twelve, so you were eight by Christmas in 1942. Uncle Sam paid us a surprise visit for Christmas. Throughout dinner, he'd talked about barracks life, the airfield, and his Kitty Hawk. He loved the American single-engine, single-seat, all-metal fighter bomber. I remember Mum and Dad hugging him in the hallway before he left to join his RAAF unit for deployment overseas. Dad said, 'Keep your head down, and come home to us when this is all over.' I remember being surprised to see all three of them in tears. I never thought to ask why. Now I know why Uncle Sam never returned."

"His RAAF Squadron was stationed at Turnbull Airstrip in Milne Bay on the far eastern tip of New Guinea. The Japs wanted to establish a foothold in New Guinea, from which they could attack Australia. Uncle Sam's plane had barely left the runway to counterattack the Japs in their Mitsubishi Zeros when his Kitty Hawk was hit during take-off and crashed into the Coral Sea."

Placing his arm around his brother's shoulder, Simon said, "History and heritage mean so much more when you realise your relatives were involved."

*

Coming through the hallway, the cigar smoke smell told them their father was home.

"Is that you, Joseph?"

"Yes, Dad."

"Can you come in here for a few minutes?"

The boys looked at each other in askance. What had Joe done now? He shrugged and strode across the formidable floral Persian carpet in muted reds, browns, and blue to sit opposite his father. William sat in his favourite burgundy Chesterfield armchair, which had a buttoned leather high back and armrests with hand-tacked studding supported by curved Queen Anne legs. His feet rested on the adjacent Chesterfield stuffed pouffe.

"How's your research going?"

"Good! I've found out where Uncle Sam's RAAF base was in New Guinea! Dad, you didn't enlist, did you?"

"Unfortunately, no. I tried, but two things stopped me. My left-footed limp was the first. Secondly, due to my work as a manager at a company that supplied American services here in Australia. You know that about a million Yanks passed through Australia between December 1941 and the war's end in 1945?"

"Yes! And I remember the slogan "Overpaid, Oversexed and Over here."

William chuckled at the memory. "You know that Australia was the training and supply base for the US troops preparing to retake the Philippines as a major step to defeating Japan?" Joseph nodded his agreement.

"The company I worked for secured many contracts to supply the U.S. troops with canned goods. Our small range of fruit salads and meats speedily diversified to add chilli con carne, corned beef hash, ham and eggs, stew, pork and beans, and roast beef with gravy. Oh, I forgot, asparagus. The Yanks liked to eat that on toast!"

Joseph took an exercise book from his school bag. "Hang on, I want to write that down. So, your company supplied canned food for the Yanks, and you worked in one of the 172 reserved industries and occupations?"

William nodded in agreement.

*

"Joe, I wanted to ask how deep or broad your research is going. You can get lost following a line of enquiry. Or you can limit your work to focus on a father-son link from one generation to the next." He said, handing Joe a list. You might like to return to Jozef Gabreski, the disgruntled Polish soldier who ended up in Tasmania to serve a seven-year sentence for stealing goods in England.

"Hang on! The convicts were English, Irish, Scots, and Welsh men and women! How did a Polish bloke become a convict in a British penal colony?"

William laughed, "Trust me, convicts were defined by where they were arrested, and so 70% of the convicts were English, another 25% were from Ireland, and 5% were Scottish, with a sprinkling from Wales. They'd broken English law and were sentenced accordingly. And so, Americans, French, Africans and our Polish relative Jozef Gabreski were punished as Englishmen and transported.

The pair sat in deep conversation until Dianne's voice could be heard from the dining room. "Third and final call! If you two don't come to dinner, I will throw your meals out!"

*

DECEMBER 1956.

Father and son had arrived early at Spencer Street station. Joe boarded a carriage of the long train pulled by the steam locomotive, The Spirit of Progress, ready for an adventure that would take him five hundred thirty-eight miles and eleven hours to reach Sydney.

Joe's parents had paid for his return ticket and five nights' accommodation at the Youth Hostel Association (YHA) in Cumberland Street, a stone's throw from Sydney Harbour. The State Library was a short walk of about two miles away. Joe would be back well before Christmas. Esmay, the state librarian in Victoria, had organised Joseph's access to historical materials dating back to colonial times, including lists of convicts and the ships travelling to ports along the eastern coast.

Joe opened his wallet to read his father's list of the generations on his paternal side.

1. Jozef Gabreski   1769-1824 Polish Jewish soldier
   Married Catharine Mc Donald an Irish Catholic (1799-1859)
   Following the father-son links only, search for
2. Joseph   1802-1899
3. William   1831-1899
4. Thomas   1853-1910
5. Simon   1873-1940
6. James   1894-1940 My drunken father
7. **William Potts, aka** Gabreski, married **Dianne O'Brien** in 1932
8. Our three boys, Thomas 1933, Samuel 1934, and You 1937

Joe smiled; let the adventure begin!"

*

A tad after 7 pm, Joe took the connecting train to Wynard Station at Sydney's Central Station and walked ten minutes to the two-story sandstone building with the YHA signage. The man at the desk was bald but sported a long, thick beard, and his forearms were covered in tattoos. He spoke with a deep baritone voice, asking, "Name?"

"Joseph Potts, I'm from…..."

"Yeah. I was expecting you. You are in room twelve."

Following the brusque directions, Joe found room twelve on the upper floor at the end of the corridor. The door was ajar. Tugging at the sticky-handled door, he found it refused to budge further open or shut. Bunk beds were set against the three walls opposite the entrance. No windows meant no access to fresh air, so perhaps leaving the open door was just as well. He approached the vacant lower bunk on the back wall. Five unwashed bodies, two of whom snored loudly, populated the other beds. The coarse grey thread-woollen blanket smelled of vomit. Joe did not undress or take off his boots, preferring to lay with his back to the wall. That felt safe. He tucked his left under his head, ignoring the grubby pad masquerading as a pillow. His right arm held his backpack tightly to his chest, his nose breathing the odours of home and clean clothes.

*

Despite taking several naps during the train journey, Joe fell asleep to the snoring symphony emitted by his roommates. Monday morning came with a cacophony of oaths as the sleeping figures woke and prepared to leave. Joe pretended to sleep as he watched the noisy youths depart. It was 7 a.m. Joe crept from the room to follow signs to the bathroom, hoping to shower.

Joe handed his blanket to the desk clerk on his way out, asking for a clean one. The tall, voluptuous woman's name badge pinned to the tank top indicated she was 'Chris'. Flicking the long-haired blond wig from her face, she took the blanket from him in a deep voice: "Hello, darling. Did you sleep well?"

Joe flushed and stuttered, "Yes, thank you," hastening into the morning sun.

'That was no woman!' he told himself. Looking around to get his bearings, he headed towards the Sydney Harbour Bridge. He remembered it took eight years to construct and was opened in March 1932. The sun warmed his spirit as he sat on a park bench in Dawes Point Park, taking in the magnificence of the Sydney Harbour Bridge, colloquially known as "the coat hanger".

*

Thirty minutes later, he followed the pencilled-in directions on the Sydney map to find the State Library on the corner of Macquarie and Shakespeare Streets. Turning into Essex Street, he saw a small delicatessen. He ordered a black coffee with a ham, cheese, and tomato sandwich. He consumed them as he walked into George and then Bridge Streets. Reaching Macquarie Street at the Royal Botanic Gardens, he saw the State Library, built in 1910, on the corner of Shakespeare Street.

Approaching the reception desk, Joe announced his arrival. The chief librarian, Mr Brown, wearing a nondescript brown suit and brown brogues, greeted Joe. The older man's beige shirt, golden tie, and bristly hair liberally peppered with grey hair added colour to his appearance. Brown pointed out the amenities along the way before depositing Joe at an empty desk marked 'reserved' in the cavernous three-story Mitchell Library Reading Room. Joe looked up in awe at the two staircases leading to the mezzanine levels, where more books were stored on the second and third levels. Brown pointed at the large cardboard box marked "pre-booked by Potts" on the desk. He handed Joe a pair of white gloves, saying, "These unique leather-bound books understandably never leave the library." Taking the first of ten volumes, he laid it open on a large book cradle. "Your gloves are to protect the pages."

"Yes, I understand. Esmay taught me the do's and do nots of reading these precious volumes."

"You may be on first-name terms with Miss Esmay Stephens; however, you will address me as Mr Brown!"

"Of course! No problem."

"These pink bookmarks may assist you in your work. Do not eat or drink in here! You may leave your desk for up to two hours at a time. Any longer, you may find these volumes stored away for the rest of the day. The library opens between 9 a.m. and 8 p.m. precisely. Please advise the reception when you leave for the day. I understand you want access for five days?"

"Yes, my train ticket to Melbourne is for Saturday morning."

*

Joe worked tirelessly until noon. He dropped into the library's café to order a salad roll and a Schweppes lemonade. 'Mother, I am eating well,' he thought as he trotted across the busy intersection towards the Botanic Gardens opposite the library. He quickly found the Governor Phillip fountain surrounded by a water fountain and several statues. Reading the plaques, he learned that the statue was unveiled in 1897. Joe chose to have his picnic lunch on the shady side, as it was a balmy summer's day of 26 degrees. He likened his brain to a saturated sponge. He needed to wring it out. Having eaten, he closed his eyes, intending to have a refreshing power nap.

Joe felt someone sitting next to him. The unshaven man wore an ill-fitting shirt, knee-breeches, stockings, and a heavy wool coat. The figure spoke with a heavy European accent, "Why are you looking for family, my secrets?"

Joe's eyes bulged as he cleared his throat, but words failed him.

"Do you think I am a ghost? I am a distant relative! Jozef Gabreski!"

Joe looked around him and asked, "Are you for real? Are you telling me you are Joseph Gabreski, born around 1770? The Polish guy generations back, a soldier who went to England after the Siege of Warsaw and Prague in 1790-something?"

"No! Not Josep! But Jozef!"

"Are you related to Jozef Gabreski, the Polish nobleman?"

"He is my grandfather. I never met him."

"Why did you abscond from the army?"

"I was young, about your age. War meant adventure. Soldiers had power. My friends and I fought battles against the enemy, young soldiers our age. I saw many terrible things done in the name of future peace. Returning to our original barracks, I walked away from that life three years later. I left the country.

"Yes, but why did you choose to go to England?"

"I crept onto a ship. I did not know where it was going. At Portsmouth, in England, I slipped off unnoticed."

"You are a deserter!"

"No! I was a disillusioned man. Powerful governments send young men to fight their political battles. Look at history: Political enemies become allies twenty years later. Soldiers are supposed to die, not come back. You say deserter; I say survivor!"

Joe nodded. Had he not been conscripted into the CMF and later into the Air Force, Uncle Sam might have been here to chat with. The pitter-patter of rain jolted Joe from his reverie. Jozef had disappeared. Joe scrambled up and raced across Shakespeare Street and back to his desk in the large reading room at the State Library.

*

That afternoon, Joe worked methodically, skimming passages, looking for keywords, words, and phrases, and drilling down to his area of interest. By 6 p.m., his tummy was rumbling; rubbing his eyes, he packed his bag and left the library to search for a meal. The metallic scent of saltwater on the cool evening breeze reminded him how close he was to Sydney Harbour. Heading that way, he soon found a fish and chip shop. Dinner and some sightseeing until it is dark, he thought.

Two hours later, Rodney, the gruff man at the YHA desk, greeted Joe with, "You didn't get lost, then? Oh, and while I think of it, Chris said to give you these." Joe smiled, seeing a freshly laundered blanket, sheets, and pillowcase, all wrapped in plastic. "No, mate, I'm pretty good with maps. Please thank Chris for me; I'm off to bed."

*

Joe stretched on his usual lower bunk. His day's work covered Jozef Gabreski's trial in the Sussex Spring Assises at Horsham in 1802. Jozef was nabbed stealing a lady's bonnet—and sentenced to seven years in New South Wales, ten-and-a-half thousand miles away. His convict transport was the 1200-tonne HMS Calcutta that sailed from Portsmouth in June 1803. Its main deck was sixty-five yards long and eleven yards wide, and her topmast was sixty-one meters tall. Two purpose-built prison rooms were fashioned below the deck as part of the refit of the four-mast, twelve-hundred-ton Royal Navy frigate.

It was dark when Joe woke. Sensing he was not alone, he asked, "Who's there?"

"I want you to meet my wife," Jozef answered in his heavily accented voice. So, this was Catharine McDonald, Joe thought. She wore a long-sleeved, ankle-length, coarse blue woollen dress buttoned at the neck. Her

Irish brogue was challenging, but he understood her better than Jozef. Each held a sleeping child on their shoulder.

"You make notes about the ship, thinking it was big?" Jozef began. "We were packed like sardines with six hundred forty people on board."

"I'm sure I read there were only three hundred convicts," Joe interrupted.

"Ugh," Jozef uttered. "You listen! Not correct me, smart boy. Three hundred were imprisoned below deck. Two rooms with one hundred fifty men in each. Stinking hellhole! Two hundred crewmen were one deck higher, and above them again, fifty-nine Royal Marines whose job was to protect the ship. Another fifty Marines and over forty civil staff were to work in the new colony."

Catharine picked up the story. "My pregnancy didn't show in June when I joined the other sixteen free settler wives and eight children, all related to one or other prisoner. Two-year-old Jozef ran wild with the other children on the rare fair-weather days when we were allowed up on deck. Captain Collins and the ship's surgeon Edward Bromley were rarely seen and smelled of rum when they did appear," she chuckled. "By October, several pregnancies were evident as we reached Sullivan Bay."

Jozef spoke of Collin's decision in January 1804 that the site where he was ordered to establish any European settlement wasn't practical. "We sailed on to reach Hobart late in January."

"Our, Catharine, was the first European child born and baptised in Van Diemen's land," his wife proudly added."

Rowdy voices announced the arrival of his new 'roommates' for the night. Joe was sorry to note that his four guests had disappeared.

*

Finding the light switch, four youths entered the room, acknowledging Joe with a nod and grunt. They dumped their odd assortment of luggage on the floor, stripped to their underwear and climbed into the bunks. They were drunk; it was midnight, and they were soon asleep. Fortunately, no one snored. Joe fell asleep, dreaming of the high seas and foul weather described in Captain Collins's ship's log. Józef's words came to him about the bitterly cold days and weeks before it became stifling hot. He wondered at the safety of children running around the main promenade deck.

*

Joe spent the days at the library and the evenings taking in the sights. His favourite time was the nights. On the third night, Catharine appeared beside his lower bunk. She was barely five feet tall, with sea-green eyes, a fair complexion, and fiery red hair tucked into her bonnet.

"I have inherited your skin tone and flaming red hair," Joe said in greeting.

"And temperament," she giggled.

"Did the smell of unwashed bodies bother you on the ship," Joe asked.

"Oh no, laddie, it was what it was. If you could smell it, you were alive and not at the bottom of the ocean."

Joe nodded. "You were granted land at Clarence Plains in 1806. Can you tell me about that?"

"Yes, it was a blessing and a curse. Few ships had reached Van Diemen's Land over the last eighteen months, so stores of wheat, vegetables, tea, sugar, and alcohol dwindled, leaving the colony starving. Collins granted me, a free woman, a parcel of land on the Clarence Plains in 1806. The hundred acres also entitled me to have one convict assigned to work for me. Jozef was released from the timber sawmills and sent to help me grow corn. I had become his guarantor, assuring the government that he would not abscond or commit a crime while indentured to me."

"Wonderful, the family was together again," Joe commented.

"Yes and no. Jozef was always a proud man—the man of the house—the provider. Now, for all the world to see, his wife ordered him around! His self-esteem suffered, and he became a taciturn man, one of few words and prone to bursts of anger."

"Oh, I thought he'd be overjoyed to have the family together.

"Aye, laddie. 'Sticks and stones will break my bones'....."

Joe finished, "But words will never hurt me! My father said that to me not so long ago. I was upset about someone who suggested I had convict blood. It turns out he was right."

"We lived on the land, from the land. Jozef spent hours on hunting trips, bringing a bounty of rabbits and more for the cooking pot."

"What about little Joseph and Catharine? Were they happy to have their father around?" Joe asked.

"Jozef was unhappy, and the children and I kept out of his way when his dark moods overcame him. It wasn't until 1810, when he was granted his Ticket of Leave, that he returned to his old self. That piece of paper lifted the convict's burden from his shoulders. He threw his back into doubling the cultivated acreage. We tripled our harvest within six years, supplying the colony and the commissariat with grain for the year with corn starch, oil, syrup, and livestock feed."

Catharine faded away as the lights went on at 7 a.m. Joe and the others were up, washed, and dressed in the breakfast room by 7:45 a.m. Chris and Rodney served eggs, bacon, and sausages. Coffee and tea were available on a self-serve basis. Bread, butter, jam and vegemite too.

*

Thus, the rhythm of days and nights in Sydney passed. Joe's interaction with the various boys who spent the night at the YHA was limited as soon as it became evident he was not on a get-drunk-quick holiday. On Thursday, he returned to the YHA in the evening. Chris and the heavily tattooed Rodney were interested in how Joe's 'work' was getting on. Joe enjoyed sitting with them in the foyer. He excused himself around 9 p.m. and went to his bed. It was his last night, and Catharine appeared.

"Little documentation exists on how children grew up in the penal colonies. Can you tell me a little about that?"

Catharine sighed. "When Jozef came to live with us, Joseph was four and

Catherine two. They'd seen little of Jozef since birth, so the man of the house was a stranger to them. Jozef was a harsh father. Their fear of his outbursts tempered their love for him. He insisted on passing on his Polish culture and traditions. I have Irish blood and have picked up some English traditions, which I also wanted to pass on. So, there was tension between us as parents, the children and us, and the colony around us. Everyone had their story and heritage, and the mix caused many a raised eyebrow."

"Mum still does the traditional English Christmas dinner, using a cookbook from her great-grandmother. And Dad has his traditional ways about him. My complexion and ginger hair led to nicknames like Paddy. I didn't like it and insulted people right back, having a go at their looks, heritage, sometimes both!"

"Och, laddie, you need to celebrate the differences. Be willing to compromise. Remember, it's what you give to others that they will give back to you. Our boy Joseph worked hard to please his father. His badgering of the Hamlet boys and name-calling often ended in bloodied fisticuffs. Jozef glowed with pride; his boy was strong. Growing up, Joseph ran amuck with some hooligans, and there were regular run-ins with the local constabulary."

Catharine stopped to wipe the tears from her eyes, and Joe leaned in to hear what she whispered next. "Our boy was barely twenty when he was hanged for burglary in 1821."

Joe didn't know where to look or what to say to comfort her. All this happened almost 200 hundred years ago. Thinking of his mother, he wondered how Dianne might feel or do if he or one of his siblings were sent to war. Or ran amuck and were sentenced to death by hanging. He realised these two women had a significant role in loving and caring for their husbands and children.

"Little Catharine soon proved herself a hothead, too. She ran off at fourteen. She came home pregnant at sixteen. I was forty-five, and we pretended that wee William was a latecomer for Jozef and me. Our daughter was his favourite 'auntie'. Fortunately, the family secret remained intact. Catharine met and married an Irish free settler, Patrick O'Malley, early in 1824. Within months, they boarded a ship bound for the settlement and founded the bay named Port Phillip after the Governor of New South Wales in 1805."

Joseph had found data confirming this but nodded, not wanting to interrupt.

"The last straw for me came in 1824 when Jozef died. We were reasonably well off; we lived comfortably in what started as our small bark hut, which was extended twice as the children grew. Jozef was fifty-five and not in the best of health. But he was a thrill-seeker and bragged about his exploits in the taverns when he'd had too much to drink. He was caught stealing cattle and died in Hobart goal, waiting for the circuit judge to arrive a month later."

"I was no longer the well-regarded wife of the man who supplied the colony with wheat. I sold our holdings for a song, and passage was booked for four-year-old William and me on the next available ship to Port Phillip. It was 1824. I was forty-seven years old."

Joe sat beside the stoic woman, barely holding back his emotions for her sake.

"Fortunately, Catharine needed someone to help her with her growing family. She had nine children with Patrick O'Malley. She treated her stepbrother as her own, and I lived with them until I died in 1855, after my seventy-eighth birthday."

She faded into the night without another word, leaving Joe melancholy as he tried to sleep.

*

On Friday morning, Joe woke up with a start. It was dark. Someone was tugging at his backpack, which was tucked under his bunk. As full awareness of his surroundings came to him, he shouted, "What the?"

"Shit, he's awake!"

"Run!" Two dark figures raced out the door.

Joe gave chase until, rounding a corner in the hall, his bag was used as a battering ram, hitting him in the face. He dropped down in stages like a falling tower. He lay there dazed.

Ripping the backpack open, one boy shouted, "Stupid kid has school stuff in here."

"I've got his watch and wallet," he said as he kicked Joe in the ribs. Far out, he only has ten pounds and small change!"

"Stop kicking him! Come on! Down the fire escape."

*

Joe pulled himself into a sitting position, holding his bleeding nose. There was blood coming from the back of his head, too.

"Are you okay?"

Joe looked at three figures who blended into one, then three before he went limp and blacked again.

"Go down to reception! Get help!" a voice shouted.

Wearing her black pageboy wig, Chris ran with the boy who came to the reception. She took Joe into her arms and asked, "Darling, are you all right?"

Joe nodded, breaking out of his momentary stupor by smelling her liberally used Chanel number five perfume. "My boots, my backpack, my research," he whispered as his eyes rolled back.

*

"Hush now, let's get you to our flat," Chris said, almost carrying Joe downstairs to the rooms she shared with Rodney. Kevin, the couple's friend, a doctor, arrived to check on Joe.

"They did a good job on him. But he doesn't need the hospital and the police hassle. He needs sleep and a good meal when he wakes up. I will write a script for some light painkillers. Call me again if he loses his balance or throws up food later in the day." He said to Chris as she walked with him as her left.

*

At 7 o'clock, Joe woke on the sofa, lying under a multi-coloured woollen blanket, unsure of where he was. Chris came in holding his washed clothes over her arm. Agh! He remembered. He'd chased a would-be thieving pair down the hallway in his singlet and jocks.

A COLLECTION OF POEMS

BY MARYANN GRIGSON

My Island in the Sun
A teardrop in the Indian Ocean,
Lies my paradise aglow,
Kissed by gentle morning breezes,
Bathed in golden sunlight's glow.

Waves that shimmer, oceans blue,
Dance and whisper on sunlit shores,
While emerald pastures, rice fields wide,
Breathe in peace forevermore.

Rivers weave through meadows green,
Where cattle graze in tranquil grace.
And misty highlands, cool and pure,
Cradle tea leaves rows between.

The warmth of smiles, so bright, so true,
Mingle with birds in joyful tune,
Sweetly humming as they soar,
Beneath the sky's embrace at noon.

"Welcome," whisper the coconut palms,
Their fronds swaying one by one.
How could I forget such glorious beauty,
My island pearl, shining in the sun?

*

The Ocean

The ocean stretches, vast and wide,
Reflecting skies in hues of blue,
It kisses shores both near and far,
A world untamed, yet ever true.

Where ships and yachts like nomads glide,
And surfers chase the curling crest.
Waves rise and crash in foamy white,
Then melt upon the golden west.

At times, it hums a peaceful tune,
Soft ripples that glide upon the shore,
But when the winds unleash their wrath,

It roars and rages with winds that blow.

Listen to the sound of the ocean,
The echoes of a million seashells,
Forever, it's in motion, like unwritten music,
A symphony in endless swells.

*

A Beautiful Garden
The garden is a realm beyond compare,
Pansies, roses, sunflowers bright.
Where blossoms sway in fragrant air,
Daisies in pink, a pure delight.
Lavender whispers in purple hue,
Heather shrubs in vibrant view.
Bees hum softly, drifting near,
Gathering nectar, gold and clear.
Butterflies dance with wings so light,
Flitting like jewels in the morning light.
A symphony of colours, soft and wild,
Nature's artistry free and beguiled.
Amidst this garden, pure and fair,
Magic lingers in the air.
Amidst this haven, wild and free,
Nature hums in harmony.

*

My Mother

A portrait rests upon the mantelpiece,
Framing a face so warm and kind,
A loving gaze that time won't fade,
A heart forever intertwined.
For more than two score years, she shone,
A soul so rare, so deeply true,
Caring, nurturing, always giving,
Her gentle strength in all she'd do.
Never a word of discontent,
Yet always there with love to spare,
A silver-haired angel, soft and bright,
My mother—beyond compare.

*

Good Friends

A wide circle of friends
Is easy to find in this world—
From childhood playmates
To teenage companions,
From fleeting hellos
To whispered goodbyes,
And even a friend for just a day.
But a faithful friend is rare,
A treasure that lasts forever.
Through joy and sorrow,
They stand beside you,
Laughing in sunshine,
Crying in the rain.
For true friendship knows no distance,

No barrier too great to cross.
Time may pass, miles may grow,
Yet strong bonds never fade—
Good friends always remain,
Until the end of time.

*

Elusive Dreams
Stars shimmer in a midnight sea,
As sleep enfolds me in its gentle tide.
Dreams unravel in silent symphony,
Soft whispers echoed deep inside.
Fingers dance on ivory keys,
Summoning melodies of love and loss.
A haunting tune from yesterday
Weaves through time, a spirit tossed.

When laughter was light, and hearts unchained.
Through moonlit veils, I float, untamed,
I wander where the flowers bloom,
Drenched in fragrance, rich with doom.

A garden bathed in moonlight's kiss,
Their perfume thick, a siren's spell,
A breath too sweet to let me go.
Was it real—or fleeting mist?
The air intoxicates, lingers sweet,
A spell too potent to withstand.
Was it real, or but a dream—
A fleeting touch of wonder's hand?

THE GOLDEN JOURNEY

BY RODERIC GRIGSON

In the quiet of a Melbourne evening, surrounded by the hum of passing cars and the distant chatter of pedestrians, Liang Daniel sat in his late grandfather's study, dust motes dancing in the golden glow of a desk lamp. The scent of aged paper and sandalwood filled the air. He had come to sort through his grandparents' belongings, but instead, he had discovered something unexpected—a leather-bound journal, its edges frayed with time.

His fingers traced the delicate Chinese characters on the cover, ink faded but barely legible: "*The Journey of Jinhai Liang*". It was his great-grandfather's journal. He had always wondered what had driven his family to leave China; now, with the journal in his hands, he was closer than ever to uncovering the truth.

With a deep breath, he opened it. The pages were filled with long vertical lines of traditional Chinese calligraphy that he found difficult to read. Daniel could make out some of the characters, but they were not the modern forms he was familiar with. He pulled out his laptop and signed into an internet site he had used before that provided translations from traditional to simplified Chinese.

The Liang family had left China with heavy hearts and desperate hopes. Taishan, once their home, had become a place of suffering. Years of war, corruption, and famine had left entire villages starving. The Qing government's taxes grew unbearable, and bandits roamed the countryside, making it unsafe to farm or trade. The land that had once nurtured them had turned against them, offering only hardship in return.

Translating the traditional forms was no easy task, but Daniel leaned in, his curiosity sharpening. Each character felt like a puzzle piece, a fragment of a story long buried. He read on.

Then had come the rumours—whispers of gold buried in the distant lands of Australia, a place called *Gum San*, the Golden Mountain. Letters from those who had gone before spoke of riches beyond imagining, fortunes lying beneath the soil, waiting to be claimed. For Jinhai, it was a chance for his family to escape their fate and carve out a new life where his sons would not grow up in poverty. It was a gamble, but staying behind meant certain ruin.

The wind carried the scent of salt and hope as the ship cut through the churning waters of the South China Sea. Aboard, crammed together with hundreds of other hopeful souls, was the Liang family—father Jinhai, mother Meilin, and their two sons, Liang Wei and Liang Jun. They hailed from Taishan, a land of rice fields and narrow, winding paths flanked by tall bamboo. Life there had been hard, ravaged by war, famine, and the relentless hand of poverty. The rumours of gold in Australia had been enough to make Jinhai trade his meagre land for passage across the sea.

Daniel's hands trembled as he turned the page. He imagined the desperation his ancestors must have felt, the weight of uncertainty pressing on their shoulders. He swallowed hard, compelled to read on. The images they were creating in his mind seemed so real. It was like he was there watching them.

Their journey had been long and arduous. Days bled into nights of rocking waves, seasickness, and the ever-present stench of unwashed bodies. Meilin clutched Jun to her chest, humming lullabies to keep the terror of the unknown at bay. Wei, barely twelve, sat silently near the ship's edge, his dark eyes fixed on the horizon, searching for a glimpse of the promised land.

"Wei," Jinhai murmured, resting a hand on his son's shoulder. "Are you afraid?"

Wei hesitated before shaking his head. "No, Baba. Just wondering what it will be like."

Jinhai nodded, his eyes distant. "It will be different, but we are together. That is what matters."

"Do you think there will be dragons there?" Jun piped up, his small fingers clutching his mother's sleeve.

Meilin chuckled, pressing a kiss to her son's forehead. "Perhaps, little one, but we are strong. We will tame them."

Daniel leaned back, exhaling slowly as he closed his eyes for a moment. His head ached from deciphering the unfamiliar characters, his vision blurred from the strain. Yet, beyond the ink and paper, he could almost feel their emotions—the uncertainty, the fear of the unknown, the weight of a journey with no clear destination. A deep gratitude settled within him for all they had endured.

With renewed determination, he turned the page. The faded Chinese characters, etched with time, only deepened the authenticity of the story unfolding before him.

When the Liang family finally arrived in Port Phillip, Melbourne, they were overwhelmed by the sights and sounds of a bustling colony. The docks teemed with ships, their sails billowing in the salty breeze as cargo was unloaded by sweating labourers. The streets were alive with a cacophony of sounds—merchants hawking their wares, the clatter of horse-drawn carriages, and the chatter of people in a dozen different languages. European settlers strode past in their stiff coats and bonnets while Chinese traders carefully laid out silks and teas on wooden carts. The scent of fresh bread from a bakery mingled with the pungent aroma of fish from the harbour.

Daniel could almost hear the clamour of the marketplace, the voices blending in a mix of foreign tongues. He imagined his great-grandparents stepping into this strange, new world, clutching their few possessions, standing on the threshold of an uncertain future.

Melbourne was a striking mix of grand stone buildings with intricate facades and hastily constructed wooden shanties. The city was expanding rapidly, and its skyline was punctuated by the rising smoke from factories. Wealthy businessmen strolled through the unpaved avenues in polished boots while ragged gold-seekers trudged past, their eyes weary with the weight of failed dreams. In the distance, the grand silhouette of St. James' Cathedral loomed over the city, its bells tolling a reminder of the passage of time.

For Jinhai and his family, Melbourne was overwhelming yet full of promise. They saw others like themselves—Chinese men bargaining in tight clusters, their voices thick with dialects from Canton and Fujian. There were tea houses filled with the scent of jasmine and fried dumplings, where weary travellers gathered to exchange news and plans for the goldfields. But there was also hostility—suspicious glances from European settlers, signs posted on shop doors that read "No Chinamen Allowed." It was clear that survival in this land would require flexibility and careful navigation.

They had only a short reprieve. They spent a few nights on the wharves amongst the barrels and bales before being herded onto another boat that would take them to Robe, South Australia. The colonial government had imposed a hefty tax on Chinese arrivals, forcing many to land in South Australia and undertake a gruelling trek to the goldfields on foot.

Daniel set the journal aside, his stomach grumbling in protest. As much as he wanted to keep reading, he needed a break. He headed to the kitchen, quickly assembling a sandwich and downing a glass of water. The simple meal satisfied his hunger, but his mind remained fixated on the journal's contents. Without wasting another moment, he returned to his seat, picked up the journal, and dove back into its pages.

The march to Victoria was gruelling, stretching over 400 miles. The red dust clung to their skin, their clothes, their very breath. They walked in long lines, carrying whatever meagre possessions they had—bundles of dried fish, sacks of rice, pickaxes, and cooking pots. Jinhai walked beside his sons, his back straight despite the burden on his shoulders. Meilin, though weary, never faltered, knowing that their future depended on her endurance.

Upon reaching the goldfields at Ballarat, they were met with a chaotic sprawl of tents, wooden shanties, and the constant clang of picks against rock. The air reeked of sweat and unwashed bodies, a mingling of languages creating an unceasing hum of desperation and ambition.

They settled in Canton Town, an enclave of Chinese diggers who had carved out a space of their own amidst hostility from European miners. The camp bustled with makeshift shops, communal kitchens, and shrines where incense burned day and night. Here, the Liang family found refuge among familiar customs, even as they were eyed with suspicion by outsiders.

Jinhai and Wei joined the gold-seekers, digging under the hot sun from dawn until dusk. The tunnels below the ground were stifling, the air thick with the scent of damp earth and sweat. Shadows flickered in the glow of oil lamps, casting eerie figures on the rock walls. The walls of the tunnels creaked and groaned, whispering dangers of cave-ins. The deeper they dug, the harder it became to breathe, the weight of the earth above pressing down on their shoulders. Some miners used cradles to sift through dirt and water, rocking them back and forth to separate gold from gravel. Others worked in narrow shafts, hammering at quartz veins, searching for rich deposits. It was painstaking, exhausting labour, but the glint of gold specks in a pan made every aching muscle worth it.

One evening, as they worked, Wei looked up at his father, wiping sweat from his brow. "Baba, do you think we will ever find enough?"

Jinhai smiled faintly, gripping his pickaxe. "Gold is not always about luck, my son. It is about patience. The earth rewards those who endure."

After a catastrophic cave-in that left many miners entombed beneath the earth, Jinhai and Meilin made a life-altering decision. They could no longer stake their future on the treacherous whims of the mines, where each day was a gamble between fortune and death. With their hard-earned savings—gold painstakingly sifted from riverbeds and pried from stubborn rock—they turned away from the darkness underground and toward the promise of stability.

With their hard-earned savings, scraped together from years of backbreaking labour, they secured a modest storefront in Ararat, a town pulsing with the relentless energy of the gold rush. Their general goods store, though small at first, became a vital lifeline for miners, both Chinese and European, who came seeking supplies to sustain them in the harsh and unforgiving landscape. Shelves were stocked with essentials—sturdy tools, thick canvas, dried meats, sacks of rice, and delicacies imported from China that offered weary diggers a taste of home.

Meilin, with her quiet strength and steady hands, transformed the shop into more than just a place of commerce. She prepared steaming bowls of broth and rice, fragrant dumplings, and hot tea for miners who arrived exhausted and hungry, their bodies aching from hours of toil. The warmth of her kitchen was a welcome refuge, a brief respite from the exhausting work in the goldfields.

Jinhai, meanwhile, built a name for himself as a fair and honest merchant. He never overcharged desperate miners, nor did he take advantage of those who had fallen on hard times. The goldfields became a distant memory, replaced by the steady rhythm of life behind the counter, of friendships forged over trade and conversation. Word of his integrity spread quickly, earning the respect of both the Chinese community and the European settlers. Slowly, their humble store grew, expanding its offerings and deepening its roots in the town.

Over the years, the store became more than just a business—it became a gathering place, a cornerstone of the community where news was exchanged, friendships were forged, and weary souls found a moment of solace. With time, the family flourished, no longer bound to the perilous goldfields but firmly planted in a life of their own making—one built not from luck but from resilience, hard work, and an unyielding belief in a better future.

Daniel paused, rubbing his tired eyes. Hours had slipped by unnoticed, and his throat felt parched. The strain of translating the ancient characters and piecing together their meaning had left his head throbbing. He pushed back his chair, stretching stiff muscles as he made his way to the kitchen. A cool glass of water soothed his dry mouth, refreshing him just enough to continue. With a deep breath, he sat back down, ready to dive back into the past.

Years passed. The gold rush waned, and many miners moved on, seeking fortune elsewhere. The Liang family, however, stayed. Wei married a young woman from the community, while Jun went on to apprentice with a carpenter. Meilin, once a woman of Taishan, now spoke English alongside her mother tongue, her hands as skilled in shaping dumplings as they were in tending the shop.

Wei's children, growing up between two cultures, attended local schools and worked alongside their parents in the family shop, which had expanded to become one of the most trusted businesses in Ararat.

When Daniel's parents were growing up, their family had long since transitioned from miners to business owners. They learned to bridge the gap between their Chinese heritage and the Australian way of life, proving their place in a community that once saw them as outsiders. His grandparents had fought hard for acceptance, ensuring their children received proper education and opportunities.

Daniel's father, Liang Michael, had grown up working in the family store, learning the importance of spirit and respect. His mother, Lin Mei, had come to Australia as a young woman, studying finance and eventually working in banking. The two had met in Melbourne, both aware of the sacrifices their families had made before them. They had instilled in Daniel a deep appreciation for his roots. However, he had never truly understood the depth of his heritage—until now.

Daniel was raised in the comfort of modern Australia, his childhood filled with footy games, weekend markets, and family gatherings where the aroma of his grandmother's dumplings mingled with the scent of freshly baked lamingtons. He struggled, at times, to reconcile his Chinese heritage with his Australian upbringing. But as he read further into his ancestor's words, he began to understand.

Daniel closed the journal, his fingers trembling slightly as he ran them over the worn leather cover. His heart pounded in his chest, heavy with the weight of the past. His family came to this land with nothing but hope and the will to survive. They endured backbreaking labour, weathered discrimination, and sacrificed more than he could ever comprehend. Yet, through sheer grit, they carved out a future, turning struggle into strength and hardship into legacy.

His gaze drifted to the framed photo on the desk. His grandparents stood side by side, their faces lined with the echoes of their journey, their eyes still warm, still kind. How many times had those hands, now forever still, toiled under an unforgiving sun? How many nights had they laid awake, wondering if their sacrifices would ever be worth it?

A lump rose in his throat as he reached out and touched the edge of the frame. His voice came out as barely more than a breath. *"Thank you,"* he whispered. *"For everything."*

The golden journey had never truly been about gold. It had been about survival, about learning to adapt in a world that was not always welcoming, about holding onto family when everything else felt uncertain. They had arrived as strangers, outsiders in a foreign land. But through determination and love, they had made it their home.

And now, Daniel stood on their shoulders, their sacrifices woven into his very being. He was not just a descendant of their journey—he was its continuation. Clutching the journal to his chest, he closed his eyes and made a silent vow.

He would honour them. He would carry their story forward.

SEMI-DIGESTED MOMENTS

BY HECTOR DAVID SOSA

Uncombed dark hair hidden under a black beret,
Silently struggling with a lack of clear concentration,
Hoping for a minute of essential clarity to purposely set in,
As a broken wave of noisy frustration furiously flows throughout.

The voluntary involvement of sharp, gothic, electronic rock music,
Dramatically opening possibilities of unique creative thought,
For the undefined unknown to fantastically come forth and play around.

My peculiar situation revolving simultaneously with the great planet,
A strange experience to be shared in other-worldly verse,
Without skipping or jumping, to instant erroneous conclusions.

Current mood is emotionally iconic,
With dry, hazel eyes wanting drops of much-needed moisture,
And unhealthy lungs craving pure oxygenated air,
While a poisonous packet steadily goes empty.

The unsatisfied procedure to momentously solve all problems ends in failure.

However, sane solutions are brought about by careful pondering,
Meaningful memories displayed in the accessible but blurry eye of the mind,
Recognising what once was and how one has been unfairly altered,

As a potential grand change for the better?
Or only an optimism derived from mediocre sources?

For the blackness is here now,
The coolness of an expiring night,
With a bright, multicoloured morning to follow,
And an infinite range of potential energy to be realised.

MOONLIGHT VISITOR

BY NORMA SAVIGE

He came to her every full moon at midnight and for the two following nights each month.

The first time, Kate had spent a restless evening, and because sleep would not come, she wandered down towards the jetty below her lakeside cottage. The lake shimmered in the moonlight, and her pathway was lit almost as clearly as in the early morning. The air was soft and warm, with the faint smell of eucalypts surrounding the cottage. The sounds of the night were familiar and comforting to her: insects, birds, and animals calling, the occasional fish rising in the lake, and the rustling of animals moving through the dry undergrowth. She had lived with these sounds since coming to the Tasmanian Lakes area several years earlier and had grown to love them. From the short path above the lake, she heard a soft thud and paused to glance around what she considered to be her own private backyard.

The sound came again nearer than before, and she noticed silver ripples on the lake not far from the end of the jetty. She stood stock still and strained to identify the origin of the sound. Her breath caught in her throat as she realised that a small boat was rocking gently in the silver moonlight on the lake's surface, and a man was flyfishing over the side. She knew there were trout in the shallows near the banks of the lake but was not sure they would be attracted to feed in the moonlight. She was nervous about approaching the intruder but was also curious to find out if he was a regular visitor to this, her sanctuary, her place of solitude and safety. She had never felt unsafe out by the lake as it was so isolated and away from the town, and this sudden visitation had unsettled her.

She felt a prickle of fear for the first time since she arrived at the cottage. She had never even considered the possibility of a stranger intruding in her haven. Stepping onto the warm wood of the jetty, she saw the boat was now at the steps. Should she speak? Should she hide? Should she tell the man to leave? How could she stop this shaking?

'Can I help you?' she whispered, then coughed to clear her throat.

'Can I help you?' she asked more confidently as she neared the boat, which was now being moored to a post. 'What do you want?'

The visitor turned abruptly, almost upsetting the boat, and spoke apologetically. 'I'm sorry to disturb you. I come here when there is a full moon to try to outwit these beautiful trout.' He gestured out to the lake, and as he turned back to her, she noticed a warm smile spread across his handsome face as smile lines crinkled around his eyes. She caught herself thinking that his eyes actually seemed to sparkle in the moonlight. He held out his hand to her as he leapt up onto the jetty. 'I'm Lars Amundsen, and I will go if it disturbs you having me use your jetty. I mean, no offence. I love it here.'

'Well, I love it too – particularly because of the peace and solitude. I don't mean to be selfish, but I'm used to having it all to myself.' She paused, 'I suppose it's fine. It was just a shock to see you here.'

She stepped down and reached out to shake his hand. He smiled and thanked her. 'I come here often when there is a full moon. Did you know,' he spoke softly, 'there are platypus in that bank?' he gestured to her right.

'I do know. They sometimes come out when I'm here in the early morning.'

They sat side by side, legs dangling over the water, watching the moon and the lake. Now and then, a fish would rise. 'They are definitely laughing at me,' he chuckled.

'Would it be OK with you if I continue to come here when there is a full moon? I promise not to intrude on you.'

She rose and smiled at him. 'Of course. You are welcome to share my refuge. Perhaps I'll see you tomorrow night.' She waved as she stepped onto the path back up the hill, wondering just why she felt she could trust this tall, strong stranger who seemed to belong in another world.

*

The next night, she met him with homemade lemonade, blueberry muffins and soft cushions. He smiled, pleased to see her, and as he tied up his boat, he broke the silence, 'One reason I love it here is that it reminds me a little of Norway, where I was born, with its mountains, lakes, wilderness and open spaces.'

She nodded. 'I love it for other reasons. I lived through a sometimes difficult and tumultuous marriage. When my husband died, I was left with more money than I needed and a longing for peace, quiet and solitude. I have found that here.'

'I'm sorry to breach that. I did not know.'

'Of course, you didn't. How would you know? Don't apologise.' She reached over and squeezed his hand, 'I am happy to have you share this with me.' He smiled, and they continued to hold hands as they watched the lake's surface rippling in a gentle breeze.

On the third night, she invited him into her bed.

Their love-making mystified her. She didn't know it could be so passionate and yet so gentle at the same time. No need for gymnastics or displays of masculine virility and endurance. Their desire was mutual, and she was completely sated, leaving her with feelings of gratitude, peace, and joy.

'You do know that I won't be here tomorrow night?' He bent to kiss her forehead. 'I come to check out the pumphouse works further around the lake a few days a month, and for the rest of the time, I look after my daughter, Elise.'

She understood he had his own routine and responsibilities. Over the following months, they slipped into a regular pattern, enjoying each other's company for three nights around the full moon. As the weather cooled, they spent less time on the jetty together and more time in the cottage. Sometimes, she was aware of his departure in the early hours, but often, she would awaken to find he had slipped out without disturbing her.

After a few months, Kate struggled as she tried to answer a curious colleague's questions. 'I don't know how to explain it to you, Barb. After he's gone, I feel content for the rest of the month. I go about my life as usual, and when he returns, it's full-on and so satisfying that I'm happy just to know he is in my life.' She began straightening up the flyers they had been distributing to the members of the local youth group. 'I would never ask him not to be with his little girl. He's a wonderful Dad. Something some of these kids here could do with, that's for sure. I admire him for that.'

'I agree, but I just don't understand how you can adore him so much but feel OK when he is not with you, ' Barb said as she called the young people back into the clubhouse.

'I don't understand it either. Somehow, I feel he is always with me, whether visible or not. He's just here.' She shrugged and turned to greet the group light-heartedly, jostling for their favourite seats in the room. She sensed he was there right then and smiled to herself as she strolled over to close the door. She knew it would be difficult for anyone else to understand their relationship but did not mind – she was happy, and, it seemed, so was he. Who cared what anyone else thought?

*

Then, one night, he didn't arrive. She waited and tried not to fret. There could be any number of reasons: his daughter was sick, he was sick, or the pumphouse owners didn't need his engineering skills anymore. For three days and nights, she paced through the cottage, down the path, along the lakeside and back to the jetty, and he didn't come, although she felt his presence at all times. 'Why can I feel you but not see you?' she cried aloud.

After another non-appearance a month later, she was spurred to act. She drove along the rutted dirt road through thick forest to the old pumphouse now converted to a boutique hotel. A flustered concierge asked her to wait while she searched for some information requested by a phone caller. 'No rush. I'm just here to enquire about Lars Amundsen.'

'What a coincidence. I'm just putting this together at the moment.' The concierge smiled as she pushed a folder towards Kate and opened it to a plastic pocket holding a newspaper article.

PUMPHOUSE ENGINEER SAVES THREE LIVES.
Two nights ago, Lars Amundsen, described as "a strong, well-built Viking of a man" by the manager of the pumphouse, was returning from a midnight fishing trip and, in the bright moonlight, had noticed three men clinging to an upturned boat far from the lake shore.

He rowed to the men who, unfortunately, admitted to overindulging in a bottle of whiskey. Their clumsy, panicked struggles quickly overturned his boat, too, and he was left with three freezing, floundering, helpless men clinging to him and his boat. Amundsen swam ashore with one man at a time, then returned to collect his own boat. He struggled for some time to right his boat and, having lost the oars, swam and pushed the boat before him to the shore.

"Those three clowns owe their lives to him but haven't been able to thank him yet as he collapsed and was carted off to the nearby Bush Nursing Hospital to recover from hypothermia and severe exhaustion," reported the manager.

Kate stared at the newspaper clipping, unable to fully take it in. *He was in hospital! No wonder he couldn't come to me.*

The concierge put down the phone and returned, apologising. 'I just looked these out today. I must have known someone would be interested.'

'He is a hero,' Kate stammered and smiled proudly.

'He certainly is. It's a tragic story, isn't it?'

'Tragic?'

'Oh, you haven't read the next page.' She turned the page over to reveal another news clipping.

DISTRICT MOURNS DEATH OF HERO.

We regretfully report that Lars Amundsen, hero of the Pumphouse Point rescues, has died after succumbing to an undiagnosed cardiac condition. A hospital spokesperson stated that the enormous strain of the rescues was too much for his heart, and he died two days after admission to care.

Tributes are flowing from far and wide as this tragic news spreads. A plaque commemorating his courage will be placed near the site of his heroic deeds.

RIP Lars Amundsen, 24.2.1956.

Kate stared at the article. She felt weak and clutched at the countertop. She struggled to breathe, and her chest was wracked with pain. *What does this mean? 1956? Last century? That's impossible. He was with me three months ago. This is a mistake.*

The concierge continued, 'This is such a coincidence. His daughter, Elise, visited his commemorative plaque now and then, and I met her two years ago. She didn't remember her father but told me she had felt his presence throughout her life.'

Kate nodded, knowing exactly what Elise meant by that feeling.

'We received news yesterday that she had passed away two and a half months ago. She was two days away from her seventieth birthday, I believe.' She shook her head. 'That's why I looked these up to include in our history display. I still need to add the newspaper photograph to the articles. A nice-looking man, I must say.' She smiled as she handed Kate a photo of Lars. 'I'll make you a copy if you like. I remember making one for Elise when she was here.'

Kate nodded as she gazed at Lars, smiling at her from the paper in her hand. He looked exactly as he had when she first met him. Her hand was shaking, and she looked up to see the concierge frowning at her as she reached for the paper.

*

Kate smiled at the image of Lars on the passenger seat beside her as she navigated the rough track back to the main road. 'I know you are here with me, Lars. I hope Elise might be here too.' She spoke aloud, 'I am so confused. I should be sobbing, grieving, nursing a broken heart. Instead, I just feel grateful for having had you in my life. I don't understand it, but there it is. I know you have gone to be with Elise, which fills me with joy.'

She stopped her car to let a pair of kangaroos cross the road. 'What a wonderful man you are. Or should I say, were,' she laughed. 'I love you, Lars, and I will never be lonely or feel unloved because I have known you. Thank you for choosing my jetty to visit.'

HOLIDAYS WITHOUT BORDERS

BY CORINNE KING

After much planning and discussion, our day to fly out of Melbourne for our Trip-a-Deal holiday in Japan was eventuating finally. We flew out of Melbourne at 6am on a Qantas flight for Sydney on 14th March 2024 to connect with our International JAL Flight (Japan Airlines) scheduled to fly directly to Tokyo, Japan, a tedious long 9-hour flight for us.

JAL (Japan Airlines) was a superb Airline, with pristine service and precision handling of their services, straight from the first step we took to check-in.

We left Sydney at 9.20am and arrived in Tokyo at 7.20pm. Tokyo is two hours behind Melbourne time.

Our 4 Groups of Trip-a-Deal to visit the "Cherry Blossoms in March were broken up into 4 Colours – Red, Blue, Yellow and Green - our group was Green, and we were met by our respective Group leaders and taken to our Prince Hotel in Shin Yokohama for the first night.

The next day - March 15th and, known as "The Ides of March", was our 49th Wedding Anniversary, and the day dawned for us at 5am with breakfast at 6.30am and out on the Coach at 8am. The usual tight schedules of organized tours, but nevertheless, the only way to travel in groups is to see maximum places of interest.

Our 15h March Friday morning start was cold as we were heading to the 5th Station of Mt. Fuji at a height of 2,300m above sea level. Travelling to Mt. Fuji was a long and tedious 4-hour drive with four stops for toilets and leg stretches. The day could not be more perfect, with sunshine, clear blue skies, and a temperature of 18°.

Overseas travel and meeting with other communities is a very exciting process as one gets to meet, greet and share a myriad of anecdotes with different communities. We found the Japanese culture very interesting. They were a kind and intelligent race of people who displayed many factors that the Western world needed to adopt in many ways.

We spent quite a fair time at the 5th Station on Mt. Fuji. We enjoyed looking at the many buses that arrived with tourists. Amazingly, many bus loads consisted of Japanese, some of them to view the grandeur of the majestic mountain of Mt. Fuji for the first time themselves. Our Driver and our Tour Guide told us that we would move on to our next destination, where we then took a short cruise on Lake Kawaguchiko to admire the scenery of the Lakes District and see Mt. Fuji in her splendour from a closer angle.

It was then that our Tour Guide informed us that her previous group could hardly see Mt. Fuji because of the thick cloud that sadly blanketed Mt. Fuji all day, and mind you, that was only just two weeks prior to our holiday trip. We were all tired after our gruelling, long flights. We looked forward to checking into our Daiwa Roynet Hotel in Hamamatsu to spend an evening of leisure with our fellow travellers.

The next day, on 16th March, we were out bright and chirpy after a good night's sleep and ready to take on yet another adventure in a delightful Country with its inhabitants equally pleasing and enjoyable to be with and be of great help to their country's visitors. We just enjoyed the hospitality and general kindliness of the Japanese people in the City of Hamamatsu. After our big breakfast, we toured from Hamamatsu to Nara to see the thousands of deer that have now become a symbol of the City of Nara to make the City of Nara a specially designated natural treasure. The thousands of deer that inhabit the incredibly large Park that is home to the deer has become a very symbolic region of veneration and following for those who believe that the thousands of deer are carriers of messages from the Gods.

These deer are considered the "Messengers of the Gods" as they bow to specific visitors passing on "a Goodwill message from the Gods." These deer wait to be fed "Deer Crackers" by visitors. We were very blessed to have two Deer bows, especially to us at different times. This was supposed to be a "Blessing from the Gods", according to the beliefs of the people of Deer Park. The two deer who "blessed us" came close to us and nodded, the symbolic way in which the message is passed on to the visitor to Nara Park. We were impressed as some of the members of our tour group were not treated to this very special greeting.

Again, the multicultural group that we had on our Tour Group on the Coach were a mixed bunch. We all got on so well, sharing "flavoursome goodies" every morning around the Coach as we boarded so we could all have "nibbles" as we travelled to our first morning stop on the way.

After this excursion, we were back on the Coach to head to the World-famous Heritage Buddhist Temple that was built in 772BC - one of Japan's most famous and historically significant temples and a landmark of the City of Nara and of the Country of Japan. The Japanese venerate their "holy" temples and give great respect to the foreign nations who visit these designated sites. The freedom and camaraderie extended to the many multicultural visitors who grace the sites of interest in Japan are numerous. We noticed many of those who were tourists were so multiculturally mixed, and everyone blended in so well, too, in a tourist atmosphere.

The following day, we continued our trip to Osaka to be in our Hotel Hanshin. A City that is known for its gaudy neon lights, extravagant signage, and an enormous variety of Restaurants and Bars.

We certainly experienced a very hectic and tiring long day. Certainly, we achieved heaps of sightseeing and long distances driven and covered by our Coach Driver, a very careful, courteous and ever so happy driver with a ton of personality. His name was Mr. Hashamoto, and he always wore a full suit and tie every morning to work as our coach driver.

Having completed the highlights of Hamamatsu, Nara, and Osaka, we widely explored the vibrance of this famous City. We took the optional extra tour to explore Hiroshima.

On the morning of 17th March, we left our hotel in Osaka, where we had checked in for two days. We travelled by coach to the Shin-Osaka train station to experience the bullet train ride for two hours to Hiroshima Station. On arrival, we were taken by Coach to the Hiroshima Museum.

We were to soon learn about the atrocities of War which were experienced by our parents and previous generations. There was not a dry eye amongst us all. The amazing recording of the horrendous end-of-life saga of over 350,000 lives that were lost on that fateful day on 6th August 1945 when that massive Atomic Bomb was dropped on Hiroshima was certainly not a pleasant experience. The disparities of War, Greed and Power displayed in a Museum in Hiroshima were astounding, where the Americans were responsible for the atrocities of the Hiroshima Bombing. However, it was a reality.

Ian and I have seen a similar in Hawaii, where the Japanese did it initially bombed Pearl Harbour on 7th December 1942. We have visited that Museum too in Hawaii and seen the destruction that was caused and the thousands of lives that were lost because of that fateful day. This, too, was a reality.

And then again, in more recent times, the Conflict of War in Vietnam between 1954 and 1975 brought destruction and loss of life - another Museum in Vietnam we have visited and seen the immense sadness depicted. Multiculturalism and harmony are now displayed in Vietnam, Laos, and Cambodia, which we visited in September 2019, a part of the World that has seen the light at the end of the tunnel.

In mid-May 2024, we were cruising the High Seas in the Torres Strait, taking in the incredible history of some of Australia's next-door neighbours and giving us a rich knowledge of the multicultural nations we have on our doorstep. As our holiday times are running "thin," we need to fulfil some dreams of our "bucket list", hence the fact that we are taking in some unusual and exotic places to visit.

The fascinating facts and figures we have learned about Papua New Guinea, The Solomon Islands, and the Country of Kiriwana based in The Solomon Sea have given us an insight into our neighbouring Countries that have been closely connected with our own Country of Australia.

Prior to our visiting the Countries of Papua New Guinea and the Solomon Islands, we were very lucky to have on board the Cruise Ship Mr John Hucknall OAM and his wife Morag, who provided us with some fascinating Seminars on Board our cruise ship.

The Country of Papua New Guinea is a Country with a population of approximately eight million. Their official language is English, but their 'lingua franca' is Pidgin English. Their very demeanour and friendliness were second to none, and one could melt to their own way of communicating with the tourist who was on their own land officially.

Papua New Guinea is a culturally stable country. It has very rich diversification in its own people and their lifestyles and general well-being. The people were very friendly and genuinely humble, and they were very industrious and capable in many ways.

The coastline of Papua New Guinea covers 5,150 kilometres in total. It is an indication of the vastness of this country, which is our neighbour, situated in the Torres Strait north of Darwin. In that country, amazingly, there are over 850 different languages spoken, indicating that there are that many cultures.

In the mountain ranges of this very picturesque and conducive country is the highest mountain called Mount Wilhelm, which is at a height of 4,500 metres. Wildlife and birdlife are plentiful and interesting for the avid mountaineer to explore and seek. The Sepik River is 1,126 kilometres or 700 miles long, and this river of Papua New Guinea provides the country with the ability to maintain its irrigation and crop maintenance for the survival of its people.

Papua New Guinea also flows the Fly River, which is approximately 1,050 kilometres or 650 miles long, and this river also provides the irrigational activities of the country.

There is evidence of volcanic movement in Papua New Guinea, where Mt. Lamington erupted in 1951 and 3000 people died around the Country of Papua New Guinea. There are approximately 600 islands, atolls and reefs, and the vastness of this country is only 260 kilometres or 160 miles from the Australian mainland.

In the ancient development of Papua New Guinea, agriculture was independently developed in the New Guinea highlands around 7,000 BCE, making it one of the earliest areas in the world of original plant domestication. The farming in those early years was mainly taro and yams. A major migration of Austronesia-speaking people came to coastal regions roughly 2,500 years ago along with the introduction of pottery, pigs, and certain fishing techniques, indicating to the World the early development style of this intriguing and interesting land of Papua New Guinea that in today's world denotes a wide and varied mixture of the "multiculturalism" that has been passed down from generation to generation since those early years.

In the early years of the development of Papua New Guinea, ancient internal trade routes were developed. Sweet potato was introduced to the country some 300 years ago, with its far higher crop yields, which transformed traditional agriculture in the land. It largely supplanted the previous staple food of taro and yams, giving rise to a significant increase in the Country's population in the highlands.

In the past, in Papua New Guinea, headhunting and cannibalism occurred. The reasons for headhunting among the tribe's people were simply atrocious and barbaric. Still, by the early 1950s, open cannibalism had almost entirely ceased. I must admit that this would have been frowned upon by the Western world when spontaneous cases of cannibalism were noted and made public.

Going back to the foreign invasion of the first Europeans In Papua New Guinea, who were probably the Portuguese and the Spanish navigators in the early 16th Century, when the Westerners were eager to explore the far eastern lands across the high seas of the Indian and Pacific Oceans. Notable mention must be made here that the "Bird of Paradise" skins were found to be traded in an Amsterdam auction as early as 1522, giving reason to believe that in the 15th Century, traders had been to Papua New Guinea and captured the "Birds of Paradise," a tropical Australasian bird, the male of which is noted for the beauty and brilliance of its plumage and its spectacular courtship display. Most kinds are found in Papua New Guinea, where their feathers are used in ornamental dress. The Aru Islanders of Papua New Guinea were known to seek and capture the Bird of Paradise to preserve its skin and sell it for high prices in the early 15th Century.

In 1914, the Australian troops in World War I occupied German territory of Papua New Guinea, which remained under Australian military control until 1921. Australia's first casualties in WWI were in Rabaul when a group of reservist naval personnel (Australian Naval and Military Expeditionary Force (AN & MEF) captured the German wireless station at Bita Paka on September 11th 1914 (Surrendered 13th September 1914).

The British Government, on behalf of the Commonwealth of Australia, assumed a mandate from the League of Nations to govern the Territory of New Guinea in 1920. The Commonwealth War Cemetery is at Bita Paka,

During World War II, the New Guinea campaign, which was from 1942 to 1945, was one of the major military campaigns of WWII. It has been recorded in the history books that approximately 216,000 Japanese, Australian, British, Indian sub-continent and other Asian Soldiers, Sailors and Airmen died during the New Guinea Campaign.

The multicultural lifestyle of Papua New Guinea is very diverse, and the descendants of those who walked on the soil of Papua New Guinea are seen in present times.

Major Exports of the Country of Papua New Guinea include Fish, Timber and Palm Oil. The resources exported are Gold, Nickel, Cobalt, Copper, and Silver, indicating that the Country is rich in these home resources.

Visiting the countries of Papua New Guinea and the Solomon Islands and making a brief stop-over at the Island of Kiriwana gave us an insight into the multiculturalism status these countries, which are neighbours of Australia, hold. We were enlightened by the lifestyles and government legislatures of Papua New Guinea and the Solomon Islands by Mr John Hucknall OAM and his wife Morag, who were certainly very experienced with the natives of the country, having lived there many years. Both John and Morag were The Government of Australia's Officers based in Papua New Guinea. Their base was well monitored, and all their work was documented.

Our return cruise in May 2024 from the Port of Cairns and back after twelve days was most educational after having been educated into the true facts and figures of the countries of Papua New Guinea and The Solomon Islands and their lifestyles. Our final stop in the Bay of the picturesque Island of Kiriwana, an island of unique scenery with pristine white beaches lined with coconut trees and azure blue seas that surrounded this unique island in the Solomon Seas north of Australia, was truly a worthwhile encounter.

MY SOLO HOLIDAY

BY DIANE BROWN

Four long years had gone since Mike died, and loneliness grew deeper in my soul as each year passed. After a time, my children constantly urged me to take a holiday, but my answer to their urging was always the same.

"Where on earth could I go, and what would I do on holiday by myself?"

After a particularly bad case of the flu, the decision was made for me, my eldest son's face beaming as he handed me a thick envelope.

"Well, you cannot say no to this, Mum," his young face looked at me in anticipation. "We all pooled together and decided to send you on a holiday."

Tears welled in my eyes, and I knew I could not use the same worn excuse. I hugged him closely, and after he left, I spread the contents of the envelope across the kitchen table. There was a return ticket to Proserpine in Queensland and a return ticket on a seaplane to Hayman Island. My eyes widened further when I discovered that I had been booked into the Intercontinental Resort for two weeks.

My children saw me off at Melbourne Airport, and after hugs all around,

I nervously boarded the plane. The trip was uneventful, and on arrival at Proserpine, the first thing I noticed as I walked across the tarmac was the humid air. It felt as if a wet blanket had been wrapped around my shoulders.

On viewing the seaplane, the butterflies in my stomach definitely decided to dance. It looked so small in comparison to the plane I had just departed, and I wondered if it was safe. My heart started to race as I contemplated what would happen if this tiny plane fell into the sea.

After climbing aboard and buckling my seatbelt, I was greeted by an American couple who were also travelling to Hayman Island.

A round, bright red face greeted me as I looked across the narrow aisle, and a broad, calloused hand reached towards me.

"Well, howdy there, little lady. Are you travelling all by yourself? My name's Jackson, and this is the little woman, Maryanne."

I smiled towards them both, noting that most of Maryanne's fingers were encircled in large diamond rings. Feeling uncomfortable as I stretched sideways to face them while we chatted, the time soon flew by, and before I knew it, I was gazing down through the small window at the most magnificent sight I had ever seen.

The pilot announced we were flying over the Intercontinental Hotel. As I gazed out the tiny window, I could see a half circle of white buildings surrounded by a huge bright blue swimming pool, with a kabana covered in white umbrellas nestling in the centre, its frontage stretching out towards the clearest blue sea I had ever seen. A thick forest of palms and rainforest trees surrounded the rear of the white buildings, the deep green a stark contrast to the whiteness of the buildings.

After leaving the seaplane and booking into reception, I was escorted to my suite. I felt overcome with emotion that my children had chosen such a beautiful place for me to stay. If only my late husband, Mike, was here. Why didn't we take holidays like this before he passed away?

My first night of dining alone was most uncomfortable. I was seated at a small table for two but dining alone. It wasn't easy to know where to look as I waited for my meal to be served, and I was thankful that the view and spectacular sunset were enough to give me something to focus on. As soon as I had finished dining, I immediately retired to my spacious room, luxuriating in a warm bath before falling into a deep sleep.

The following day passed quickly, spending most of my time relaxing by the pool, even managing a swim, before burying my head in a book for the rest of the afternoon. As evening approached, I once again became apprehensive about dining alone again. I hoped that perhaps I would bump into the American couple, and they would invite me to eat with them.

Dressing carefully, I smiled at my reflection as I brushed my hair, pleased to see that my cheeks were rosy from my afternoon in the sun. Again, upon entering the dining room, nervous flutters floated around my stomach as I was shown to the same table for two on the terrace overlooking the sea. Studying the menu as I sipped a glass of wine, a deep voice broke my concentration.

"Madam," the voice momentarily paused. "May I join you."

I did not know whether to be relieved or concerned. Still, my instincts told me to risk the liaison, so I quietly answered that I would be delighted to have his company.

What a wonderful night followed. Our conversation flowed with ease, and this beautiful man named Antonio swept my breath away. He walked me to my room, holding my hand to his lips as he bade me goodnight, asking if I would join him for breakfast the following morning.

The next day was even more delightful as we walked hand in hand through the nature reserve, relaxing over a salad lunch in the kabana and ending our day on the sunset cruise. That night, as we walked past his room, he reached out his hand and asked me to stay. This beautiful man named Antonio held me close, his lips lightly brushing my throat, his dark velvet eyes searching my face, telling me that he wanted more. It was so wonderful to feel wanted again, and as I wrapped my arms around him, I knew I was going to stay.

We spent my remaining holiday together, and as I boarded the seaplane for my journey home, he touched my cheek.

"Promise me you will return at the same time next year."

I did return the next year and for the next 15 years after that. During our year apart, Antonio and I never communicated. Still, in my heart, I knew he would be waiting for me. Each summer, when I returned, I would find him seated at our special table, always with a red rose on my table napkin. As we aged, our love for each other deepened. I understood when he explained how he could never leave his disabled wife, and I cherished the short time each year that we spent together.

On the 16th year, I arrived as usual. However, as I walked into the dining room, I immediately saw that Antonio was not there. As the waiter held the chair out for me, I noticed a white envelope resting underneath a red rose. I knew before I even read the letter that Antonio had died, and upon reading the letter, my instincts were correct. He had been ill for most of the past year, but before he died, he had organized for this letter to be placed on our table.

I sat alone that night, as I had that very first night all those years ago when I arrived on Hayman Island. I was no longer worried about dining alone. As I sipped my wine, memories of how nervous I had felt about taking a holiday alone flooded my mind. That first holiday had given me a lifetime of memories. Everywhere I looked, I could feel Antonio, the warmth of his arms, the gentleness of his caress and the depth of his passion.

I again returned in years 17, 18, and 19 before I became too old to travel. Each first evening of those solitaire holidays, I would find a red rose resting on my table napkin. When I queried the maître d' how that came about, he explained that when Antonio forwarded his letter to the hotel, he had also forwarded instructions that whenever I visited, a red rose was to be placed on my table.

I treasured those nights sitting alone, sipping my wine as the fragrance from the red rose drifted around the table. Those nights were full of memories, memories so precious that they reminded me of the beautiful love Antonio had given me and how those short two weeks each year changed my life forever.

THE FREE FRYPAN FALLOUT

BY JANE E. WOOD

The woman drove her green Nissan station wagon into the parking spot opposite the supermarket. Her sons in the back seat released their belts and hung over the seat in front.

"Do we have to do this now? Can't we just go home?" the older boy had been repeating this mantra over and over again on their fifteen-minute drive from school.

"I'm hot, and I'm tired, and I'm hungry, and I've been at school ALL day." That was the younger boy's contribution said almost as many times as the above.

Mother's response: "I'm hot, and I'm tired, and I'm hungry, and I've been at school all day too!" Hard to argue this one; their mother was a teacher.

"Come on, boys," she cajoled, "this won't take long. I just have to get milk and a few other things, and I've got enough points to get a free fry pan. I really want to get it before they're all gone."

The supermarket had been running a reward program where customers collected points for every five dollars spent in the store. When they had enough points, the customer could choose a frypan. There were five different sizes, and the woman had her sights set on the largest one.

As they entered the store, the older boy, resigned to being helpful so they'd get home faster, collected a basket for his mother to load her purchases into. It didn't take long to get the few items she wanted, and then they arrived at the frypans, which were located just before the 'ten items or less' checkout.

What might have been neat stacks of fry pans on the floor at nine in the morning were anything but at a quarter to five in the afternoon. There was no order at all.

"You hold the basket, Billy," the mother said to the younger boy, ignoring his eye roll, "and Freddy, you help me. We're looking for one that says it's 32cm. That's what we're after."

Freddy, being the helpful boy that he was, immediately followed his mother's example and dived into the piles.

A triumphant Freddy was soon holding a frypan above his head.

"Got one!"

His mother grabbed it from her son's hand and looked at it.

"No, not that one, Freddy, wrong size! That's a 30, we need a 32."

Disappointed, they bent into the task, but both continued to pull out the wrong sizes from the muddle on the floor. Frustration was building when….

"I've got one."

"Here's one." They yelled at the same time as the mother lifted up the frypan from the ground, and the boy bent down to pick it up.

The unpleasant sound of steel hitting flesh coincided with a loud yelp.

"Ouch!" the boy straightened up. "Mum, you hit me. Look!"

His mother looked at the blood that was rapidly falling from the three-centimetre-long gash above her son's left eye. His royal blue school tee shirt was now mottled, a rust-coloured trail spiling down to his shorts.

His mother thought for a moment; she really did want that frypan, and it had been hard to find….

"Come on, we'll just buy these things and then head to the doctor's." Billy gave his mother a strange look as they joined the check-out queue in front of them. Freddy was looking a bit wobbly by now, but there were only two people ahead of them.

"Mum, I don't feel all that good." The blood was still flowing.

"Look, it's our turn now." The mother turned to the check-out teenager who only had eyes for her bleeding son.

"What happened to you, mate?" he asked, his voice full of sympathy.

"Mum hit me with a frypan." The teenager's head swivelled to the mother.

"Is that so?" Disgust was written all over his face. Was it the mother's imagination, or had the temperature in the shop dropped ten degrees?

"Ah yes," muttered the mother, "we were just looking for a frypan and …."

"That'll be $20," the cashier snapped, wanting them gone.

The mother paid, and they made a hasty exit.

"To the doctor's, boys." Impressed by all the blood, the younger son made no objection.

Shopping stowed on the front seat, and they drove off to the nearby surgery. The mother noted that the blood flow seemed to have eased as she shepherded her two sons into the practice waiting room.

"Can we see the doctor, please; my son's had an accident?"

"Oh dear, what happened to you?" the very sympathetic receptionist asked the boy.

"Mum hit me with a frypan."

No more friendly receptionist.

"Come this way," was her stern directive.

They were ushered into a room and joined by the doctor shortly afterwards.

"What happened to you, young man?" she asked after viewing the wound. "That's a nasty one."

"Mum hit me with a fry pan." He was really enjoying this.

The doctor drew herself up to her full height, which was quite considerable, "I see."

Not liking the direction this was going, the mother babbled, "No, no, you don't. It was an accident. We were in the supermarket, and we both grabbed at the frypan we wanted, but he was going down as I was coming up with the pan in my hand, and his head collided with it."

"Is that what happened?" The doctor focussed on the boy. "You're in a safe place here. You can tell me, or I can ask your mother to leave if you feel more comfortable."

The mother held her breath. He wouldn't.... would he?

"No, I'm fine. That is what happened."

The doctor resumed normal height, and the mother breathed out.

On closer inspection of the wound, the doctor said she wasn't able to stitch or glue it shut and sent them on their way to the emergency department of the local hospital.

The younger one's patience was running out, and he certainly wasn't happy with all the attention his older brother was receiving.

"Where are we going NOW?" There was no mistaking the message in that word, 'now'.

"We have to go to the hospital," his mother told him.

Mutinous fists balled at his sides. "No!" and he stamped his feet.

Desperate for cooperation now. "Macdonald's, you can have Macca's if you stop making a fuss." The mother knew she'd regret this as soon as the words were out of her mouth, but then she thought, "Needs must."

In the emergency department, the triage nurse asked Freddy what had happened to him.

"Mum hit me with a frypan."

An instant shortcut to being seen by a doctor, apparently.

The doctor was all business, "Now, what's this about your mother hitting you with a fry pan," she asked while inspecting the wound. The suspicious look on the doctor's face relaxed as the mother relayed the facts as quickly and succinctly as she could, but only after the boy nodded his agreement.

The wound was glued and dressed, and the family headed home without being called for child protection services, much to the relief of the mother.

In the boy's classroom the next day, his fellow students gathered around him.

"What happened to you?" they wanted to know, the sight of the wound generating much excitement.

"Mum hit me with a frypan."

Twenty-five pairs of astonished eyes swivelled as one looked at his mother, their teacher.

The boy waited a beat.

"But it was an accident", he added gleefully and smiled at his mother.

WHEN THE FLOWERS BURN

BY MARIANNE ACTON

She lay among the tall grass, watching the flowers sway. A fallen ember caught in the breeze sizzled the petal to the bud. A floral ashiness perfumed the wind. Sitting up, she reached for the leftover pollen. The stem decaying at her touch.

Flocks of birds screeched a warning to the animals landbound—the hollow rumble of stampeding wildlife sprang from the brush, flattening the field around her. Turning toward the inferno, plumes of smoke swallowed the horizon. The blaze devoured tree trunks, the weighty creak of splitting lumber thumped hard against the scorched earth, and the tremor echoed underneath her.

She stood, rapid breath pumped through her lungs, each inhaling heavier than the last.

Heat prickled the back of her neck. Without a second thought, she followed in the animal's wake.

Skirting the forest, she crouched down and touched her palms to the ground. A desperate pant sounded among the crackling woods. Her fingers weaved through the charred grass, a burst of green colouring the blackened earth. Another pant broke her concentration, the drab sucked back into the turf, wilting it in an instant. She stood, taking a tentative step, feeling the dying flora shiver through her body. Her teeth gritted, and she walked on.

The deeper she travelled, the more ferocious the fire appetite became. Smoked bodies with singed fur, matted onto tan bones, were strewn on the ground. Burrows lay among the corpses of those quick enough to seek refuge underground. The noise got louder, and she spotted a fawn pacing before a felled log.

A gamey sulphuric smell blew past her. Her stomach lurched, and her weight snapped a twig underfoot. The fawn stopped in its tracks, and big, glassy eyes stared back at her. Bounding forward, the fawn nudged the cheek of a laying doe. Wedged beneath the trunk and the earth, its head flung back, its ribcage collapsed to its backbones, blood and visceral wept from its erupted gut.

Slow as she dared, she approached the fawn. The tips of its ears plastered in soot, its white patches dusted grey. On lanky legs, it stomped a hoof hard against the coal-covered ground. She held her hands out in front of her, head bowed, and she sneaked closer. The fawn yipped louder, stomping again. It stood between her and its mother.

She remained still and waited. The air around them became thicker, the heat getting denser. Kneeling before the deer, she plucked a fallen acorn from the rubbled landscape. She dusted off its smoked shell and held it out, letting the acorn balance on the edge of her fingertips.

With wobbly steps, the deer bumped the acorn from her hold. It fell back to the earth and rolled to a stop at its hoof. Their snout brushed against the seed, lips curled around it, and a loud crunch sounded from its mouth. She shifted herself closer, sliding a hand over its head. She rested her palm between its twitching ears. She scooped its back legs underneath itself and cradled the fawn against her bare chest, coming to a steady stand.

They waded through the hot waves, and she came back to the forest edge. The once vibrant pasture was now chewed up by the inferno. She stumbled through the smog of cremated flowers, the fawn bucked against her. Hot rocks clung to the skin of her feet. The fawn tucked under her arm, she balanced herself on one leg, flicking away the stones. Its hooves struck her rib cage, and pain radiated through her torso. She bent too close to the ground. The fawn wriggled free and disappeared into the cinder-coloured fog.

A dry yell slipped past her parched lips. She tumbled over herself and gave in to the hunt.

The torched terrain soon gave way to mud, feeling the soothing sound of the river before seeing it. Smoke rolled over the surface. The sparkling reflection that once shone with sunlight now mirrored the dull darkness around her. Beside her footprints, small pools of indented hoofs lined the bank. Hearing a familiar yip, she tracked after it the smouldering bark accompanying its call.

The fire crept closer to the water. The whine of timber spit from its trunk and careened forward. Landing on the shore, it cut the fawn's escape.

She plunged her legs into the riverside, dragging handfuls of slit up her shins and over her arms. Head down, she walked through the fire.

The fawn cowered on the small patch of earth left. Picking it up, she spun on her heel. The flame encircled them. Heat dried the dirt and flaked off her person. Her flesh bubbled under the torch.

Back up against the log, she wrangled the deer in front of her. Bent down, she slapped her hands down against the wood. The simmer singed her skin to the grain. Furrowing her brow, the brown of the bark bloomed back to life. The ash itched to suffocate the lush she reared. Sweat beaded down the sides of her face, the fibres peeled apart a narrow gap opening to peak at salvation on the other side.

The fawn looked at her. Mustered strength, skinned her hand free from the tree and shoved the fawn through. The sound of splashing water trilled above the crackling blaze.

With a sigh, the black seeped back. She leaned back against the log and closed her eyes. The wildfire, once again, ate her whole.

GRANDDAD BERT

BY NORMA SAVIGE

Granddad Bert was vexed. He sometimes wondered if he was just too old to understand this modern world. He'd been around the block more than a few times and knew a thing or two but was worried he was now being left behind.

It's not as if he hasn't taken on board all the changes so far. Long ago, he learnt that his favourite TV commentator, Stan Grant, did not have a touch of the tar brush and that Mario next door was not a wog. He is proud to be able to go to the footy and not call a player who missed an easy goal a pansy (or worse) and yell at him that he plays like a girl. He even acknowledges that it is nicer at the footy now and a better place to take kids and women, with better language and fewer brawls.

But a new lesson came one night when he sat with his daughter, Leanne, to watch the final of her favourite show, Dancing with the Stars. It's not his sort of thing at all, but they were the only ones at home, and she had asked him to join her. And what would it hurt?

Thank heaven they were the only ones there because when the eventual runner-up came on the screen, he couldn't help himself.

'Wow! She is gorgeous. She looks just like a blonde Gina Lollobrigida but a bit less curvy. What's her name again?'

Leanne turned to him and, with a straight face, told him, 'That's Courtney Act.' She smiled, 'You should look Courtney up on Google.'

He took out his fancy smartphone, looked her up and discovered he was admiring a drag queen; he felt totally sucked in. His son-in-law would probably have a field day with that if he knew. So would the blokes at the pub if they found out.

He flopped back on the couch and sighed, 'Gender-fluid! What the heck is that? I feel such a fool.'

'Why? She is gorgeous. I wouldn't mind having her looks and glamour. Don't be embarrassed; everyone loves her. And boy, can she dance.'

'But it's a bloke. What if a bloke asked her on a date? How would that go?'

'Well, Courtney would happily take him up on the offer.'

He just shook his head and spent the rest of the show thinking of all the implications of what he had discovered. This world is finally leaving him behind, for sure. Until the show's end, he sat totally bemused, now and then shaking his head or sighing.

'I'd appreciate it if you didn't tell anyone about this, Love,' he said as he struggled to drag his bung hip out of the couch, 'I'm off to bed now.'

'Night, Dad. Thanks for watching the show with me.'

A few days later, he had a new problem. His granddaughter, Tracey, was in her room studying with her friend Fee, and he was worried again.

'I'm just going down the back for a while,' he told Leanne.

'O.K.' She knew that meant he was going down to talk to the chooks. That's where he solved many of his problems. Good luck to him. At least he did try to work things out and move on.

'You alright?'

'Yes, all good. Just need a minute.'

As he nursed his favourite Isa Brown, he smoothed her feathers and told her what was on his mind. 'That Fee seems nice but wears overalls and has a tattoo on her neck. She's as tall as me, and her hair is as short as mine.'

The hen changed position on his knee, moving to put her face in the sun. She closed her eyes and murmured to herself.

'Granddad, I'm heading off now.' Tracey ducked her head as she entered the chook pen. 'I'm going to stay at Fee's to finish this project. I'll see you tomorrow.' She bent to kiss the top of his head and patted the hen in his arms.

'Hang on a minute,' he put the hen down, 'That Fee seems to be a nice person, but is she? Are they? Do you know if …?'

'What, Granddad?' She frowned. 'I've got to go. What is bothering you?'

Frustrated, he blurted out, 'Are you sure she's a she? What if she's a he? I mean, take a look for a minute. I think you might be being misled.'

She shrugged and stepped back. 'What? What difference would that make? We are doing our project, not getting married, you silly old duffer.' She shook her head, kissed him on the cheek and walked away.

He sat back on the tree stump he had rolled into the pen when he cut down an old pine years ago when he first bought the farm. It was his favoured spot to sit when he had some serious thinking to do. He had solved many a conundrum there, often adopting the pose of Rodin's Thinker. He looked down and asked the hen, 'Did you hear that? It doesn't matter if it's a boy or a girl! How can it not matter? Don't we need to know if we're talking to a male or a female? I mean …' There was no answer. The hen just turned her head and looked at him with one beady eye, then fluttered to the ground, where she spotted a grub.

'How can a fellow guess about everyone and get it right? Or do I have to start asking everyone what to call them?'

The next day, his mates in the Men's Shed listened to Bert and mulled over his problem as he knew they would.

'I reckon,' Johnno, his oldest mate, stood up and cleared his throat, 'I reckon it doesn't matter. For months, when I went to collect my pills from the pharmacy, I tried to figure out whether the person behind the counter was male or female. It nearly did my head in. One day, I asked my grandson to go in for my scripts and, while there, to figure out what was what below the counter, so to speak. He looked at me, shook his head and burst out laughing.'

Johnno looked abashed as he continued. 'He patted me on the head and asked if I wanted him to buy the pills or to ask them out on a date with me. He called me a silly old bugger.'

Bert looked around at his mates in the shed and saw his own struggles with wokeness reflected back at him. He sighed and said, 'Well, fellas, it looks like I need to move on yet again and come to grips with this rapidly changing world.'

They applauded his decision, and as he turned to go to the sink to wash his coffee cup, he looked back with a cheeky grin. 'By the way, I hope I didn't offend anyone just then when I called you all fellas. I guess I could be wrong about one or more of you. If so, I apologise.' I'm getting more and more woke every day. Go me!

HEALING HANDS FROM AFAR

BY RODERIC GRIGSON

I never thought much about the people behind the masks until I found myself in a hospital bed, grappling with an illness I didn't fully understand. As an older Australian with a chronic heart condition that had required open heart surgery twenty-one years prior and a history of metastatic colon cancer in the past seven years, I'd grown used to frequent trips to the hospital. But this time, something was different—not just in my body but in the faces of those around me.

The first few days were a whirlwind of confusion and discomfort. I was admitted to the hospital with unexplained chest pain, lightheadedness and severe shortness of breath, a combination of symptoms that defied easy diagnosis. My initial care involved an intricate dance of six specialists, each from a different corner of the globe, trying to solve the mystery of what was wrong with me.

First came Dr Haran, from Sri Lanka, who had been my GP for over 30 years. Trained as a cardiologist in the U.K., his calm demeanour belied the intensity of his scrutiny. Dr Haran ordered a barrage of tests—an echocardiogram, blood work, and an angiogram—and explained each step with patience that put me at ease.

"Your heart is like an engine," he said, his Sri Lankan-English accent lending a certain rhythm to his words. "We need to check every part to make sure it's running smoothly."

Next was Dr O'Malley, a pulmonologist from Ireland, who had a twinkle in his eye even as he asked me to cough into a spirometer and undertake lung function tests. He was thorough, poring over the X-rays and scans of my lungs with the precision of a detective.

"The airways are your lifeline," he said. "We need to ensure nothing's obstructing them." His Irish lilt made even medical jargon sound like poetry, momentarily distracting me from the anxiety gnawing at the edges of my mind.

Dr. Chen, a neurologist from Singapore who had lived and worked in the U.S., joined the team to rule out any involvement of the nervous system. She was brisk and efficient, her questions piercingly precise.

"Have you had dizziness? Numbness? Any unusual headaches?" she asked, her sharp eyes scanning my responses. Her focus was unrelenting, as though every detail was a potential clue to my condition.

Then, there was Dr Theron, a Gastroenterologist from South Africa, whose warm voice filled the room as he gently probed my stomach. He spoke of acid reflux and bloody stools and ordered an endoscopy and a colonoscopy.

"Once we look inside and gather all the information, I'll explain what's happening in your digestive system and what might be causing your symptoms," he explained, his tone rich with empathy.

Finally, Dr Ibrahim, an infectious disease specialist from Iran, rounded out the team. She was meticulous, asking about my working for the United Nations in various hotspots around the world and more recent international travel, my dietary habits, and my exposure to animals. Her Persian accent gave an air of authority to her words, but it was her compassion that struck me most.

"Sometimes, the smallest pathogen can cause the biggest problems," she said, her brow furrowing as she analysed the results of a blood culture.

When initial tests raised questions about the possibility of malignancy, Professor McKenzie, an Australian oncologist, joined the team. He had treated me when I was diagnosed with colon cancer, and his presence was calm and reassuring. His voice measured as he explained the next steps in investigating the nature of my symptoms.

"We need to rule out all possibilities, even the rare ones," he said, his tone imbued with quiet authority. "But I want you to know that whatever we find, we'll face it together." His expertise and kindness reassured me during what could have been an incredibly frightening time.

Each of these doctors brought not only their expertise but also a piece of their homeland's medical traditions and approaches. Their discussions were a symphony of accents and ideas, each contributing a unique perspective to the puzzle of my illness. They huddled together, sharing scans, debating possibilities, and collaborating in a way that felt almost magical to witness.

In the end, it was a collective effort that revealed the culprits. A gastrointestinal bleed caused by the long-term use of low doses of medicated aspirin as a blood thinner had brought my blood count down to critical levels, putting my heart under stress to process the reduced levels of oxygen. This resulted in a dangerous build-up of pleural fluid in my lungs, which was affecting my breathing.

In addition, the extensive CT scans showed a 2cm nodule on my lower left lung, which turned out to be primary lung cancer after a follow-up needle biopsy.

"The biopsy shows that the cancer is at a very early stage, and since you are a non-smoker, the chances of it having spread elsewhere is very low," Prof Mckenzie said, studying the pathology results. "I will schedule a brain scan to be sure as these types of cancers first reappear in the brain stem when they metastasize."

This new diagnosis was sobering, but I felt an odd sense of relief knowing that these brilliant minds had come together to find the answers.

With the diagnosis in hand, my care shifted to a broader team of specialist surgeons and nurses, anaesthetists, radiologists, pathologists, pharmacists and therapists who planned my treatment and care in the hospital with military-like precision.

The gastrointestinal bleed was attended to right away by the application of a medicated mesh by Dr Theron, during a gastroscopy, which stopped it immediately. The excessive pleural fluid was drained by the use of a hollow needle inserted between my ribs into the pleural cavity. After several blood transfusions and an iron infusion to correct my low blood count, I was allowed to go home feeling like a new man.

It didn't end there. Prof Mckenzie referred me to a renowned thoracic surgeon, Mr. Darling, who was an Australian from Bendigo. When I saw him a few days after being released from the hospital, he sat at his desk studying a CT scan of my upper body displayed on a large screen next to him.

"I have studied your file and believe I can help you," he said. "You are very fortunate the cancer was caught so early", his eyes fixed on the image. "It's localised to only one area of the lower left lung."

Mr Darling looked at me over his rimless glasses. "A couple of years ago, I would have had to remove the entire lobe. But thanks to modern surgical advances, we have found that excising only the section of the lung closest to the malignancy gives the patient a better quality of life."

Pushing the screen away, he turned to face me, assessing me carefully. "It's still major surgery. Any procedure involving the lungs is. But you're in relatively good health now that your other issues have been resolved," he paused to glance at his laptop. "My team is available, and there's an operating theatre slot open next week."

Mr Darling tapped the laptop screen with his pen before leaning back in his chair. "Shall we schedule it?"

I nodded without hesitation. I was never one to delay the inevitable.

"You're making the right choice," he said reassuringly. "We'll use keyhole surgery, so the procedure won't be too intrusive. You should be back on your feet in a couple of days."

The days leading up to the operation passed quickly, consumed by a whirlwind of medical preparations—filling out admission forms, undergoing further blood tests, a lung function test, and another MRI scan.

Undergoing a major surgical procedure was not new to me. After being admitted to the hospital around midday, I was wheeled into the holding cubicle outside the operating theatre, where I felt a strange sense of familiarity.

A masked anaesthetist nurse leaned over me. "I see from your file that this is not your first major operation," she said, her sparkling blue eyes warm with reassurance while sliding a needle into my forearm with practised ease. "You'll just feel a little prick…"

"That went well," she said after fastening a cannula to my arm. "I'll now give you something to help you relax…"

Darkness swallowed me.

I awoke in the recovery room to the blurred outline of a nurse hovering over me, her face partially obscured by a mask.

"How do you feel?" she asked. "Take some deep breaths and try coughing a few times if you can."

"How did the operation go?" I croaked, my mouth as dry as the parched deserts of the Sinai—a place I knew well from my time spent with the UN.

"Your surgeon will be here soon to give you the details, but by all accounts, it went well," she replied, her Irish lilt a soothing melody to my ears. "Here, suck on these slowly," she said as she held a small paper cup full of ice cubes to my mouth, and as the cold liquid trickled down my throat, it felt like liquid gold.

My care shifted to a succession of nurses who looked after me until I left the hospital days later.

Among them was Priya, a nurse from Kerala, India. Priya's presence felt like sunlight breaking through storm clouds. Her voice was calm and steady, her accent infused with the lyrical rhythm of Malayalam. She often spoke of home, painting vivid pictures of Kerala's lush backwaters, swaying coconut palms, and bustling spice markets.

One evening, as she replaced my IV fluid bag while chatting about her family, I asked her why she had come to Australia. She paused, then smiled wistfully. "Back in Kerala, being a nurse is about more than just a job; it's a calling. However, opportunities for growth can be limited. Here, I can learn more, provide for my family, and still do what I love—taking care of people."

Priya was more than just skilled; she had an intuition that made her seem almost prescient. When I felt overwhelmed by pain after major surgery or consumed by anxiety, she seemed to know before I could say a word. Her kindness extended beyond her professional duties. She would often bring a thermos of spiced tea during her breaks, offering me a small sip as though sharing a part of her culture to comfort me.

Then there was Win, a student nurse from Burma, whom the staff affectionately called "the vampire." Early every morning, like clockwork, she appeared at my bedside, syringe in hand, ready to draw yet another vial or two of blood. She always had a mischievous smile and a joke at the ready. "It's for science," she'd say with a wink, her Burmese accent adding a melodic quality to her words.

Win's precision was unmatched; I barely felt the prick of the needle. Despite the monotony of her task, she carried it out with an enthusiasm that was oddly contagious. "Back home," she said one morning as she labelled another vial, "I used to work in a rural clinic in a remote area. We didn't have half the equipment we have here, but we made it work. Coming to Australia has given me the chance to learn, become an RN, and help more people."

Her humour and warmth made the repetitive blood draws feel less like a chore and more like a strange ritual of connection. Even on my worst mornings, her cheerful banter lifted my spirits.

There was also Linda, the Australian Charge nurse who travelled from the Mornington Peninsular every day; Maya and Grace, both experienced nurses from the Philippines; Shelley, a trainee nurse from Bendigo; and Anna, a senior physiotherapist from the UK, each with their own stories and approaches to care. Maya's gentle presence was a balm, while Anna's firm encouragement pushed me to take my first steps after surgery. And then there was Finau, an ICU doctor from Tonga, who sat by my side on my first night after the operation, his calm presence helping me navigate the storm of fear and uncertainty.

I began to notice more accents—Nigerian, Kiwi, South American, Egyptian, Vietnamese, and Scottish, among the many Australian ones—each attached to someone who seemed genuinely invested in my recovery. These healthcare workers had left behind their families, their homes, and the familiarity of their own countries to fill critical gaps in Australia's healthcare system. They worked long hours, often under immense pressure, yet approached their roles with unwavering dedication.

One morning, as Priya helped me take my first independent steps, I found myself tearing up—not from pain but from gratitude. "Thank you," I whispered, my voice cracking.

"For what?" she asked, genuinely surprised.

"For coming here," I said simply. "For being here."

She smiled, her face lighting up with quiet pride. "We're all in this together," she replied.

When I finally left the hospital days later, I couldn't help but reflect on the patchwork quilt of humanity that had cared for me. The hands that healed me came from every corner of the globe, stitched together by a shared commitment to service. They had brought with them not only their skills but also the rich tapestry of their cultures, infusing the hospital with a sense of connection and hope.

Australia might have its struggles, but in the faces and hands of its Australian and international health workers, I saw a nation's heart beating strong—an unspoken promise that we could grow stronger together, one healing touch at a time.

A BOY CALLED TENNIS

BY STEPH WEBB

Teunis Stoffelberg sat alone on the steps near his classroom, eating his lunch out of the blue expandable cooler lunchbox. He liked the cheese-spread sandwiches his mother packed for him every day. He preferred Marmite on his sandwiches, but the Marmite in Australia didn't taste the same as the one he was used to. He tried Vegemite, too, but thought it was too bland and tasteless. He looked to see if his mother had packed a little treat wrapped in aluminium foil. It was his favourite snack. Biting into its tough texture and tasting the familiar spices gave him comfort and transported him to happy memories. He quickly placed his sandwich back inside his lunch bag. Picking up the foil-wrapped item, he unwrapped it. It was a small offcut of a piece of biltong. It was like jerky but spiced with black peppercorns, white pepper, coriander, salt, onion powder, garlic powder, and a good sprinkle of Worcestershire sauce. He had helped his father make and cure the delicious staple snack many times while they lived on the farm.

"Yuck! What are you eating? Is that rotten meat? Eeww!"

Teunis looked around to where the voice was coming from, only to see a group of four boys from his class standing just behind him. Their noses wrinkled in disgust, and one begins to smirk.

"What's your name again?" the leader of the group asked.

"Teunis", he mumbled as he wound the crinkled aluminium foil back over the biltong to hide it from sight.

"Tennis! What kind of name is that'" the boys chortled mockingly.

Teunis didn't know what to say. He just sat there holding onto the lunch box. He swallowed the big lump of sadness that felt like a hard pebble in his throat. The sound of the end of lunch break chimed over the school speakers, and the group of boys ran off as if nothing had happened between them.

As the children gathered at their desks, his teacher, Ms. Donnelly, called the roll.

"Tennis Stow-full-berg", she called out. He heard the same group of boys sniggering behind hands cupped over their mouths. Every time someone said his name, it just sounded so strange, with a different pronunciation.

"James, Archie, and Thorn! What is so funny? Care to share with the others, please?" Ms. Donnelly asked rhetorically.

The boys sat up straighter and feigned innocence as their teacher kept a steady eye on them in warning.

Later, in the classroom, he found it difficult to follow Ms Donnelly's instructions or to keep up with the others in his class, as he barely understood a word of English. It was all new to him. His teacher talked too fast for him to try to make sense of the few English words he knew. He forgot that no one understood the language he spoke, including Ms Donnelly, and had to face blank stares when he asked where he should put his completed written work in his word book. His attempt at English words sounded wrong, even to his ears. He tried to roll his words his tongue around the second language words he needed to use. He tried mimicking the Australian accent to make the words sound more familiar to others. It felt as if he was making it worse than ever.

He waited for his mother outside of her classroom after she finished her day as a grade two teacher in the same school. He thought of his dad, a former farmer with a degree in agriculture, now working in a caravan manufacturing company in Dandenong. If it hadn't been for all the farm murders in South Africa, they would still be on their farm. The neighbouring farm had fallen victim to farm crime, and even they had a close call with a house invasion. His throat tightened, and hot tears began to gather under his lower eyelids. He swallowed, breathed in deeply, and focused his eye on the tree near where he sat, waiting for his mother. Soon, they would all be at home, gathered in the kitchen, and his mother would cook the evening meal. It would all be much better then.

The classroom door opened, and his mother stepped out.

'Hello Ma', he said with a shy little smile and eyes fixed on her familiar face.

'Teunis, hello, my boy! How was your day?' he could see the delight on her tired face. He stepped closer to her to help her carry some of the items. She was trying to balance in her arms as she pulled the door closed to lock it.

'Thank you, Teunis. Baie dankie my kind (thank you very much, my child),' she said.

Just hearing his mother tongue spoken warmed his heart and caused him to grin.

That evening, he helped his parents to cook dinner. The three of them used this time to be together and talk about the day as they prepared the meal together. His father sprinkled steak spice, salt, and pepper over the chops and popped them into the oven. Teunis helped to peel the potatoes with a potato peeler, carefully directing the cutting strokes away from his body as he had been shown to do. His mother put the rice in a rice cooker to cook. Back on the farm, they would have eaten mielie pap (maize porridge cooked to a firm consistency). Mielie pap was a staple of their Afrikaans farming culture. Rice was usually only served on Sundays with rice and vegetables. After moving to Australia, they have found they are adapting to doing things a bit differently. They were a meat and three or four-vegetable-eating family, continuing the familiar meals as closely as possible in their new country.

Around the dinner table that night, his dad told the same jokes he used to express at gatherings with family and friends around the campfire, down at the dam on their farm. This usually led to the telling of hunting stories, hilarious encounters with native bush animals, or run-ins with an angry bull on the farm. They laughed until tears rolled down their cheeks. One couldn't tell if they were tears of amusement or tears of sorrow. The sorrow of a life and people left behind weighed heavy on each of their hearts. Family and friends are much loved, and they are now on a faraway continent under a hot African sun and dry African bushland. A land of rolling hills and flat plains where brilliant colours and khaki blended in art, fashion, and décor. A land of contrast and extreme.

As Teunis lay in bed that night, he heard the quiet sobbing of his mother in her bedroom and the deep, comforting murmur of his father's voice. He began to think of how much he misses his Aunty Marie and her tennis club sandwiches that she made neatly trimmed and stacked together like concertinas. He missed the family and friends who gathered around the open fire on their farm some weekends to cook meat on open fires. In his memories, he travelled back and saw the laughing faces and could hear the singing of songs, accompanied by uncles playing on guitars, concertinas, and mouth organs. He saw the couples jumping up and spontaneously choosing partners from around the seated group to do long-arm dancing sokkie dancing (a two-step mixed with quick fox-trot dancing). He imagined himself sitting around listening to the familiar retelling of the stories about life in the bush, on the farm, fishing stories, hunting stories, and joining in the loud, raucous laughter. With these images drifting through his thoughts and memories, he finally drifted off into a deep sleep.

One day, they followed another in much the same pattern and routine for some time until the day they found the flyer in their post box. It was about a cultural day that was going to be held at the local community centre. They decided it might be something interesting to attend together.

The day arrived, and Teunis and his parents came to see tables laden with food from different nationalities. Musicians played a variety of instruments, people dressed in traditional dress, and dancers performed at various times. He and his parents wandered around, noticing that there were so many nationalities originating from around the world and interacting with one another. This made his heart ache even more because of their familiar traditional food, boere music (folk music), and the sound of their home language. As if an answer to silent prayer, he heard someone saying,

'Ai man, hierdie samosa is baie lekker' (oh man, this samosa is lovely).

He looked up at his parent's startled expressions and noticed they had heard the same thing. The three of them looked at one another in utter surprise and then looked around to see who was speaking their taal (language). An older couple was standing close by, eating samosas and laughing with the people at one of the food tables. They tentatively approached them and asked if they were South African.

'Yes'.

Quickly, a conversation struck up as they each shared where they originated from and how long they had been in the country. The older couple introduced themselves as Brenda and Frank Nel. Next, they introduced the family at the food stand, who they had just met earlier while buying samosas. It wasn't long before they discovered the family had immigrated from India a few years ago, but they had relatives living in South Africa, too.

Another family group stopped by, greeting the older couple.

'This is our neighbours,' Mrs Nel informed them.

'We just met the Stoffelberg family. They have only been in Australia for a couple of months. 'They are from South Africa too,' the couple stated as they made introductions.

"We were both born in Sri Lanka but used to live in Botswana for a while, and we travelled to South Africa often. Roshan got a work transfer to Australia fifteen years ago, so here we are", the cheerful wife told Teunis' mother.

Soon, they were all talking about cricket and rugby as they tucked into the various tasty foods at the table.

'How about joining us for a 'bring and braai' next Saturday, we can watch the rugby together. There is a match at 6 pm. We can braai at about 3 or 4 pm, before the game', Mr. Nel suggests. Their mutual knowledge of the South African culture for a 'bring and braai' needed no further explanation. Each of them would need to bring meat to cook on the barbeque and a salad to share. Someone would bring a dessert. Everyone would supply something to drink. It was the South African way. Soon, everything was arranged for who would be making desserts and which salads.

Teunis' mother laughed as she shared the story about a very embarrassing moment at a work luncheon for a colleague when she was asked to bring a plate. She wondered if there weren't enough crockery for everyone to use. It was a strange request, but she had complied and brought along an empty plate and a spare in case someone needed it. Everyone laughed, and Mrs. Nel talked about how she and Mr. Nel had been invited over for tea by a business associate the first week of their arrival many years ago. It was a very strange time as it was so close to their dinner time.

Nevertheless, they ensured they had their dinner a little earlier. They took along some pastries to contribute to the tea, as was their custom. They arrived to find out that 'tea' was a full meal and not a cup of tea with cake or savoury snacks.

'We have been there too!' was the consensus between the little group of immigrants as they laughed about the misunderstandings they all shared.

That is when Teunis's life began to change.

All week, he could think of nothing other than the braai and rugby match at the Nel's home. He smiled a bit more at school and lifted his head higher. He still didn't speak much. He was still struggling to keep up with the others in class because he was a bit slower in understanding what was being said or expected of him.

Soon, Saturday arrived, and Teunis was amazed to see more new people had been invited to the 'Bring and Braai' event. There were a few children who he recognised from his school. He was thankful none of the bully boys were there.

The open fire had been prepared, and the coals had burned down enough for the meat to go onto the grill within about half an hour of everyone arriving. The trestle tables were laden with bowls of salads of various kinds, bread rolls, and sandwiches made of cheese and onion. These were the first to go into the metal grill frames and toasted over the fire. They were carefully turned to prevent the bread from burning. These were put onto large platters and passed around as soon as they were ready. The children were served first, as usual. Teunis enjoyed the strong, stingy melting cheese and slightly over-toasted bread with the strong taste of cooked onion. His eyes almost closed as he bit into his 'braai broodtjie' (barbeque toastie). He sat next to a few of the children and their parents until someone decided to start playing games and invited him to join, too. He felt a bit shy at first as he didn't know anyone. Playing hide and seek was easy because he didn't have to try to speak English. He could count to twenty in English. After that, the children played a few different games while the adults cooked the meat and enjoyed stories and jokes together. He began to relax and enjoy the games they were playing together.

He could see his mum and dad enjoying themselves as they were included in the conversations and began to find the things they each had in common.

By the end of the evening, Teunis and his family found themselves invited out to dinner by other guests. Teunis heard his mother talking about his birthday being in two weeks and inviting everyone over to join them for yet another 'bring and braai' to celebrate the event with them. This is the South African way. Everyone was welcome.

At school the next week, during breaks, Teunis began to join another boy he met at the 'bring and braai' on Saturday. Although they weren't in the same class, they were in the same year level. As the week progressed, Teunis made a few more friends. They didn't mind that he spoke differently or stumbled over his words. They found ways to communicate without always having to use words. He found he was better at understanding English. He was keeping up with his schoolwork during class more and gaining the confidence to join in a little more than before.

He was looking forward to his birthday and told Aunty Marie all about his party plans and his friends at school when they had FaceTime on Friday night. As he talked, she laughed and cried. He wasn't sure if they were happy or sad tears. Maybe they were both. He could relate to that. Being happy and sad about life in their new country was bitter-sweet.

A FICTIONAL TALE OF CHRISTMAS 2024

BY BERNIE WEISS

The diminutive woman walking to the front door spends Friday regularly with her daughter in Noble Park. The door opens on her second knock. The tall, blond woman in a Carer's uniform greeted her.

"Hi Lucinda, go right through. She's eating breakfast. I've just got the mopping to do, and I will be out of your hair for another week."

Today, Lucinda is accompanying Maranda, who uses an electric scooter, to shop for Christmas presents and enjoy lunch in one of the local cafes. Neither drives a car, but the mother has a Multi-Purpose Taxi Program card (MPTP) that enables these outings at vastly discounted fares. Today's outing became problematic when Maranda's scooter battery failed just as they intended to return to the Nelson Street assisted living unit. They sat in a café drinking coffee during the two-hour delay before assistance arrived. The battery had reached its' 'use-by date' and was replaced. This maintenance cost was expected in the bigger picture of scooter ownership. However, the timing today was unfortunate. Arriving at Nelson Street at four-thirty, Maranda called for a taxi for her mother's return.

The heavy-set, black-bearded driver of the metal-grey 13-cab was feeling the strain of his busy day on the road. This, he promised himself, would be his last fare. He had focussed on the younger woman's instructions, 'Blue Hills, in Cranbourne,' tapping it into the GPS unit. The secondary instruction, '214 Periwinkle Drive,' went unnoticed.

"Merry Christmas, Mum!" Maranda waved as the Toyota SUV cab drove away. "Don't forget to call me when you get home!"

"Well, I've had quite a day. How has your day been?" Asked Lucinda, who loved chatting with anyone who gave her the time of day.

"Good afternoon, madam. Please do not start a conversation with me. I need to pay attention to the busy evening traffic conditions. Furthermore, I must also watch the GPS, which guides me to the destination," answered the red-turbaned driver.

"Don't you know the way? I can help you with that." Lucinda offered.

Trying to hide his agitation, he answered, "Please sit back and enjoy the drive. I am not used to driving in peak-hour traffic conditions yet."

Feeling chastised, Lucinda sat back to enjoy the ride despite Mohamid's terse response. She had heard him yelp in pain while putting her walker and shopping bags away, and now his angry red fingers attested to what had occurred. She wanted to ask if he was okay but looked the other way and kept her mouth shut.

*

The 22-km drive via Heatherton Road and South Gippsland Highway was typically a 30-minute relaxed drive. However, today's journey was hampered by heavy peak-hour conditions as workers jockeyed for position along the Monash Freeway to get home quickly. Additionally, there was a seven-car pile-up at the merge with Stud Road, and the traffic lights at the Pound Road intersection were faulty, leaving the local constabulary to keep traffic moving. The stop-start journey had taken 90 minutes, during which Lucinda nodded off to sleep.

Looking into the rear-vision mirror, Lucinda noticed a build-up of sweat drops forming on the driver's brow. She wondered if this was due to the uncomfortably warm afternoon. An answer of sorts presented itself when a phone call came through. A woman's voice admonished him for being late for dinner. Mohamid smartly turned the sound down and shot a stream of unintelligible responses at the woman before ending the call. He looked in the rear-vision mirror to check on his passenger. To his relief, he saw her feined asleep. Lucinda did her best not to smile, having understood the gist of the exchange between the driver and his wife. She recalled how her late husband, James, would air his frustrations If she dared call him while driving home from work. With happy thoughts of her time with James, she slid back into the oblivion of sleep.

"Thank you for your custom. Your share of the share is $23, please," Mohamid said some twenty minutes later as he pulled the cab over.

Lucinda woke with a start, not recognising her surroundings. "But this isn't 214 Periwinkle Drive," she said.

The driver's large brown eyes bulged as he spun around to check the GPS. "The address given to me was Blue Hills; that sign says Blue Hills! Now hurry up; I am running late!"

Not fully awake, the 88-year-old paid her fare and waited for the cabbie to bring her walker to the passenger side.

"Well, get out!" he said in a huff.

Looking into his large brown eyes, Lucinda noticed the spittle formation on his lips. She reminded him of her walker and shopping bags in the boot.

Blushing profusely, Mohamid battled with the contraption the woman used to carry her shopping bags. Lucinda was confused by the man's gruff attitude. It was Christmas time. Where was his good cheer?

The stones along the shoulder of the tarmacked just missed the woman as the taxi's spinning wheels raced off, leaving her surveying her surroundings. The heavy traffic rushing past her on the double-lane, two-way bitumen road amazed her. When had Periwinkle Drive become a main thoroughfare? Grappling with the red walker and shopping bags, she turned to enter the colonial-style double-wrought iron gates set into the tall, high brick fence line. The signage was clear; it was Blue Hills. Lucinda's relief was short-lived as she passed a tennis court, followed by a beige-maroon rotunda to her left, the circular driveway, and the tall flagpole.

'Perhaps this is the new access point for my retirement village,' Lucinda thought, 'I can call reception if I can't, Periwinkle and my two-bedroom residential unit.'

Something wasn't right, but she couldn't say what had her heart racing. Three couples, walking arm in arm, approached from her right, greeting her cheerfully in passing.

One woman called to her. "Been out shopping again, lovey?"

Lucinda did not recognise them, but they knew of her Friday routine, shopping and visiting her daughter. She smiled in answer, realising she must be amongst friends, and shuffled on after them as they headed off towards the well-lit foyer of the administration building. Seeing the reception desk through the windows, Lucinda considered getting help to complain about her cabbie's attitude with the 13-cab company and ask for a buggy ride home. It had been a long day; she was tired and confused.

Moments later, as she entered the foyer, she stood captivated by the enormous Christmas tree dressed in baubles, bells, colourful tinsel garlands, and sparkling lights. This was familiar in an unfamiliar sort of way. Gazing upward, the petite white-haired woman smiled at the angel suspended at the tree's apex. A tide of well-turned-out people converged around the tree, sweeping her into a well-appointed restaurant.

While they all headed off to greet friends at pre-determined tablets, the thought struck Lucinda, 'I don't know where my table is; I can't see my friends.'

Noticing her dilemma, staff helped her sit at a round table set for eight, with her stroller and bags placed against the nearby wall. Overwhelmed and shy at not knowing her table companions, Lucinda lowered her head, letting her hazel eyes dart from left to right, admiring the familiar damask tablecloth, dinnerware, and table decorations. Her table companions tucked into their main course, and they wished each other a 'bon appetite.'

The waitress, carrying two dinner plates, rushed over and asked Lucinda what she had ordered: "The Battered Flathead or the Chicken Schnitzel?" As no response was forthcoming, she said, "Never mind, lovey, here have the Schnitzel." Later, as the desserts came out, Lucinda cheerfully accepted the Christmas Pudding with custard, happy not to have the trifle offered to every second diner.

A tall, dark-haired man distributed raffle tickets to everyone at the tables for 'the door prize.'

"I hope I get a prize this year, Bill," said the woman in the red bolero jacket over a well-fitting green dress.

"My job is to hand out tickets, Mavis; what you win, and if you win, is beyond my pay grade!" Bill laughed as he moved on.

Lucinda giggled along with her table companions. The banter between residents was all so familiar, in an unfamiliar sort of way.

Having enjoyed her meal, Lucinda conversed with the man on her left, who thought she was a new resident. "No, I've been here ten years," she answered.

The man looked at her with greying-bushy raised eyebrows. He'd not seen her before in the twelve years since he'd moved in with his late wife.

Lucinda could not put a name to his face, let alone anyone else's at nearby tables, 'Oh, well, it's Christmas, don't worry about it,' she thought.

After adjusting the microphone and clearing his throat, the tall man on the small stage introduced himself as Shane. He wore his thick, pepper-and salt-coloured hair tied in a ponytail, while his long ginger sideburns hinted at the fashion for men in the 1970s. His ruffled tuxedo shirt front, silver cummerbund, matching plain bow tie, over pleated black trousers added to his seventies' look.' He welcomed everyone to Christmas dinner, explaining he was standing in for Jaques, who would have been their singer tonight. However, he had tested positive for COVID-19.

"My repertoire this evening focuses on the hit parade songs of the seventies, hence the retro-look attire."

Then, in a deep baritone voice, he began.

So, this is Christmas

And what have you done?

Another year over

And a new one has just begun.

"Shane!" finally, someone I know, thought Lucinda, as the singer invited everyone to join in.

And so, this is Christmas

I hope you have fun

The near and the dear one

The old and the young

Between verses, Shane waved the residents onto the dancefloor.

A very merry Christmas

And a happy New Year

Let's hope it's a good one,

Without any fear.

Most couples at her table moved to the dancefloor; Lucinda Rose made a bee-line towards Shane to the strains of,

And so, this is Christmas

For weak and strong,

For the rich and the poor,
The world is so wrong.

Shane smiled at Lucinda, wondering why she was here and not over the road at Blue Hills Rise, where she lived. He gestured her to the microphone.

"Will you join me?" he asked.

"Yes, this is our duet, after all," she answered. Shane smiled with relief; his singing partner was here by invitation. Handing her the mike, he stood back to admire her well-modulated contralto voice as she carried the lyrics on...

And so happy Christmas
For black and white
For yellow and red ones
Let's stop all the fight.

Grabbing the other mike, Shane joined in for the final verse. The two trained voices harmonised a velvety rendition of John Lennon's 1971 hit as the hubbub of conversation died down, and the dancers stopped to sway to the melody.

A very merry Christmas
And a happy New Year
Let's hope it's a good one.
Without any fear.

The singers held hands as they bowed to the audience and each other. The diners and dancers showed their appreciation by giving loud applause, catcalls, and wolf whistles.

IN THE MEANTIME---

Maranda reported that her mother was missing!

"Mum hasn't called me to confirm her safe arrival home. More worrying," she said, "Mum isn't answering her telephone or mobile."

The emergency admin team at Blue Hills Rise raced to the Periwinkle

Drive address. Had Lucinda fallen inside her unit? Was she unable to press the alarm for assistance?

As the call-out team arrived, they noted that the lights were off, and no one answered the doorbell. Using the passkey, they entered the unit. The resident's walker wasn't there, and the breakfast dishes were in the drying rack. Had Lucinda even arrived home? Where was she? What had happened to her?

The local Police Station were advised of the octogenarian's disappearance. On contacting the 13-cabs company, they soon learned the name and address of the cabby that had taken the fare from Noble Park around 4.30 pm. A police team, accompanied by someone from the management team, visited the given address to question the cabbie. Mohamid nearly passed out when he opened his front door to the tall, uniformed constables scowling at him.

After helping the shaking man to a sofa, the officials leaned over him,

"What have you done with Lucinda?"

Mohamid's eyes were wide open, his eyebrows raised, and his jaw dropped open. He exclaimed in a croaking voice, "Nothing!"

When various versions of the same line of questioning failed to satisfy the constables, the man was handcuffed behind his back and marched out to his cousin's taxi, parked in his driveway. Mohamid was able to bring up his journey log. He swore he'd dropped the old woman, her walking device and shopping bags off at the address shown in his GPS, 'Blue Hills.'

At this point, the police and Blue Hills Rise's management realised the errors often made. They alerted their sister retirement village, Blue Hills Residences, across Berwick-Cranbourne Road, to look out for the lost Lucinda.

Back on the stage

Shane and Lucinda were finishing their sixth song together and announcing they would take a short break. Bronwyn, the office manager at this retirement village, approached the singers on stage to converse with them both in whispered tones. Hugging the white-coffered woman, she took a mike to introduce Lucinda. She explained with great relief that family, police and village staff had spent an agonising couple of hours looking for the 'lost' but now-found woman.

Lucinda took the mike to wish everyone a Merry Christmas, expressing relief in realising why she had not known anyone at the early Christmas Dinner. Looking at Shane, she thanked him for letting her sing for her supper. Then, turning back to the diners, she said

"Thank you for having me. It has been wonderful to see how *the others over the road* celebrate Christmas. The welcoming atmosphere has been familiar in an unfamiliar sort of way," she giggled. "Now, can someone please take me home?"

FROM DESERT SANDS TO CITY STREETS

BY RODERIC GRIGSON

THE PROMISE OF THE OUTBACK
In the 1860s, Australia's untamed wilderness—its vast, unforgiving desert—was the final frontier. The British had ventured into the heart of the continent, building telegraph lines and searching for gold, but they soon realized that the harsh, sun-baked outback had more to offer than just its mineral wealth. It offered its challenges, a never-ending horizon of sand and scrub, and distances too wide to cross on horseback.

By the time the British settlers had arrived, Australia was already home to a multitude of Indigenous cultures, each of which had adapted to the land's harsh rhythms for thousands of years. But for the European settlers, it was a different story. Their horses, though strong, struggled under the burning sun. They had no solution to carry goods across the vast distances of the outback. The answer, however, came from across the seas—from the dry plains of Afghanistan.

THE ARRIVAL OF THE GHANS

The British, accustomed to the hot, dry regions of India, had been familiar with camels for centuries. But to navigate the heart of Australia's deserts, they needed more than just the animals. They required skilled Afghan camel herders—men who had spent their entire lives in the harshest, most remote landscapes in Central Asia, mastering the art of navigating with camels as both transport and companion. These men, known as "Ghans," had a deep connection to the creatures, understanding every facet of their needs and behaviour. They were the keepers of a tradition, passed down through generations, of survival in the most brutal environments.

The first wave of Ghans arrived in Australia in the 1860s, brought by the British colonial authorities to work as camel drivers for the overland telegraph project. It was a dangerous and arduous task to string wires across the wild, unpredictable terrain of the outback, and the Ghans' camels—capable of going without water for days—became the perfect solution. They hauled heavy loads of supplies, food, and materials across deserts that had once seemed impenetrable.

Among the first Afghan herders to land in Port Augusta, South Australia, was a man named Mohammad, who had spent his youth trekking across the rugged, mountainous landscape of his homeland. His father had taught him everything there was to know about camels—how to speak to them, how to read their subtle body language, and how to navigate the desert with nothing but the stars as his guide.

Mohammad, like the others, was brought to Australia under the promise of work and adventure. He arrived with little more than a small caravan of camels, a few fellow herders, and a heart full of hope. The sight of their camels—a long line of towering, strong creatures with thick lashes and broad, leathery feet—was as much a statement of endurance as it was a symbol of a long-standing way of life.

Upon their arrival, the Ghans quickly set to work. They became the lifeblood of the outback, creating the famous camel trains that would travel across vast distances, bringing supplies to towns and outposts that were otherwise inaccessible. The work was gruelling and often dangerous. The Ghans had to contend with extreme heat, storms of dust and sand, and treacherous terrain, all while maintaining a deep connection to their camels and navigating their way through uncharted territory.

LIFE IN THE OUTBACK

It wasn't just the work that was tough; it was the isolation. The Afghans were far from home, in a strange land, surrounded by people whose culture and language were completely foreign to them. In Australia, the Ghans were often met with suspicion. Their long robes and turbans marked them as different. They were strangers in a strange land, and at times, even their fellow settlers viewed them with distrust.

Mohammad had experienced this firsthand. The white settlers, having little to no understanding of his background, often called him and his people "Afghans" in a generalised and sometimes derogatory way. The term, though applied broadly to all camel herders from the region, did not reflect the diversity of their origins. They came not just from Afghanistan but from regions that spanned the length of Central Asia—from the mountainous edges of the Hindu Kush to the deserts of Baluchistan.

Despite the harsh treatment, Mohammad and his companions persevered. Over time, they established small communities in outback towns like Alice Springs and Port Augusta, where they settled, their livelihoods forever tied to the land. The camels, too, adapted, finding a new home in Australia. Many of them escaped, eventually forming wild herds that still roam the outback to this day.

In the evenings, after a long day of work, Mohammad would sit by the campfire, gazing at the stars. The vastness of the Australian sky, so similar to the one he had known in Afghanistan, filled him with a quiet sense of peace. Sometimes, when he spoke to his fellow herders, they would reminisce about their homeland. They spoke of their families, of the way, the mountains in Afghanistan had once seemed to touch the sky, of the smell of fresh bread baking in the streets of Kabul, and of the bustling bazaars where they had once bought spices and fabrics.

But this new life in Australia had its own rhythm, and Mohammad found solace in its routine. The days were long, and the work was difficult, but there was a sense of purpose. He had become a part of something larger—a network of people who were bound together by a shared task. He and his fellow Afghans were helping to tame the wilderness, building the infrastructure that would allow Australia to grow.

One night, as Mohammad sat with his camel, watching it graze on sparse patches of grass, he heard the distant sound of hooves. Another herder was approaching with a new caravan. The man dismounted, his tired face breaking into a smile as he approached Mohammad.

"Peace be upon you," the newcomer said in broken English, extending his hand.

"And upon you peace," Mohammad replied, shaking his hand firmly.

"More camels to carry the load. We'll need them for the new telegraph line."

Mohammad nodded. The job, though exhausting, was essential. With each new mile of telegraph line they built, the vastness of the Australian outback became a little smaller, a little more accessible. But there was still much work to do.

As the years passed, the Afghan herders played an integral role in shaping Australia's history. They traversed the country, laying the foundations of communication and trade that would help connect the isolated corners of the continent. The work they did was largely unsung, but it was vital to the country's growth.

THE DECLINE OF THE CAMEL TRAIN

As the 20th century dawned, the world changed in ways that the Afghan camel herders could never have anticipated. The rise of motorized transport, particularly trucks and trains, made the camel caravans less necessary. The camel trains, once so essential to the movement of goods across the outback, began to fade into history. The Ghans, too, found their role diminishing.

Some returned to their homelands, while others settled in Australian towns, where they began new lives. But the legacy of the Afghan herders remained. Their camels, still roaming wild in the deserts, are a living testament to the contributions they made to Australia's development.

Though the Afghan herders had once been strangers in a foreign land, they had left an indelible mark on the Australian outback. Their camels helped tame the wilderness, their hardiness helped connect distant communities, and their presence—though often overlooked in the larger narrative of Australian history—became a symbol of endurance, survival, and adaptation.

Even now, the descendants of those Afghan camel herders remain a part of Australia's multicultural fabric. Their contribution to the story of this land is still felt in the camels that roam the outback and in the quiet spirit of the people who once walked alongside them, leading their camels across the vast, sun-baked expanse of the Australian desert.

THE REFUGEE CRISIS: A NEW JOURNEY BEGINS

As the century passed and the waves of migration shifted, the story of the Afghan people in Australia didn't end with the camels. In recent decades, another chapter in their migration journey has unfolded—a chapter that has seen a resurgence of Afghan communities moving to Australia, with many settling in urban centres like Melbourne. This migration is distinct from that of the Afghan camel herders of the 19th century, but it carries with it echoes of the past, as it too involves the pursuit of a new life in a foreign land, the quest for safety, and the hope of a better future.

The story of the Afridi family spans continents, cultures, and decades, a tale of migration, struggle, and eventual settlement. From the dusty streets of Kabul to the vibrant, multicultural city of Melbourne, their journey is a testament to resilience and hope, the legacy of generations striving to find peace and opportunity in a world that often seems unforgiving.

It was in the late 1980s when the Afridi family—comprising father Ahmad, mother Amina, and their two young children, Tariq and Laila—first faced the dire conditions in their homeland. Kabul, once a city of beauty and history, was rapidly transforming under the pressures of conflict. The Soviet invasion of Afghanistan had left the country in ruins. By the time the Afridi family realized that their safety was no longer guaranteed, the city had become a battleground.

Ahmad, a respected schoolteacher, and Amina, an aspiring doctor, had always dreamed of offering their children a future where education and opportunity were within reach. But with the Taliban's growing influence and the constant threat of violence, their dream seemed increasingly out of grasp. Every day in Kabul was a risk—whether from the shifting frontlines or the growing desperation among civilians. They knew they had to leave, but the path out was uncertain, treacherous, and filled with danger.

As the war raged on, Ahmad and Amina began making secretive plans, whispering about the possibility of emigrating to a country where their children could be free from the daily threats of war. They had heard stories of people finding safety and a new life in distant lands, but which land could they turn to? It wasn't until the UNHCR (United Nations High Commissioner for Refugees) offered asylum programs to those fleeing Afghanistan that their hope finally turned into action.

The evening was calm in Kabul, the kind of peaceful dusk that painted the sky in soft purples and golds. Ahmad sat with his son Tariq on the roof, their feet dangling over the edge, looking out across the city where the minarets of mosques towered above the old buildings. The distant rumble of conflict was becoming a constant presence, but for a moment, they could pretend that life was as it had always been.

Tariq had grown accustomed to hearing gunshots echoing in the distance, but tonight, he was silent, staring at the fading light.

"Dad," Tariq asked, his voice barely a whisper, "Do you think things will get better?"

Ahmad's hand rested on his son's shoulder, a sad smile on his face. He had always been the strong one, the protector, but now his resolve was waning.

"I don't know, son," Ahmad replied softly. "I wish I could promise you it would get better. But sometimes, in life, we must make the hardest choices."

Tariq turned to his father, his brow furrowing. "Are we leaving?"

Ahmad looked down at his son, the weight of the decision pressing heavily on him. "Yes," he said, his voice steady. "We're going to find a place where you and Laila can be safe. A place where you can grow up without fear."

Amina, his wife, joined them on the roof, her eyes red from the tears she'd hidden earlier. She had been packing. The family had made their decision—it was time to leave, to flee the city before it became completely unsafe. The Taliban's presence was growing stronger by the day, and the future of Afghanistan was uncertain.

"Ahmad, is this really the right choice?" Amina asked, her voice trembling. "What will happen to our home? Our family?"

Ahmad pulled her close, his face tight with the weight of the decision. "It's the only choice we have. For them." He looked at Tariq and Laila, who had come to join them on the roof, her small hand holding onto her brother. "For all of us."

THE LONG ROAD TO REFUGE

The Afridi family's journey out of Afghanistan was not a simple one. In the mid-1990s, they fled Kabul, joining the thousands of other displaced families heading toward the Pakistani border. The trip was perilous—fraught with the fear of being caught by the Taliban or soldiers from warring factions. They crossed treacherous mountain passes, their bodies and minds exhausted by the ordeal. Along the way, Ahmad kept up a brave front for his children, telling them stories of a better life they would one day live.

Arriving in Pakistan, they found themselves in a refugee camp in Peshawar. In this sprawling settlement, thousands of Afghans lived under the constant strain of uncertainty. The camp was overcrowded and unsanitary, but it offered a modicum of safety. Here, in the midst of the thousands of tents, the Afridi family lived for several years. Their lives became a routine of survival—tending to daily needs, seeking food and clean water, and doing their best to adapt to the new environment.

In their small tent, Amina prepared a meal of rice and lentils, her hands moving with the practised ease of someone who had done this countless times before. Tariq, now a teenager, sat by the edge of the camp, staring into the distance. His mind wandered back to Kabul, to the life they had left behind. He could still remember the cool breeze on his face as he ran through the streets with his friends before the world changed.

"Are you okay, Tariq?" Amina asked, noticing her son's faraway gaze.

He didn't answer immediately. Instead, he ran a hand through his hair and sighed.

"I miss Kabul. I miss everything. I don't even know how to talk to these kids here."

Amina set the bowl of food down beside him. "You will learn, son. And remember, this is just a chapter. We have survived the hardest part already. We will keep moving forward."

"I know," Tariq muttered. "But... it's hard."

Meanwhile, Laila, always the optimist, had made a few friends in the camp. She ran over to her mother, excitedly waving a small picture she had drawn on a scrap of paper. "Look, Mama! I drew a house like the one in Kabul. But with flowers. And birds. And..."

Amina smiled softly, stroking her daughter's hair. "It's beautiful, Laila. You always know how to find the beauty, don't you?"

Laila nodded, her eyes bright with hope. "Yes, Mama. Even when the world is sad, I can still see the flowers."

In the camp, Ahmad and Amina were determined to keep their children's education alive. Ahmad would often gather groups of children, teaching them basic reading and writing. Amina, with her medical training, volunteered at a makeshift clinic, helping with the basic healthcare needs of the refugees. These small acts of resilience kept the family going. But the dreams of a brighter future were never far from their minds.

One evening, after years of waiting, the family received a message that would change everything. They had been accepted for resettlement in Australia, a country that had long welcomed refugees and offered the possibility of a new life.

In 2001, the Afridi family was granted UNHCR refugee status and relocated to Australia, where they were assigned to Melbourne. This city was known in the camp for its cultural diversity and vibrant immigrant communities. The Afridi family arrived full of hope yet also full of uncertainty. They had heard stories of the opportunities Australia offered. Still, the reality of settling in a new country—especially one so far from home—was daunting.

ARRIVING IN MELBOURNE: THE NEW WORLD

The journey from Peshawar to Melbourne was a strange and unfamiliar one. The Afridi family had heard of Australia—of its beauty, its opportunities, and the promise of safety—but the reality of arriving in a land so far removed from Afghanistan was overwhelming. The moment they stepped off the plane at Melbourne's Tullamarine Airport, the air felt crisp and unfamiliar. The hustle and bustle of the airport—people moving quickly, the language so different—left them feeling out of place.

They were greeted by a government official who spoke to them in broken Dari, a language they knew. Still, the reality of starting over in a strange place quickly became evident.

"Hello, my name is John. I'll help you get settled here," said the man, smiling warmly but speaking in a way that felt so alien to them.

Ahmad nodded, though he felt a twinge of fear. "Thank you," he said, though his accent made the words sound unfamiliar to his own ears.

Amina looked around nervously. "Is this... is this where we will live?"

John pointed toward the exit. "Yes, we'll take you to a place in Dandenong. It's a neighbourhood with lots of families like yours. You'll feel more at home there."

As the family drove through the streets, Tariq sat by the window, watching the unfamiliar cityscape unfold. The houses were neat, the streets lined with trees, and everything seemed too perfect, too far removed from the dusty, war-torn streets of Kabul and the crowded refugee camp in Peshawar.

"I don't think I'll ever fit in here," Tariq muttered under his breath, feeling a wave of homesickness wash over him.

"You will," said Ahmad, his voice calm yet firm. "It will take time. But we are here now. This is our new beginning."

Everything was new: the language, the customs, the food, the way of life. Yet, unlike the refugee camps, this was a place of promise. The wide, tree-lined streets, the fresh air, and the organized chaos of a modern city—everything felt like a new beginning.

Their first few years in Australia were challenging. Ahmad struggled to find work in his field. Though he had a university degree in education from Kabul, his qualifications weren't recognized in Australia, and he had to start over. He took on a variety of low-paying jobs, from working in warehouses to driving a delivery van, all while continuing to study and improve his English. Amina faced similar struggles in her medical career, as her qualifications were not easily transferable. But she, too, took on whatever jobs she could find, eventually working as a caregiver in an aged care facility, a role she could perform with her experience and compassion.

Tariq, now a teenager, was enrolled in a local high school where he found the transition particularly difficult. He had been separated from his friends in Kabul and had lost so much in the journey—his home, his community, and his country. Yet, the school provided an environment where he could slowly rebuild his confidence. Tariq's first few months in Melbourne were filled with confusion, isolation, and uncertainty. He would come home from school, his face a mixture of exhaustion and frustration. English was still a hurdle; the culture felt alien, and the kids in his class spoke too quickly, laughed too loudly, and often seemed to forget he was even there.

CRICKET: THE BRIDGE

One warm Saturday afternoon, as he walked through the park near their new home in Dandenong, he noticed something that stopped him in his tracks. A group of boys were gathered around a large tree, playing cricket.

Tariq had watched cricket on TV back in Kabul with his father—his family would gather to cheer for their national team, but he'd never played it himself. However, there was something familiar about the game, something that made him feel like he could belong. The ball flew through the air, and the kids shouted, laughing and calling out to one another in thick Australian accents. It was the kind of scene he hadn't experienced since his childhood in Kabul.

Curiosity tugged at him, and before he realized it, he was standing on the edge of the field. One of the boys, a tall teenager with a wide smile, waved at him.

"Oi, mate! You want to join us?" he called out, holding a bat in one hand.

Tariq hesitated. He wasn't sure if he could join in if he even knew how to play properly. "I, uh... I've never really played before," Tariq replied shyly.

The boy grinned. "No worries! We'll teach you. It's just like hitting a ball. You can't mess it up."

Tariq's heart raced. This was his chance to break through the wall that had kept him feeling like an outsider. He nodded, stepping forward tentatively.

"Name's Ben," the boy said, tossing him a worn bat. "And you are?"

"Tariq," he replied quietly, feeling the weight of the bat in his hands.

"Alright, Tariq. Let's see what you've got."

Ben bowled the first ball, and Tariq stood there, staring at it as it came toward him. It wasn't as fast as he expected. The ball was smaller than a soccer ball, but the motion of the game, the fluidity of it, felt oddly comforting. The moment the ball approached, he swung the bat instinctively.

"CRACK!"

The ball flew off the bat, soaring through the air, high and long. Tariq stood there, stunned for a split second. His eyes followed the ball, and then, in a blur of movement, one of the other boys dashed and caught it mid-air.

"Nice shot!" they all cheered. "First try! You've got some skills, mate."

Tariq grinned, his face flushed with excitement. For the first time since they had arrived in Australia, he felt like he belonged, like something in this new life made sense. His heart still raced, but now it wasn't from the uncertainty of being in a foreign land; it was from the adrenaline of the game, the rush of playing, and the camaraderie of the kids around him.

"You're up to bowl next," Ben said, tossing him the ball. "We'll show you the ropes. Don't worry about messing up."

Tariq stood, his feet planted firmly in the grass. He had always been a soccer player back in Kabul, but this felt different. There was an energy in the air, a spirit of shared purpose. He gripped the ball and tried to focus, remembering the matches he'd watched with his father. He bowled the ball to Ben, who expertly struck it, sending it flying once more across the field.

Over the next few weeks, Tariq found himself meeting up with Ben and the other boys nearly every weekend. The game of cricket had become his bridge into this strange new world. He learned the rules, figured out the best way to bowl, and even started developing a competitive streak. But more than that, he made friends.

One afternoon, after a particularly exciting match where Tariq had scored his first fifty, helping his team win the game, Ben slapped him on the back with a grin.

"Mate, you've got a real talent for this. How long have you been playing?"

Tariq laughed, his smile wide. "This is my first time. Ever."

"First time?!" Ben looked at him in disbelief. "You've got the natural instincts. You should play for the school team!"

Tariq paused; the idea of actually playing cricket in school was both thrilling and terrifying. He wasn't sure he was ready for it, but the more he thought about it, the more he realized he wanted to try.

"Maybe I will," Tariq said, looking around at his new friends. He wasn't sure what his future in cricket would hold, but for the first time, he felt a glimmer of belonging in this new land.

That evening, Tariq came home to find his parents sitting at the dinner table. Amina had cooked a hearty Afghan meal—rice, lamb, and a salad of cucumber and tomatoes—and the scent filled the house, grounding him in the familiarity of home. His younger sister, Laila, was already talking about her new friends from school. As always, Ahmad was reading the newspaper, his face a mix of concentration and quiet joy.

Tariq set his schoolbag down and sat at the table, still grinning from the game.

"How was school today?" Ahmad asked, his eyes soft with the ever-present concern of a father who had seen his children grow up too quickly in the midst of upheaval.

Tariq paused before answering. "It was good. Actually, better than good. I played a cricket game today—some of the boys from school. We won. I think I'm getting better at it."

Amina raised an eyebrow, her smile both proud and curious. "Cricket, huh? You know, your father used to love watching cricket back in Kabul. You'll have to show us some time."

Tariq's heart lifted at his mother's words. For a moment, it felt like Kabul wasn't so far away. He could still share his world with his family, even in this unfamiliar place.

"You should try out for the school team," his father suggested, his voice filled with quiet encouragement. "It might be a good way to make more friends here."

Tariq looked down at his plate, his mind racing. The thought of being on a school team, of playing for something bigger than just a weekend game, made his stomach flutter. He hadn't imagined it would be possible, but now, it seemed like a real possibility.

"I think I will," he said, smiling to himself.

As he helped clear the table that evening, Tariq's thoughts swirled with excitement. Cricket had given him something new—a language, a game, a group of friends—and, most importantly, it had given him a sense of belonging that he hadn't felt since arriving in Melbourne.

At home, Amina and Ahmad noticed the change in him. He was more confident now, more open. He shared stories of his new friends, of cricket matches, and how he was slowly learning the language. Tariq had never imagined that the key to his new life in Australia would be something so simple—so Australian—as a game of cricket.

"You're not the same boy who came here with us," Ahmad said one evening, his eyes filled with quiet pride. "You are becoming Australian, Tariq. But you will always carry our heritage with you."

Tariq smiled. "I am both," he said, looking at the cricket bat leaning against the wall. "And maybe I can teach my friends how to play soccer."

A few months later, Tariq stood at the edge of the cricket field at school, dressed in the school's cricket whites, his bat in hand. It was the first match of the season, and the butterflies in his stomach were almost unbearable. The students from his class, now his friends, clapped and cheered as he walked to the pitch.

Ben waved from the sidelines. "You got this, mate!"

Tariq nodded, his grip on the bat tightening. This was more than just a game—it was proof of how far he had come. From the refugee camp in Peshawar to the cricket field in Melbourne, he had found his place. The game wasn't just cricket; it was a part of his journey, a symbol of his strength, and an affirmation of his new life.

As the bowler came charging toward him, Tariq smiled, his heart pounding. The ball came at him, fast and sharp, and instinctively, he swung the bat.

The sharp sound of the ball hitting the bat was sweet—a perfect shot. The crowd erupted into cheers, and for the first time in a long while, Tariq felt truly at home.

At that moment, he wasn't the shy Afghan refugee anymore. He was Tariq—the boy who had found his place in the game, on the field, and in the world.

THE INTEGRATION

Laila, still a child, adapted more quickly. She excelled in her studies, picking up English at a rapid pace, and promptly became the bridge between her parents and the Australian community. She translated for them, helping them navigate the complexities of the healthcare system, the education system, and the labyrinthine paperwork that came with being a new migrant family.

As the years passed, the Afridi family began to build a life in Melbourne. They settled in Cranbourne, a suburb known for its cultural diversity, where many other Afghan families lived. The area offered a sense of connection to their homeland and provided a network of support. The Afridi family participated in Afghan cultural events, shared meals with other refugees, and celebrated holidays like Eid and Nowruz in the same way they had in Kabul—except now, it was in the comfort of their new home, surrounded by new friends.

Ahmad, now more fluent in English, was able to secure a teaching position at a local school that specialized in providing education to migrant students. His students were often children of refugees, just like Tariq and Laila, and he brought a deep sense of empathy to his work. Amina, after many years of studying and completing additional certifications, became a nurse in a local hospital, where she was able to care for others and give back to the community that had embraced them.

Tariq, now an adult, had overcome the challenges of adolescence in a new country. He graduated from university, earning a degree in engineering and played cricket every weekend at the local club level. He was no longer the scared teenager who had fled Kabul; he was a confident young man with a future in front of him. Laila, too, had found her calling, studying law at university with the hope of becoming a human rights advocate. She often spoke at community events, sharing the stories of refugees and the importance of multiculturalism in Australia.

The Afridi family's journey from Kabul to Melbourne is a story of transformation. They arrived in Australia as refugees, scarred by the violence of their homeland. Still, they rebuilt their lives with the help of their community, their resilience, and their deep connection to their Afghan roots. Though they would never forget the hardships they had endured, they found strength in their new identity as Australian citizens—blending their Afghan heritage with the opportunities offered by their new home.

The Afridi family is just one of countless stories that shape the multicultural mosaic of modern Australia. Their journey is a testament to the power of migration—how people, displaced by war and hardship, can find new beginnings in places far from home. As the Afridi family moves forward, their children, now fully integrated into Australian society, carry with them the rich traditions and stories of Afghanistan, ensuring that the sacrifices of their parents are never forgotten.

A DAY WITHOUT MY MOBILE PHONE

BY DIANE BROWN

"Hurry up, Di," Norm called from the car. "The traffic's horrendous with all the roadworks, and if we don't leave now, you'll miss your train."

Grabbing my handbag, I hurried into the garage, feeling slightly out of breath as I slid into the front seat. Norm was right; the traffic was crawling, and we arrived at the station with only a few minutes to spare.

Breathing a sigh of relief, I settled into my seat, and as the train departed, I rummaged through my handbag. This cannot be right. I thought to myself as my hand turned over a hairbrush, my money purse, a packet of mints, my lipstick and quite a few tissues. Where on earth is my phone?

Realization hit me as I recalled the happenings of the morning. I had placed my phone on the charger whilst I was getting dressed, and with Norm yelling at me to hurry up, I had raced out of the house without it. Drat!!

What on earth am I going to do now? It's a 55-minute trip into the city, and I don't have my phone. I stared out the window, looking at the meaningless scenery. Graffiti-covered fences flashed by, houses with gardens, houses with no gardens, houses half-built. It was all so boring. My hands seemed to take on a mind of their own as my thumbs moved up and down in their usual dance that was so familiar on my train trips.

I was becoming tense. What if someone needed me urgently? How would they contact me? What was I missing on Messenger, and what was happening on Facebook? And were there any new reels? One of my favourite pastimes during train travel was looking at the reels. I loved watching the antics that cats got up to, the dogs that spoke, the babies trying their first solid food, and little children mixing up their words as they tried to string sentences together. It was an enjoyable pastime, and now I am sitting here with nothing to do but listen to the various telephone conversations that other travellers were engaging in. Some spoke in languages that I did not understand. It did make me wonder who was on the other end of the line, as the caller on the train seemed to talk non-stop without even pausing to take a breath.

At last, the seat beside me was taken, and to my relief, the first thing the young man did was take out his phone. My eyes were immediately drawn to his screen as I leaned slightly forward, and my thumbs started their familiar dance. I was so absorbed in watching his screen that I did not notice the young man frowning at me. Within a few minutes, he left the seat beside me and re-seated himself further down the carriage. Good heavens, I thought to myself. It was not as if he was watching something confidential.

The long journey eventually came to an end, and I soon found myself in David Jones, my favourite store. I had recently received a birthday voucher, and today was the last day I could use it. After trying on a particularly expensive silk blouse, I thought, What the heck, as with the 30% off from the voucher, it would make it more affordable.

I carefully handed the beautiful blouse to the woman at the checkout, explaining that I did have a birthday voucher, but unfortunately, I had left my phone at home. The woman's face, which originally held a friendly smile, immediately turned frosty.

"I am most sorry, Madam, but unless you can produce the voucher, I am not at liberty to offer you the 30% deduction."

I stared at her in horror. "But surely you can look up your records and find that I am a member?" I queried.

"Madam," the frosty voice continued, "Surely you must understand that we have thousands of members, and it is just not possible for me to look up your name. I'm afraid you will need to pay the full price for this lovely garment."

I walked away, feeling desperately downhearted. Who did she think she was, that old duck with blue hair and pink lipstick that looked far too young on her. And honestly, did she think she looked fashionable with her glasses hanging around her neck on a fake gold chain? And what was with the haughty, put-on accent, acting like she was royalty rather than just a shop assistant.

Feeling despondent, I decided to head home, only to realize that Norm would not be able to meet me at the station, as I could not text him as to what train I was on. I managed to find a public phone box, and after carefully wiping the handpiece with my clean handkerchief, I began to dial Norm's mobile number, only to discover that I did not know what it was. When I dialled from my mobile, I just pressed the symbol of a phone displayed under Norm's photo, and I never really noticed what the number was. Oh well, I thought to myself, I will just have to get the bus home from the station.

I purchased a newspaper to read on the train trip home. However, each time I turned the page, my elbow dug into the side of the rather large person sitting next to me, so after hearing him mutter a couple of times, I eventually gave up. At last, we arrived back in Cranbourne, and I was pleased to discover that I had only a 10-minute wait before the bus arrived. As I climbed aboard, I was concerned to see that the bus was crowded with noisy school children, one who was kind enough to offer me his seat. As I sat down, I was surrounded by a group of loud young boys, some sitting beside me and some standing in the aisle. There was a definite odour of smelly sneakers. Each time the bus turned a corner, the boys who were standing would reach upwards to hold the rail above their heads, which released a strong waft of body odour. My God, could this day get any worse!

After alighting the bus, I staggered home, footsore and weary. As I entered the house, Norm looked up from his computer and commented, "Oh, Di, did you know you left your phone at home?"

Following a much-needed cup of tea, I grabbed my phone from the bench and flopped onto the couch. I couldn't wait to check my messages and see what had happened whilst I had been offline. As usual, there were no texts from the children, and no one urgently needed me. The new promotions were the same as normal: Kogan, Everyday Rewards, Flybuys, etc. They all encouraged me to purchase their wares. Nothing much had even happened on Facebook. Its contents were now full of more and more advertisements. But as Norm yelled from the kitchen that I was to rest while he organized dinner, I flipped through to the reels. There they were, the newly added ones, detailing methods on how to look after your indoor plants, videos of dogs barking at cats, cats hissing at dogs, a man singing with a cat, and most importantly, pianists that get your attention by playing half a piece, before it abruptly stops, and the piece starts playing from the beginning again. My day suddenly became a whole lot better.

THE CHAOTIC CLUSTER OF QUEBEC

A SURREALIST POEM BY HECTOR SOSA

"'Surrealist automatism' is a method of art-making in which the artist suppresses conscious control over the making process, allowing the unconscious mind to have great sway." — Wikipedia.

This is another exercise in surrealist automatism or automatic writing. I wrote it like a poem, forming verses freely with minimal conscious control.

Ubiquitous silence surrounds the grand stadium,
Ambiguous mechanoids respond refusively at the giant encounter,
Never have they severed such an atomic platinum,
For whoever spites the broken fence with decaying objects,
Is ruled by the straight darkness of minuscule adornments.
Despite the ever-emerging success of the long-lost city,

Wide multicoloured forests shy away uniformly from enslaved confrontation.
May there be an inspiring switch sort of lots,
To lock the assemblage left and out,
Into distinct oblivion and alchemically far beyond,
The insane broad borders of controlling fear-based forces.
Whether there are any enduring contentions to describe of,
The deep matter consistently emanates playfully from conducive without,
Within the full point energy that is released in huge bright clusters,
Depriving the solid solution from being out-configured,
To ignite certain euphonious destruction on the chaotic mistakes,
Those that ignore the wasted inhibitions of the latter, sober employees.
At the instant minute of the second guest being closer,
Ludicrous displays of fantasia revolves around the circus,
Performing unusually intensified plates of common,
To elucidate the very fabric of the auspicious entity.
Pretending to be numb is absolutely efficacious,
To put gorilla teeth munching within the gourmet of yesterday,
And devour the lust of the present, momentous serving.
Actively inviting the eternal bunch out of hot sauce,
And salute a well-spoken doctrine of distortion.
Duels fought between resilient space beings and duplicating robots,
As the unity binds, the epiphany rings out at the last record button,
Struggling to convert any empty spirit within its grasp.
Forever haunting the space between ligaments and pests,
A pariah guides forth from explicit hiding,
Into the well of tomorrow's heavy breakfast,
With fried ripe bananas and soft chocolate milkshake,
Satisfying the absence of moving marble statues.

For whom it may not last,
First, as much as the previous cast,
Together, in horrendous ideological progression,
Inspection of new horizons below,
Above the conventional pillars of kinetic structures.
Impulsive neuroplasticity evolves further into the fiery tunes,
Hot and affected by the acidic nature of fierce indulgence,
Rapidly manoeuvring into the yellow-belly oceans,
With chaotic currents flowing the all of nothingness,
Manufacturing sets of cylindrical wheels of concrete.
One may not die disrespectfully,
Two may attain a liquid state,
But none may await away the pain endured by half a century.
Thousands of ages into cycles attributed to dominion,
Here lies the fate of the tremendous efficiency of new dawn mechanics.
Dangerous habits fill the silver air orbiting all around,
Poisonous fumes eradicate the purple garden,
The deterioration of parts portrays injustice,
And the lives of gizmos carry the rubbery leaf aloft.
An antique cottage full of cheeses,
Endeavours to emulate the vast cosmos,
Into a crunchy ideal of insinuating prosperity.
For the pale tomorrow may gradually sight off the plain figures,
While the distant past dissolves instantly,
Today, it remains the tropical hybrid of evergreen delights.
Let there be an occasion of vivid vision and exclusive thunder,
And a lightning of speedy wonder.
The radiant rain may hold the key piece of revulsion,
Encrusted with sizable collector's items,
All over the spec of unpredictability.

A FORESTED LAIR

BY STEPH WEBB

From her vantage point, Sorcière stood surveying the forest below. Her tall, lithe frame blended in with the towering trunks of the Mountain Ash trees. Close to her, on a branch, perched Branoc. Together, the womanly creature with tall-branched antlers rising from her silver-white head and the large iridescent-black feathered raven surveilled the forested mountain range. The slope of the mountain provided an impressive view of the vast, dense rainforest.

Dusk had begun painting the sky in hues of pink and violet. The sprawling canopy of trees rippled like a living sea in the evening breeze. The air was thick with the scent of damp earth, eucalyptus, and moss. This place, Sherbrooke Forest, had become their new home- though the memories of another, vastly different forest still lingered in Sorcière's mind. Finding the forgotten, secret portal had been fortuitous.

It had been the strangest sensation stepping into the swirling mist of colours inside the portal. At first, the rainbow haze disappeared, and blackness surrounded her. It was rather unnerving until the swirling vortex returned, and her feet stepped into a strange new land.

Light-headed and nauseous, Sorcière took her first hesitant steps with Branoc, her raven, tucked under the deep purple sleeve of her velvet cloak. He appeared equally affected as he took his first bumbling steps, and she chuckled as he shook his head and stumbled unevenly across the unfamiliar terrain. Branoc responded by fluffing out his feathers and sneezing in disgust at being the source of her amusement. She loved the strong bond between her and her *familiar*. Thankfully, their effects soon wore off, and they ventured further afield to explore their new abode.

Gazing about her in wonder, her thoughts once again gathered, she considered the magic of this land. Through her studies and research, Sorcière discovered the mystery, magic, power, and sorcery in the ancient continent of Australia to be relatively unknown. Within the ancient world maps used by mystical beings, this continent at the bottom of the chart was originally called The South Land, and to many, it remained known as just that.

'*The magic may be hidden*', she had contemplated during her darkest days. '*It may be more powerful than any I had ever encountered.*' The intrigue captivated her imagination, charting her destiny. Her mind steeled. Fate sealed. The journey to Sherbrooke was planned in meticulous secrecy. The rainforests in the South Land were believed to be inhabited by fae of many kinds, some as old as the land itself. It was rumoured that some of the fairies, elves, merfolk, and the like were travellers along with the humans who voyaged the land and seas from other lands. The faerie beings, as believed, were followed out of curiosity, banishment, or exile from their lands of origin. Some journeyed unseen, along with humankind, while others found portals to step between places to the next. It was also rumoured that the faerie of the South Land was the most peaceful of all the continents.

Sorcière had been intrigued by the discovery that South Land was known to be different- having dreamtimes, song lines and people who were deeply rooted in their love of the land on which they lived.

'There is magic here,' she acknowledged, but there was none she felt threatened by. 'I am prepared to fight if need be! I am powerful! - and trained in my arts of magic and warfare. This seems to be a good place to begin my new life. This is where I have planted my feet. This is where I choose to build my army and my stronghold. '

Branoc, her raven companion, made a soft, raspy sound, startling her for a second. He always sensed when she needed a little reminder to stay focused. He had been her faithful companion and servant for numerous decades. Fixing her large fae eyes on him, she briefly reminisced on their journey together. Branoc was an abandoned, helpless fledgling in Europe when she found him huddled amongst the forest debris. It was on the first anniversary of her clan's annihilation. The pain and loneliness of being an orphan and the sole survivor of her clan at the tender age of thirteen was particularly wretched that day. Memories of caring for Branoc in his infancy and their bonding ceremony by a Polish magician had solidified their close and trusting relationship. As she had grown in wisdom, so had he. Always her servant, ready to do as she commanded.

'That was then. This was now' Sorcière voiced loudly as she suppressed the memories of the past into a dark, hidden corner of her mind.

"This is the place, Branoc. Here, we will build our lair," she announced.

Branoc's piercing ice-blue eyes regarded the trees surrounding him. He cocked his head, peering this way and that.

A pale dark purple light began to radiate from Sorcière. She lifted her skeletal arms and began to whisper words in an unknown tongue. Her face and arms- pale, glowed as magic swirled around her bony structure. Long silver-white strands of hair, now seemingly with a life of their own- infused with magic, took on a purple hue as they flowed around her body. Magnetic energy charged the air. Golden light glowed through Sorcière's elongated branched antlers slightly above her pointed ears. The forest became frozen in a deep slumber. Silence blanketed the mountain range as birds and creatures hushed, suspended in time. Nothing moved except for that which she commanded to move.

The trees began to bend and twist under her command. Their branches laced together, making three platforms for a forest dwelling. The silent twisting and turning branches were undetectable in the vast forest as the weaving of the lair took place. She spoke, and chunks of fallen tree trunks and storm-damaged fallen branches spirited away from various parts of the surrounding forest, and timber platforms arranged themselves.

A dense screen of trees around her lair hid her spacious dwelling in the trees at the top of the forested mountain peak. There would be no prying eyes here where she chose to live. The steep terrain and difficulty of getting to this wooded area ensured that none would come near. It was perfect for hiding a three-level abode amongst the cluster of trees.

Sorcière added a screen of glamour to ensure it was well and truly hidden from sight. She created open verandas, ornate wooden staircases, and a lavish kitchen with a small, cosy meal nook. Arched doors and windows added opulence to the structure. She desired a comfortable and well-structured lair. She appreciated beauty and comfort in her surroundings as most faeries did.

On the top level, Sorcière decided to place her bedroom. Harnessing the energy from the air, she worked her magic. Forest green, midnight blue, and indigo light flowed from her hands as she enchanted a huge bed to take up a third of the room. Sorcière crafted a canopy of leafy wood vines, with purple and blue flowering creepers, to materialize over the bed. Soon, soft transparent drapes hung from the top frame, and the bed was circled. Reminiscent of a cosy but luxurious hedge burrow. Parts of this reminded her of the many safe places that had been her refuge while she was fleeing the Snow Forest in Europe centuries ago. The forlorn, barren, and grimy hovels had been her 'home'. None were as picturesque as this, although she had always used her craft to beautify the most basic shacks she was forced to live in.

Sorcière relished the thought of isolation and freedom her lair would give her, A place to plot and plan against the woodland elves who presently dominated the lands surrounding her below. She was confident the woodland elves would be no match against her shrewdness, power, or tricky scheming.

Sorcière smiled, cold and satisfied, as she studied her lair. Her eyes, one blue eye and the other tawny brown with starry silver specks glowed with pride.

Branoc watched her, his ice-blue eyes gleaming.

"What do you think Branoc?" she asked.

The raven let out a low, warbling croak. Sorcière threw back her head and laughed- a dry, knowing sound.

The draining effects of using forest magic wore on Sorcière's body. Rest and recovery are what she needed. Sorcière dragged herself up a gnarled spiral staircase to her bed. As she sank back on the voluminous cloud-like bed, Branoc appeared on the bed beside her. In his beak, he carried a scrap of bread he had scrounged from somewhere near the village earlier in the day. Branoc had kept it hidden within the foliage of a silver wattle tree near the lair. He dropped it on her chest and nudged her with his strong black beak.

Sorcière reached to retrieve the bread from her chest. She looked at the offering before gratefully accepting the nourishment. It was dry and crusty but still edible. She was too exhausted to care much for food. Her thoughts connected with his as she thanked him for his gift.

Branoc hopped off the bed and strutted across the floor towards a slightly opened window. He flew onto the windowsill, and then, with a little hop, he dropped out of the window opening. Within a twinkle of time, he returned holding a small plastic water bottle. The day before, he had picked it off a picnic table at the campgrounds a distance away. It had no lid. He had examined it closely. It was almost half filled. Picking it up with his beak was ease as he carried it to a nearby tree. From there, he had managed to use his beak to grip the bottle at the opening and fly with it for short distances. Branoc gradually got it up to the top of the mountain through sheer persistence. He hardly spilled a drop in the process.

Sorcière's eyes were closed in a deep slumber as he propped the bottle against her skeletal hip, near her hand. She moved slightly but didn't open her eyes. He pecked at her hand, shoving it closer to the bottle. She opened her eyes and looked to see what he had brought her. Seeing the bottle, she sat up, inspected it, and took a grateful sip. She held it out to him to have a drink, too. Although it wasn't enough to quench their thirst, it revived them sufficiently. Next, both settled in for a deep sleep. Sorcière buried herself under the bedcovers, and Branoc perched on one of the woody vines on the bed frame.

They slept for hours and only woke up the next day. The sun was high. Its rays streamed across the bed. The golden midday sunlight tickled between Sorcière's long eyelashes- stirring from her sleep. Branoc sensed her waking. His ice-blue eyes snapped open. He stretched his legs and wings. Sleep began to fade from his body like a fleeting memory. Sorcière threw back her bed covers and, with quick, fluid movements, extracted herself from the bed.

Stretching her long, bony limbs, Sorcière strode to the window. She gazed down across the forest, her antlers casting long, sharp shadows against the walls.

Then, her lips curled into a sinister smile.

"Go," she hissed to Branoc. "Find the woodland elves. Learn their weaknesses."

As Branoc flew through the forest, Sorcière and he were as one. His eyes and ears communicated the sights and surroundings. She saw what he saw. It was as if she was flying in his body. As Branoc's wings cut the air, her long, pointed ears twitched.

Branoc spread his black wings, leaping upwards, his body stretched in flight. Glossy plumage reflected iridescent greens, blues, and purples in the autumn sunlight. He flew horizontally from the lair before changing course to fly higher. He soared high above the tree canopy. He performed a few aerobic movements through the air. It was as if he was a high-flying acrobat. Branoc dove and rolled. He flew upside down and turned his body from one side to the next. He sped along through the air with liquid-like strokes, gliding and weaving. He sailed, and he soared. Wind currents and slipstreams graced his flight. He was playful. A paragon of the air. At times, using the air streams to glide effortlessly through the sky.

After this playful performance, Branoc silently glided down toward the lower part of the forest. He turned this way and that as he flew down to the crown of trees below. His course led him purposefully towards his mission. As he flew lower, he darted through the tree branches. He swerved to avoid the many boughs and extending tree limbs, which jutted at different angles. Down, down, down he went. Lower and lower until he spied movement below. A clearing.

Finding what he was looking for, Branoc landed on a sturdy tree limb with a light two-footed landing. His sturdy black feet folded over the woody bark. Strong black toes gripped tightly onto a sturdy perch. Sharp black talons tipped his jet-black toes. He took a few side steps along the bough and leaned forward slightly, peering at the scene below. Still too high to see clearly. He dropped further down, falling silently like a black shimmering dewdrop. He landed effortlessly on a lower scaffolding limb. Staying in the shadows, he spied a group of woodland elves in a clearing amongst the woodlots.

Sorcière smiled with deep satisfaction. *There they are! Well done, Branoc! I have found their abode. Soon, they will all be in my hands. I will make them bend to my wishes.* She chuckled at the scene in the forest down below, at the foothills of the mountain.

Unsuspecting that they were being observed, elven children played in groups. Elven forest guards and families mingled in the clearing. It was the scene of a typical day of the carefree woodland elves.

The sorceress and the raven silently watched. Waiting.

Authors Note: A Forested Lair is an excerpt from the novel 'Farynn' that is in the process of being written.

SURVIVING THE STORM

BY JANE E. WOOD

BERWICK AUGUST 1991.
Ellen shoved another red gum log into the Coonara, grabbed her coffee from the mantelpiece, and sank onto the couch. The heat of the fire brought warmth and comfort as the weather raged outside. Her children asleep, Ellen had a short break to recoup for the evening rush. The dogs spied their opportunity, jumped onto the couch and snuggled up to her, glad of a respite from the ministrations of the two children who loved the dogs but were relentless in the attention they gave.

They were all so tired of the cold, wet weather. It felt like it had rained every day for weeks, which was actually the case. It had been not easy keeping her 21-month-old and four-year-old sons entertained. They loved to be outside playing in the puddles, sliding in the mud and pushing their trucks around. She didn't mind the filthy clothes but was only prepared to wash mud-laden tracksuits once a day. The dogs, too, ended up with mud up and down their legs and bellies every time they went outside, necessitating drying them with a towel and creating nearly as much washing as the boys.

Today seemed worse than usual; the wind was howling, driving rain against the windows. The house lay on a north-south axis, and with the prevailing weather coming from the northwest, it meant some of their largest windows were bearing the brunt of the elements, including those in the two rooms in which the boys slept.

Ellen had barely finished her coffee when her older son appeared beside her. Michael climbed up and over the dogs and inserted himself between the older dog and his mother. Disappointed with having her snuggle time interrupted, the dog headed to her bed on the floor.

"Did you have a good sleep?" Ellen asked her son, who'd brought a book with him for her to read.

"It's a bit noisy, Mummy."

"It is, isn't it? Let's read that book now."

The book Michael had with him was called Wombat Stew. Ellen got as far as the first chant. "Wombat stew, wombat stew, ooey, gooey, wombat stew." When she stopped, the noise of the wind had changed. It was no longer howling; it was roaring and getting louder as if a train was headed straight for the house.

Seriously alarmed and acting on instinct, Ellen grabbed Michael from the couch, yelling for the dogs to follow and darted into the small hallway in the middle of the house that ran between the boys' two bedrooms. She shut the doors at both ends, securing dogs and child in the space, raced into her younger son's room and swept the sleeping child into her arms, terrified that the wind could shatter the glass in the window beside his cot. Ellen backed out into the hall, shutting his door, the bathroom door, and the toilet door. They were now cocooned in the little hall, the wind growing impossibly louder and louder. Ellen's arms wrapped around her sons' small, frightened bodies, and she spoke in soft, reassuring tones.

"It's just the wind. We're safe here. It'll be okay," she repeated over and over, not sure she, herself, believed what she was saying.

Above the noise of the rain and wind, another layer of sound, things were sliding and bouncing across the roof. Ellen knew it must be tiles being ripped out. What else could it be? She said nothing to the boys, just continued to cuddle and reassure, but they'd heard it. Of course, they had, and their trembling bodies showed it. The dogs were whining, afraid of the noise and feeling the fear in the little hall. No one moved. They just crouched together up against the wall, waiting for it to pass.

And then it did. The movement of tiles stopped the roar of the wind, and the rain became a howl, which then, moments later, ceased altogether. Ellen could feel the frightened boys relax in her arms, but still, they turned onto her shoulders and sobbed. She held them tighter and tried to stroke the dogs to reassure them, too. Slowly, the crying eased, and when they were calm, Ellen told the boys, "Stay here. I want to check if it's safe for you to come out." They nodded uncertainly.

She stepped out of the hall, leaving the dogs and children behind, and into the kitchen, not sure of what to expect. Her heart was pounding as she walked through every room in the house but found no broken glass. She returned to the hallway.

"It's alright. You can come out now." The boys and dogs warily followed her back to the warmth of the fire. With Ellen's encouragement, the children scrambled up onto the couch, and the dogs followed.

"Now, I need you to stay here while I have a look outside. You have to stay on the couch. Michael, you need to look after Robert. Can you do that?"

"I want to come with you," Michael cried.

"I don't know that it's safe for you to come. Please stay here. I need to see what's happened. Once I know, you can come and look with me."

Ellen slipped out the sliding door onto the deck. The table and chairs that should have been there weren't; they were fifteen or more metres away across the yard. From what she could see, even from that distance, they were never going to be used again.

She stepped off the deck. At her foot was a roof tile, driven into the dirt at 45 degrees. As she walked along the east side of the house towards the front, she found tile after tile, ridge tiles and flat tiles, all broken and wedged in the dirt. Just beyond the kitchen window, she stopped and looked up. It took Ellen a moment to process what she was seeing. There were two holes in the roof, one about a metre square and the other a little smaller.

Holding her panic at bay as best she could, Ellen looked across her paddock to her neighbour's house. Their garden shed was gone, and in the distance, across the road and into a far paddock, she could see that a path of destruction about ten metres wide had been wrought on the stand of hundred-year-old conifers.

Filled with trepidation, Ellen continued her journey around the front of the house, terrified that any one of their five small sheds might have gone the same way as her neighbour's.

On reaching the other side of the house, Ellen breathed deeply, very relieved to see all sheds still standing upright. But the chooks, had they survived?

Ellen's hens were free-range in a yard that surrounded the middle shed. Fearful of what she would find, Ellen opened the gate in the yard. To her right, wedged firmly up against the thick grass that grew along the wire fence, was one of her hens. Her eyes were closed.

"Are you alright, Rosie?" Ellen dropped to her knees to scoop up the animal. At her touch, the bird opened her eyes, but she seemed unable to move her trembling body. "Come on, Rosie, you're safe now." And Ellen stroked her back, feeling the bird slowly relax. After a few minutes, Ellen decided she could return the hen to the pen to join the three that had had the good sense or good fortune to ride out the storm in the comparative safety of their shed. Ellen found another bird not far away from the first. It, too, was trembling with fear, and like Rosie, she calmed down after some care from Ellen. Ensuring they had food and water, Ellen then closed the hens into their pen, securing them for the night, even though there were a couple of hours of daylight left.

Back inside the house, Ellen told the boys she would show them what had happened outside after she had made some phone calls, the first being to her husband, who worked more than an hour away, and the second to the S.E.S.

It took the S.E.S until 11 pm to arrive; they had been very busy, they said. The volunteers secured a huge plastic orange cover over the roof. They told Ellen that her house had sustained the most damage of all the jobs they had attended that evening. She later found out what she had suspected since the roaring 'train' first approached the house; a mini tornado, about ten or so metres wide, had swept up the barely populated Hallam Valley, damaging everything in its path. It was unfortunate that its path just happened to take it from the northwest corner of her house, across the roof to the southeast corner, removing much of the roof.

The neighbour's shed was found about ninety metres away.

They all came through the storm safely, but not without some psychological impact on Michael, who developed a fear of storms for some years after it happened. Oddly, about six days later, another mini tornado struck about four kilometres north of Ellen's house, this time in a suburban setting, causing damage to the roofs of many homes, Ellen's parents included.

THE GRANDMOTHER EFFECT

BY MADISEN WHITE

A family folklore that is not my own. But it is my own. Our cultures are woven into the fabric of our lives and perhaps into our very bones.

Enter the Grandmother Effect, a distinctly human theory of adaptation. It suggests that as fertility declines, women retain their strength of body and mind to assist in raising their grandchildren. However, the benefits of the Grandmother Hypothesis extend beyond the survival of future generations. According to this model of adaptation, the act of grandmothering is believed to extend the human lifespan itself.

It is key not only to human survival but to the survival of knowledge and culture.

Everyone has a story and a culture, and with it comes the choice—and the privilege—to keep it alive. Its story is told through corny aphorisms, the swelling of nostalgia, the "I remember whens" and the "Have I ever told yous." It is stitched together and carried forward through the choices and lived experiences of generations.

*

Iris Joy nuzzles into the dog in my arms, and a lump catches in my throat.

We sit side by side on the bench outside her home, listening to The Seekers after a day out. It has been a long day for her—longer than usual. She was once the plump, American "Gramma" with a larger-than-life personality. Over time, her body has shrunk, and her spirit has distilled. Her hair is even whiter than I remember, and her frailty makes her seem almost gnomish and mystical. Yet she remains familiar, her corny Midwestern accent unchanged.

Still the quintessential matriarch.

She is nearly ninety now.

The haze of passing faces and overlapping voices floats around her. Sometimes, they are her family. Sometimes, strangers. Some days, they are one and the same. Her sharp blue eyes drift from face to face with a faint air of knowing, nodding along to the humdrum of conversation. But every so often, when a familiar song plays or a familiar gaze meets hers, a mischievous twinkle sparks to life.

Throughout my childhood, she took great pride in her ability to get along with anyone from anywhere. A hospitality queen, she managed the Southern Cross Hotel after moving to Australia in the sixties with her young family. As her family grew, she ran the local shop at the foot of the Dandenong Ranges—mother, businesswoman, and storyteller.

On many a lazy Sunday afternoon, she would regale me with tales of her restaurant days. Of the ditsy server who spilt chicken soup, of the middle-aged customer who stood irate, a lone noodle comically dangling down his face. And of my grandmother, maintaining her "professionalism" and "sincerity" while barely containing her laughter.

Her stories were always grand and theatrical in their telling, the details shifting slightly with each retelling as if they, too, had taken on a life of their own. I suspect she enjoyed embellishing them just as much as she enjoyed the memory itself. Even the most mundane moments became a saga in her hands, shaped by her voice, her expressions, her uncontainable laughter.

As I grew older, I realized her knowing air was not just an innate skill but a desire. A desire not just to understand others but to know everything about everyone—and to weave it to her advantage in her own mischievous, artful way.

Swapping names on wedding seating charts after one too many tipples. Whispering over dinners, subtly nudging in-laws against one another—just for the drama, of course. She played her cards close to her chest, revealing her hand only when it best suited her with a flourish.

She was the kind of woman who could talk her way in or out of any situation, who could smooth over conflict with a knowing smile or stir it up with a single whispered word. Even in her old age, even as her memory fades, there are glimmers of this woman still—the glint in her eye, the half-smile that suggests she knows something you don't.

The grandma of my youth lived by the motto, "Fake it 'til you make it." And boy, did she make it—up as she went along.

She goes by her middle name, Joy. Never Iris.

As a child, I sometimes wondered if Joy was an alter ego. A chosen alias, a talisman of radiance and positivity, summoned to stave off the darkness.

Recently, I learned of her divorce, long-forgotten and long-concealed. I understand now how these truths were woven together as Grandma Joy crafted a new life for herself.

Her second husband, my beloved Grandpa Rusty, passed away from a heart attack. The first words I could make out between sobs and phone crackles were:

"I knew. I knew it would be today."

Her voice was steady and certain as if some part of her had sensed it and braced herself for the inevitable. I wonder now if that was part of her magic, too—the ability to see the twists of life before they unfolded, to carry that knowledge quietly within her, shaping the world as she saw fit.

WHEN HEADS COLLIDE

BY STEPH WEBB

The black spiked gates between the hand-hewn grey boulder gateposts were shut and locked. Only night creatures moved behind the metal barricade. A sigh whispered through the trees, over the lawns, brushed past rose bushes and tickled the waters of the ponds within the botanical gardens. Day-time visitors with their chatter, kids in prams, dogs on leads, picnic baskets, and lattes were long gone. Homes nearby were lit by the glow of interior lights and flickering television sets and lined up in neat rows of lamp-lit streets—the night sky above, inky-black and silent. Something dark moved overhead in the brooding night sky, fruit bats on their nightly hunt. A black rat scurried through a gap under the fence and quickly disappeared into the dark interior of the gardens. Everything went quiet as if the night sounds had been simultaneously muzzled. The night air, now cool and slightly damp, stilled in expectation as if holding its breath.

In this hush - on the edge of the hill, inside the gardens, a pale, wispy fog began to take shape. It gathered in density, and the churning and twirling of vapour moved as it expanded. Tones of grey, blue, and green light flickered and swirled within. A shadowed figure, bulky yet lean, began to emerge within its foggy interior.

Lesnik stepped out of the swirling vortex that twirled in icy shades of white and cold blue light. His solid, broad, yet narrow-waisted frame silhouetted darkly against the misty shimmer of the portal behind him. The Black Forest faerie king planted his feet solidly onto the gravel path that snaked its way through the park from its entrance towards the hilltop. Behind him, the polar swirling mass flashed and glowed blindingly, then glimmered briefly before it evaporated as quickly as it had appeared. The royal faerie ring had been vibrating again, starting a few weeks ago, and he had been tracking its location, which led him here. He had to return it to the Black Forest and thereby regain the power that had been locked since it was stolen.

Lesnik cast his cold blue eyes around as he assessed his surroundings. Thickly branched antlers crowned his head, poking through long silver-mauve hair that framed a gaunt chiselled face, and flowed down almost to his waist. He cast his eyes to his left to the towering trees and, to his right, over a vast open space with rooftops below. In the cloudless night sky above him, on the dark hilltop, a group of large fruit bats flapped as they passed overhead, looking for nourishment.

He sensed the movement before he identified its source. A tall, slender, kilted warrior with immense wings stepped out from amongst the trees. Sláine, the sneaky, thieving scoundrel who had raided the Black Forest fortress while he was attending to matters elsewhere. He seemed to be on his own. Where was his band of fae warriors? Or was he on his own?

'What do you want here?' declared the confident Scot as he stood with one arm across his chest, gripping the hilt of his sword.

'You know well enough' was the calm and confident retort.

'It sure took you long enough to catch up to me. What's the matter? Getting a bit old now, are ye?" laughed Sláine.

Lesnik shot hateful looks like daggers at the smirking Scot as he spat out contemptuously, 'Where are your mutts?'

'About.' was the sneering response.

'I have come for what is rightfully mine. It is not yours to hold or own. It belongs to the Black Forest throne and heirs of its kingdom.' His voice thundered with fury as lightning flashed around him. His anger rose further as the Scottish fae king threw back his head and laughed at him.

'If you hadn't been so negligent of your duties, going off and leaving your precious fortress unprotected, it would have saved you the thousand-year hunt for the ring. Your guards were easy to overpower. Asleep they were.' Sláine trailed off as his opponent's eyes glowered at his mocking.

'And they paid for it with their lives!' Lesnik spat back. And I paid for my laxness by losing the power that is linked to the ring, he thought with deep regret at his careless flippancy to believe that no one would dare to loot his fortress in his absence. Since then, the ring has emitted vibrations from time to time, in varying intensities, from various parts of the world. Unfortunately, Lesnik always seemed to be a step behind the ring and its captor. Until now, that was.

Dark clouds began gathering around above them as their tempers rose in readiness to do battle. Rolling thunder grumbled and growled as the two fae kings faced one another, hands on swords and eyes ablaze with warring intent. Each one sizing the other as this was the first time either of them had laid sight on one another. Their reputations were fabled and talked about as legends of their strength, cunning, and mystical powers had increased with each telling.

Lesnik stepped forward, eager to get on with his task, and drew out his sword, holding it in readiness. Sláine followed suit, and soon, they were engaged in battle. Swords clashed, and sparks flew from the magic each of them held. Fierce winds began to howl around them and find their course, tearing through the surrounding streets and homes. Huge trees swayed and tottered as leaves were stripped and scattered far and wide. Branches cracked and splintered as they broke off and smashed down on parked cars or house roofs. Here and there, fences were flattened, and debris of all kinds was dragged along in the foray. Rain lashed out over the suburbs as people huddled inside seeking shelter. Only the very brave or very foolish ventured out to secure fences, rescue toppled beehives, trampolines, and garden huts, or look for pets caught unprepared for the sudden storm that raged around them.

Through the wind, rain, and flashing thunderstorm, the two kings stabbed and parried at one another. Forward and backwards, clashing and colliding, striking against one another, they danced and swung with lightning speed in combat. A thrust, a slice, a lunge. A cut on a cheek, a slice on a bicep, a nicked ear. The night zig-zagged with blinding white light and flashes of bluish-white electricity as the elements participated in the duel. The clashing clatter of swords pealed through the din of the storm. The battle between two fae kings rang through the air. Louder than the deafening sounds of the storm, terrifying the surrounding inhabitants and animals who were seeking shelter in homes, hollows, or trees being ravaged by the storm.

Suddenly, the sky darkened as if blotted out by an eclipse. A gargantuan shadow hovered over the two warring kings as lightning flashed over the top of the hill. Neither paid it any heed in their determination to annihilate one another. The shadow blotted out the dazzling streaks of lightning as it plunged, and two giant taloned feet of a gigantic eagle snatched up the sword fighters.

Shock and surprise rippled over their faces as they were lifted high into the air. The talons, like steel, caged them in their grip. Driving rain pelted down on them as the giant eagle flew out towards the sea. Below them, the water was dark and ominous. On and on it flew, clutching the helpless fae kings in its powerful claws. They were trapped within its steely grip. Not even fae magic could help them. It headed towards the land of the big white cloud. As it flew over the ocean, the ring tumbled out of the Sláine's pocket and fell into the sea below. Its vibration rang out like a cry to Lesnik, the Black Forest fae king. He watched in horror for the short time that he could see it, glinting as it tumbled away, out of reach. He heard its high-pitched wail until it was cut off abruptly by the deep, dark ocean below.

The eagle flew over the cloudy headland and dropped the tartan-kilted fae king. He tumbled to the ground relatively unscathed, except for his pride and nursing his injured wings. As he looked up, he saw the eagle fly further, still clutching Lesnik.

The eagle flew on until it reached the land where ice and glaciers abound, and there it released the Black King to tumble onto the icy land below. He stared up at the eagle as it soared away in the skies above him and headed back from where it had come from.

The eagle flew home, rid of the ancient fae menace that had come to its ancient land and its people—home to Australia. Its powerfully skilled wings carried it as it soared over the ocean, gliding through slipstreams and navigating its path homeward. It slowly flapped, sailed, or adjusted its angle to steer itself towards its destination.

The moon was brilliantly visible as it headed back to where the battle had first summoned it from its rest. Below, the gates of the park came into view as they seemed to welcome it back. The sign read Wilson's Botanical Gardens as the moonlight from a clear night sky illuminated the lettering. The eagle landed on the high hilltop in the middle of the park. It looked out across the trees and rooftops. Its huge golden-yellow eyes scanned over the City of Casey from the left, the view of Beaconsfield, to Cranbourne and Clyde on its right. It turned to scan Dandenong Ranges behind its back before turning around and rotating its head once more to survey the peaceful neighbourhood as dawn breaks and mop-up crews arrived to clear and repair the storm's debris.

All was well again under its protection and care.

LOVE, HATE RELATIONS

BY ROBYN KING

Ten years ago, in 2014, I had a year I would choose to forget as it involved my Cousin Rhonda and her mother, my aunty Helen, my husband and my parents. In January of that year, my husband told me that he no longer loved me and he was in love with someone else. It devastated me. I kept asking myself. "Did I see the signs? Who was he in love with? How long had he rejected me and allowed another woman in?

He was fifty-five, and I was fifty-four. Intimacy was spread evenly across the month. It was not something we had at the forefront of our minds. I asked myself. Was that a problem? We could have talked about it. I was happy to kiss him whenever we would pass each other. I was happy to tell him every day that I loved him. He would respond with. "Love you more."

I just did not see this coming. Was I walking around with blinkers on?

I had to talk to him. I was desperate. I wanted him to stay. I didn't want him to go anywhere. I hated his snoring and the way he would never cover his face when he sneezed. But I have lived with it for so long that it became something that I chose to ignore. On the wedding anniversary before he left, he paid for an all-expenses paid trip to the Gold Coast hinterland for a four-day spa and wellness treatment. He was always so thoughtful that way.

I was really scared to be left alone. Looking back on our lives as a married couple, I see that our life together was exciting. We would go hiking. We both loved the outdoors. Fishing was one of our favourite pastimes. We hired a boat once, and I caught five whiting and five flatheads. I was very happy with myself. All he caught was an old boot. I told him that if we went back to that spot again, he might catch another one, and he would have a set. We called it a bootfish. He took it in his stride as he thought it was funny also. We still laugh about it.

In 1982, my gynaecologist told us that we could not conceive as a virus I had contracted while in Borneo on a hiking trip affected my ovaries. I was never the same after that trip. We had tried for some time to conceive. I believe in miracles, and she said there was a 15% chance I could get pregnant. But alas, it wasn't to be.

It was a Wednesday, and I was at work. My husband rang me and said he had been to the house and took all his clothes and his tools. He paid for the second TV, so he got it, and he also got the gym equipment. He was moving out today. I asked him who is this woman that he was moving in with?"

He told me it was his secretary. Janis Paper. Fancy a secretary named Janis Paper. It didn't seem real.

"I asked him why? He loosely fluffed around his answer. I wanted to know what she had that I didn't have. He gave me some compliments. That didn't fit the question.

He was being an idiot. I had to work it out myself. She was younger, uneducated and very superficial. Everything was fake. Her lips, fingernails, her boobs, her eyelashes, and I was told a little while later she had butt cheek implants.

I couldn't believe it. He would be the laughingstock of the office.

Then it dawned on me he loved the fact that he could manipulate her into his way of thinking. If she said something silly, he could just smile and be happy that any intelligence that she didn't have would make him seem uneducated. He was always telling me he wished that his memory were as good as mine.

So he left, and they are still together to this day. I don't know if he is happy or not. I don't see him. They moved away and live in Townsville. I never found another. I am happy to live on my own with my two Maltese terriers and a moggy.

In that same year, in March. My wonderful, beautiful father collapsed in the garden while pruning. Fell off the ladder and landed on the garden's birdbath.

He didn't slip. He had a heart attack. My mother found him after he heard the crack of his head hitting the birdbath. He was conscious when the ambulance arrived but fell unconscious on the way to the hospital and died that night.

Dad was eighty and lived a happy and prosperous life with Mum. He worked as a gardener for years. He called himself. A leafy manicurist. He was very proud, and his garden did not have a flower, shrub, or leaf out of place. People would walk past our house and stop to chat. He loved telling them the difference between perennials and Annuals. The difference between introduced and natives. He would explain the bird attracting trees. He would leave a box of lemons and oranges from our trees in the backyard for all who appreciated them. Never asked for anything for them. Occasionally, he would be given tomatoes and cucumbers in exchange.

When Dad passed away, Mum found it hard to cope without him. She would stare for hours into the distance while sitting on their favourite garden seat. The garden wasn't the same, and she would hire someone to cut the lawn. But it was never the same. She died exactly six months later. I saw her body during the viewing, and she seemed to have a smile on her face. I wonder if she was actually happy again. I thought about that smile for a long time after that day. I miss them both. I miss my husband, too, in a funny sort of way. I'm still angry at him, but I accept that I have learned a lot since all my family has gone. I know myself really well, and I can handle more situations now than ever before. As I think of my parents, I think I will still be with my husband, and we will get old together.

By the beginning of 2015, a couple of days after the new year. I received a phone call from my solicitor. I thought he would still be on holiday after Christmas, but he explained to me that he had such a backlog of paperwork that he had to come in early to sign off some affidavits and make some phone calls. And mine was one of them.

I am an only child. He wasn't telling me something that I didn't know.

Well, he received an email from a lady named Helen Smithe.

I thought to myself that I knew that name. That's the name of my mother's younger sister. I listened carefully. I didn't want to sound presumptuous, but what does she want. Money, I suppose. I thought it was money with everything and everyone. I am my parents' daughter, and I should be entitled to everything they have. No one else is legit. I became angry even before the solicitor explained what the email was about.

"Please continue," I said.

Your aunty Helen claims that her daughter, Rhonda, is your father's daughter. She is of a similar age to you, and she is putting in a claim for any money or property that should be hers as she is a descendant of your father's.

"My father never mentioned Rhonda being his. I remember her. But where has she been? I haven't seen or heard of her since I was a child. She can't be dad's. I'm his only child. You mean to tell me he went to bed with Aunty Helen?' "I call bullshit to that. Sorry for the swearing. Is there any way you can prove this is the case?

Well, your aunty Helen says your father has been paying amounts of money for years. Right up until he died. She sent me a copy of all money transactions.

"How does that work? She's the same age as me, and she shouldn't get money forever. Well, she has cerebral palsy and your father, being such a kind man, says, and I quote ... "Rhonda will need care for the rest of her life as she has cerebral palsy".

Your father claims her as his own. His money paid for hospital bills, medication, and her upgraded wheelchair. He bought her mother a van, which was installed with hydraulics to lift and hold a wheelchair.

I couldn't believe it. I was furious. I didn't want to share anything with her. I didn't want her to be born. I hated them. I wish she would just shrivel up and die.

I wanted to know if there was anything I could do. The solicitor said. "No"

I called him useless. When I got off the phone, I opened Google and found another solicitor. I rang for an appointment.

When I spoke to her. She said we should be able to fight. But Rhonda will have to get something. I eventually softened to the blow. I questioned how much she was entitled to, but the solicitor said that would be up to the judge. But She was going to recommend a lump sum, and the houses were to go to me. I could live with that as I was going to fight for the houses. That is what I wanted. I still wanted to go to the coast and stay in our holiday home.

One day, when I visited the solicitor, she told me that Rhonda would like to meet me.

I told her, "Not in your lifetime. I hate the girl. I don't care about her. I hate my aunt Helen. I remember the fight my mother and father had when I was about six. Yeah, you tell her. It must have been when mum found out that the baby was dad's, as I heard Aunty Helen's name mentioned. I never saw her again after that. She broke my mother's heart. I don't want anything to do with any of them.

The day of the court case, the heavens opened up, and it rained for days. I guess it was my mother telling me to fight, as Aunty Helen deserves nothing. She was a conniving double-crossing bitch.

I got the house, and Rhonda got the cash. It was less than what my solicitor thought. One hundred thousand dollars. I thought my parents had more than that. It didn't matter in the end. My father paid more than enough through the years, and the judge said Rhonda was well off.

I love my houses. I miss my parents, and I miss my husband.

As the last ten years have passed by. I have had some sickness. But I'm okay. I go to the Balla Balla community centre for morning melodies on Thursdays. I joined their knitting group, and I sing in a choir on Sunday mornings at the local Methodist church. There, I'm surrounded by kind, loving people who have taught me to forgive and to love myself. And to accept what I can't change.

I realise I held a lot of bitterness since I lost my husband and parents. For my own well-being, I need to loosen the ropes and the chains that made me so angry with Aunty Helen for screwing my Dad and having an illegitimate child. For my mother, who put up with my dad's infidelity. Without letting it out. Then, it made her sick, as she had a lot of sickness over the years. And I am even angry at her for not being here to talk to me. I am angry at my Dad for being sucked into that wench. He should have been smarter. Then I am angry at my ex-husband. That's the first time I have called him my ex. He was always my husband.

Not that long ago, my aunty Helen was looking for me. She came to my house while I was out. She left a note under my door. She says that she was so sorry that I refused to meet up with her and Rhonda.

Rhonda wanted to meet me. Then, the note said Rhonda passed away in 2020. She was forty-nine. Her last words were, "Tell Catharine that I love her."

I gulped. I had a lump in my throat. That has haunted me ever since. I was nasty. I said things that I never realised were so hurtful. It was unjustified. I judged Rhonda, and I took it personally. I wasn't the reason everything went pear-shaped. It was life. Rhonda was the one who suffered the most from her sickness. She didn't ask to be born. I made things worse for her. I should have handled it better. Every night, I say a little prayer, and I tell her that I am so grateful that she tried to reach out. I wish I had met her. I should have been more humble and chose my words better. I hope Rhonda is in a good place. And she forgives me.

This is my story of things that I wish I had known ten years ago.

GARRY

BY NORMA SAVIGE

'For God's sake, Jason, it won't hurt you to mow your grandfather's lawn this afternoon. It will only take up an hour of your precious time, and then you and Jonno can go off and do your own thing.'

'Yeah, yeah, Mum, I should have known you brought us here for breakfast as a bribe. It wouldn't be out of the goodness of your heart.' Jason's face was flushed and angry. 'Do you know how embarrassing it is to have a mate see me treated like a child and bossed around like this?

Jonno shifted uncomfortably in his seat and smiled at Mary. 'It's fine, Jase, really. It won't take us long,' he said.

'It's not fine. Just because Pa has a bit of a sore knee, I'm expected to jump to and do whatever he needs, whenever he needs it. It's not fair. I'd like to know what he'll do when I go away to uni in the new year. Who'll run after him then?'

Mary shook her head and sighed. Her father had done so much for her and Jason while she struggled as a solo parent. They both owed him big time. She loved Jason but worried that he still acted like a spoilt child at times. She had tried to raise him to be a kind and respectful person and had thought she had done so until lately. She wondered if, deep down, he might be anxious about going to university in the city by himself. *I'll need to sit him down and have a heart-to-heart with him to find out just what's going on with him.*

An awkward silence followed as the three of them focused on their chosen breakfasts: waffles for the boys and a croissant for Mary. She liked this café on top of the hill in the small town where she had grown up and looked around, recognising many of the other diners. They were locals who knew her family well. She hoped they couldn't overhear Jason's complaints about helping his grandfather.

They had just started to tuck into their breakfasts when Jason looked up and nudged Jonno breaking the silence, 'Get a load of this old codger,' he smirked, 'He's got his slippers on. Silly old coot.'

Mary turned to see Garry, an elderly man from the town who lived independently with a little assistance from social services. As she watched, he shuffled slowly into the café, gripping a twenty-dollar note in his hand.

'Morning, Garry,' called the café owner behind the counter with a wide smile and a greeting. 'The usual, Darl?'

'Yes, thanks, love. Toasted sandwich and coffee. Breakfast of champions.'

'Pop back out to your car, and we'll bring it to you when it's ready.'

'Thanks, love,' he said and turned to leave but wobbled on his feet.

Mary leapt up and grabbed his arm. 'Take a seat for a minute, Garry. Is the old blood pressure not too good this morning?'

'Nah, love. I think I might be a bit dehydrated with this hot weather, that's all.'

'Jason, hop up and get Garry some water. Jonno, move over so he can have your seat.'

Jason stood at the water table, staring. He was mortified. Sitting in full view at their table was the scruffiest person he'd ever seen. The man had long, wild white hair, about a week's growth of stubble on his face, a checked flannelette shirt inside out and old, worn blue slippers that looked two sizes too big. Everyone was looking at them.

He was trapped. He knew his mother would make him stay and converse politely with this old bloke. Jonno will never come out with us again, that's for sure.

'Did you know your shirt is inside out, old fella?' he smirked as he slid back into his seat, grinning at Jonno.

With Mary's help, Garry removed his top, turned it right way out, and held out his arms to put it back on. 'Whoa! You've got a tattoo. You're a cool dude,' Jason taunted. Mary kicked him under the table. 'What? There is one on his arm.'

'It's just my blood group. We had it done to go to Vietnam.' Shrugged Garry.

'You were in Vietnam? Did you have a gun?' Garry nodded. 'Did you kill anyone?' Garry didn't answer. 'Bet you did. What was it like?'

'That's enough!' Mary slammed her knife onto the table. 'Have some respect, will you? I'm not sure what's got into you lately, but I've had enough. Just shut up.'

Jonno had sat quietly throughout these last few minutes. He leaned towards Garry and spoke gently to him. 'Sir, I had a great-uncle who died in Vietnam. And I know it wasn't fun,' he gave Jason a withering look, 'What was it like for you?'

'Well, young fella, it was a hell of a lot of heat and a hell of a lot of waiting, never knowing when the action might start. I had a mate, Macka, from this town who was there with me, and we played lots of card games and listened to all the latest music from America. It was great to have someone with me that I'd gone to school with and who knew all of our town. We shared a lot of good …' he stumbled over his words, '… good times. But …' He stared at the local park across the road and fell silent.

Mary put her hand on his arm.

He looked at her. 'I still can't believe it, you know. One minute, we were creeping through the long grass looking for the VC, and the next, all hell broke out.' His eyes were filled with tears, and he didn't try to wipe them away. 'Macka was screaming and calling my name. I crawled over to him and saw straight away that his leg was blown clear off, and he was bleeding out. He was begging me to help him, but there was nothing I could do. I got behind and wrapped my arms around him to hold him up. I was bawling my eyes out like a baby. I told him he'd be OK, but he knew that wasn't true.'

Jason and Jonno stared at the man openly crying at the table, and when he lifted his eyes to them, they looked away from his pain.

Garry cleared his throat and continued, 'He said, "Tell my mum I love her, will you, Mate?" and I said I would. I hugged him and told him I reckoned she was right there with us. He smiled then. I told him I could see her standing there holding the big wooden spoon she chased him with when he played up. He actually laughed then and said, "Oh, Mum," and died with a smile lingering on his face. I sat there holding him and sobbing until the choppers arrived and took us back to base.'

After a long silence, Garry looked at the people around the table before continuing. 'I came back to Oz two weeks later, and I felt so guilty for surviving, but when I went to see his mother, she was lovely to me. Told me she was glad he was with me when he died. It's fifty years tomorrow since he died. I used to sit with him at the cemetery on that day and look after the grave a bit, but I haven't been able to go for the last two years.' He looked at the two boys and shook his head. 'We were about your age. Bloody disgrace it was.'

All four of them sat silently, pretending they hadn't noticed the others' tears until Garry's food arrived at the table. Jason sprang up to take it from the server. 'I'll take this out to Garry's car for him,' he said and turned to Garry, 'Is there anything we can do for you, Garry? ' He looked at Jonno, who nodded. 'We're going to mow my Pa's lawn today. Could we do yours, too?'

'Your Pa's lucky to have you to help. Who is your Pa?'

'Charles Miller.'

'Ah, Charlie. Good bloke. He went to 'Nam the year after us. Got a nasty leg wound, if I remember rightly.'

Jason stopped and stared. 'I didn't know he was in Vietnam. He told me that was an old football injury,' he said, turning to his mother, who shook her head and looked away.

'Yeah, it's hard to talk about sometimes. I'm not sure why I spilt my guts to you today. I guess because the anniversary is coming up, and your mother's kindness to me opened up the floodgates.' He stood to go, and Jason took his arm while Jonno rushed to open the door.

'You know, Garry, Jonno and I can help you get there tomorrow and do some tidying up too. Mum has lots of nice flowers we can take too.' He looked at his mother, who still couldn't speak but nodded in agreement.

Mary felt numb while waiting for the boys to return to their half-eaten breakfasts. One thing she knew for sure was that her son would be a different young man than the one she despaired of earlier this morning. Offering up a silent prayer of thanks to Garry, she looked up and smiled as they returned to the table.

'I guess two new hot breakfasts wouldn't go astray?' They nodded with relief. 'It sounds like you're going to need some extra energy for a busy couple of days ahead of you,' she added.

Jason turned to Mary and said, 'We're really lucky, aren't we, Mum?'

'We all are love. We all are.'

SWEET DELUSIONS AND FAMILY FOLKLORE

BY MADISEN WHITE

Not the kind we read about today,
but something softer—corny nostalgia,
a lump in your throat,
glorious choral Christmas carols,
Pumpkin pie that never quite tastes as good
as the memory of it,
As the mothers and fathers who made it long before us,
Better in our minds than it ever was on our tongues.

Airs and graces,
reminders of proper etiquette,

good posture, effortless hospitality—
Bestowed upon children, grandchildren, and local waiters alike.
Yet never quite aligning.
with their tracksuits dusted in pet fur,
the stray stain on their sleeve,
the emboldened request for another glass of wine,
despite their adult children's cautious disapproval—
The one they swear they didn't already drink.

Their sly hands in any game of cards,
proud rule-explainers, shameless cheaters,
Feigned innocence wrapped in a mischievous grin.

Good, God-fearing Christian folk,
but never ones to deprive their grandchildren of Halloween,
of apple-bobbing and sickly sweet desserts,
of witch costumes and exaggerated moles,
Of *"Go on, Rusty, tell them a spooky story."*

Of magic and tradition, passed down,
or clung to—
Because they were lucky enough to have it,
Or because they never did.

A quiet enchantment laced through their stories,
Woven into their heritage, their culture.

My grandmother's grandmother,
the first daughter of the first daughter,
a tiny, wizened medicine woman

Who foretold her own death?
And lingered through spiritual mediums and tarot readings.

My grandfather's family—
A single mother of three,
His father, a soldier? A vagrant?
In absentia, nonetheless.
Another history carried in his deep brown eyes,
his high cheekbones and prominent nose—
Owlish features, a quiet legacy.

A family folklore,
A culture I cannot claim,
But one that hums beneath my skin all the same.

THE COURT OF MANY COLOURS

BY CORINNE KING

I start my story from the beginning, and this highlights my background and the diversity I have grown up with over the years. I originate from a background of a diverse nation of many cultures. From this alone, I have a great history that goes back three hundred to four hundred centuries. This has been a part of my cultural background, of which I am very proud.

I am a descendant of Dutch and German on my maternal side ancestry. On my paternal side, I have British and Portuguese - a mixed bag or, to say, a "Heinz 57".

Growing up with these cultures instilled into me has been interesting as I recall the German and Dutch food always displayed on the table when it was Christmas and Easter when we visited my Maternal Grandparents' home in the 1950s. The same applied to the festive seasonal visits to my

Paternal ancestry home, where we savoured the Portuguese and British delicacies.

I talk of the Country of Ceylon (formerly known as Serendib), now known as Sri Lanka, where my initial background in the multiculturalism way of life begins. I attended a school in Colombo where I had friends with Indian and Muslim heritage, and we also knew that we were the "offspring" of many cultures ourselves.

This tiny island set like a "pearl" in the Indian Ocean south of the Country of India was a nautical base for the ancient sailors of the high seas who ventured from the West to the East to seek "trade of value," as they risked lives and families in the process. The high seas have been brutal to many, a "nautical fleet" that consisted of pioneer adventurers and seekers of a new start in life in the East.

The richness of living in a "multicultural community" made my integration into the Australian way of life easier when I migrated with my parents in the very early 1970's. There was a time when Australia opened its doors to migrants under "The White Australia Policy", and this was changed to permitting migrants to enter the shores of Australia only if they had families that had settled down earlier. There was a calling for new migrants to be educated and work-orientated so that they could give their talents to the country of their choice to live in.

In the 1950s, 1960s, and 1970s, we did not hear of "Refugees" or "Asylum Seekers"; these new migrants to Australia were never heard of then. The country's policies on migration have since changed, and we have been able to deal with a new kind of migrant that has been accepted into this country of Australia. The numerous Wars between Nations and the internal unrest in individual countries have contributed to a wider scale of "multiculturalism" in this Country of Australia, which many of us now call "Home." However, a huge majority of people refer to the "country of their birth" as the "Motherland" unless they were born here.

I, too, have, as a migrant, married my husband Ian, who was British and an early 1970s migrant from England. We married and bought our home, which was a luxury to possess in the mid-1970s. Of course, in that era, we had to have a sizeable deposit to place on the choice of a home that the State Bank would sanction according to our working status and the nature of our loan.

We wisely chose our home in a brand-new pristine housing estate that would reap many benefits in the ensuing years we would live in our choice of home and area. My dear late Dad always told us in those early months of marriage, "To cut our coat according to our cloth." In other words, do not "borrow over the top" and find it hard to meet financial commitments. So, we followed his advice and acted accordingly. It worked perfectly as we met our goals comfortably. We find that this policy does not quite meet with the cultural changes we have around us and the Government's financial assistance given to many new migrants.

We married in 1975 and have one daughter, Karen, who was born in 1981. She has always said how proud she has been to say that she has a "Curry & Chips" background. Many find this a fascinating description of her explanation of a mixed background and cultural complexity.

During the primary years of Karen's education, there was a great multicultural mixture of kids that Karen grew up with. She was certainly enriched with this great advantage over the years, broadening her outlook on the changing scenarios that she faces in the professional duties she encompasses in her present employment. Ian and I have lived forty-eight-plus years in our own home. For this, we are so humbled by the simplicity of our lifestyle and the way we have embraced the "multicultural scene" that has enabled us to grow in "thought, word and deed" in this manner.

When we bought our home in early 1976, we were termed the "Seniors of the Court" - this referred to our small Court that consisted of four houses. We were in the middle years of our twenties, and the other new home buyers were twenty-one plus to twenty-five years old, while we were both twenty-six-year-olds.

Ian and I, too, were exemptions to the rule as we were both migrants. In contrast, the others were Australian-born and the children of migrants and consisted of a good mix. Meeting with the parents of each homeowner was in itself very interesting as we became familiar with the Greek and Italian community cultures and traditions.

Ian and I loved the "International" blend that existed within our little Court "fellowship", as Ian is British. I, being Sri Lankan, created a rich mix of culture, food and tradition sharing. We also gained a very close bond with the parents of our neighbours. They, in turn, enjoyed meeting and sharing their respect and love for my parents, who were, in turn, both older than all their parents at the time.

I am very passionate about sharing that as we were all owners of new homes in the 1970s, the homes came as bare shells to the buyer. We had to start from the very beginning by dressing up our homes. We had to buy our tiles for floors and walls, and we also chose our floor coverings – in the mid-1970s, vinyl, cork, polished boards, carpet, or tiles. These were the customary floor coverings of that era. When the other neighbours went shopping on the weekends, they would all bring back samples and come over to our home to share their discoveries with us and ask us for our opinions for guidance. This happened with the other neighbours in our Court. It was a great atmosphere and "bonding of fellowship" that was building so strongly amongst the four young couples of a four-home Court.

Our four homes had no fences, and we would place picnic mats and sit on our front lawns, which were overgrown weeds in the early days until we all decided to get our front lawns "rotary hoed" by the one guy who was an Irishman. He was so happy to get a big job for himself as he was also building up his finances to pay for his new household needs and young family. He was Jim Kelly, and he hails from Carlow, Southern Ireland.

Every "tradesperson" that was employed by one of us was also "hired" by the other homeowners in the Court. This saved us all individually from going through the "Yellow Pages" that we all had home-delivered in the early days. These big Telstra books carried the names of businesses of virtually every kind. A common expression in those early days of our lives was to "let our fingers do the walking." In other words, we hired our "tradespeople" through the "Yellow Pages" as they were the most recommendable, as we were made to believe.

*

Ian and I often recall how our neighbours, who were all a maximum of six years to a minimum of two years younger than us, had such great respect for us that they would even consult us about purchasing a wheelbarrow, lawn mower and garden tools. The closeness we all shared was incredible. Quite often, we reminisce about this quality that existed in the mid to late years of the 1970s. This kind of "fellowship" amongst new neighbours would not exist in present times as new homes come to buyers of first homes with every imaginable modern convenience and gadget supplied, plus the tiling and floor coverings all pre-chosen and provided by the home builder. The pluses of new home building, compared with the way new homes were presented to home buyers in the 1970s, were very different.

The early years of our lives as a newly married couple were simple. The rest contemplate having their families early in life, once they have completed their new homes, to give them that "dressed up look." Curtains and window coverings were the next items on the agenda, and this, too, was yet another adventure for us all. Again, we all shared samples of material and laces for opinions on our window dressings. "Bonding" again.

We were all so very closely bonded together as we all shared the one interest of establishing our homes to start our young families. There was no competition shown with purchased items or goals attained.

Amazingly, the other three couples started their families at the same time, and Ian and I had different plans. Our plan was our choice, although we did get the occasional hint from the older generation of family and friends, "When are we going to have the pleasure of the pitter-patter of little feet?"

There was no doubt that this comment annoyed us immensely as we had plans to visit each other's countries. Ian was very keen to visit Sri Lanka as it had changed its name from Ceylon to Sri Lanka since I had departed its shores. Ian was eager to meet with the numerous people I mentioned and received letters and cards from for my birthday and for Christmas and New Year.

I, myself, was keen to visit England, a Country I had always wished to visit and become familiar with as I had a penfriend who resided there. Our pen-friendship originated when we were single-figure years old, and it is still maintained so richly as we are both in our seventies. I was also keen to meet with my new British family, who were very accepting of me right from the early days of our friendship prior to marriage.

Visiting England in 1979 was exhilarating, to say the least, as there was not such an influx of the Middle-Eastern, Indian, and Asian communities residing in the country yet. My presence amongst Ian's family, friends, and penfriend's parents and in-laws was well received, and I felt very warmly accepted into the British culture. I was truly in the midst of this. My blending with the English people was so easy as they all enjoyed listening to all the anecdotes and snippets I readily shared. I was also keen and eager to introduce some savoury dishes into their rather bland food diets.

I started off with a very well-combined stir-fried chicken and vegetable dish with egg noodles all tossed into one dish. This laborious process was well accepted by the family unit in which we were residing in Ian's hometown in England. I then ventured to prepare a mild butter chicken-style curry. I made savoury rice with a yellow lentil vegetable. Add to the array of dishes with a tossed salad for good measure. My efforts did go down well, as it was very well accepted and considered palatable for the bland palate. I felt I had conquered the English bland palate and the in-laws in their efforts to venture bravely into the flavoursome change of food types.

My interest was even furthered when I went with Ian to a local Indian Food Store and made friends with the Indian Storeman. He was most courteous and realised I was keen to purchase curry condiments that were of Sri Lankan origin and flavour. He was most obliging by informing us that he was going into London the next day to purchase more stock for himself and that he would buy some condiments with Sri Lankan flavours, especially for me.

We went back to his Store the next day. I ended up purchasing a wide range of mini spices to take with us when we visited a classmate of mine in Bracknell who was keen to have me come to her cosy home to prepare a full meal. At the same time, we chatted in the kitchen, and our husbands went through decades of chatter. Of course, my friend had purchased the meats, the rice, and the lentils but was eagerly awaiting my cooking to flavour them.

I was so happy with my culinary efforts as we both cooked up a storm. When we opened the kitchen window, we sure got the aromas of food wafting through the air of the cul-de-sac my friend lived down. We had such a chuckle about the new aromas that had hit the town of Bracknell. We sat down around 6.30pm to a very flavoursome meal that I had cooked in my friend's kitchen.

We ended up having a tin of fruit salad and ice cream for our dessert, with a sweet liquor to wash it all down for the night. Then Ian had to gear himself up for the long drive back to our base accommodation.

The multiculturism that existed in the late 1970s was not so evident in the townships in England as they are now. I must, however, confess that in the Supermarkets, it would have been rare to see many Asian and Middle-Eastern cultures around. There were the Indians and Sri Lankans in plenty, but certainly, they were to be found in pockets around the townships.

Our 1979 tour covered a three-day visit to Hong Kong and a three-day visit to Singapore, where we met with a cousin and were introduced to the culture of the area. We thoroughly enjoyed the blend and flew on to Rome for a four-day tour and visit to the Vatican on the most auspicious day in 1979 in the Vatican calendar when the newly elected Pope John Paul II was to meet with the "common people" for his first Mass after having been elected to the position of Pope. We were so honoured to be amidst this massive crowd of around 90,000 to 100,000 people who had gathered for this celebration. We ended up joining an "English" speaking group and squeezed our way into the Church of St. Peter in Rome.

When this incredible experience was over, we flew into Zurich and stayed in the delightful Hotel Zurich, where we covered so much during the four days and three nights we were there. We took day tours to the summit of Mt. Titlis, termed the highest mountain of the Uri Alps in Switzerland, with a summit of 3,238 metres. It was truly an adventure as we first took the express Gondola to the middle station and then the cable car to the summit. We also took a coach tour of the entire township of Zurich and a cable car trip to the snow-capped ranges of the Swiss Alps. In the evenings, we socialized with Swiss families that we were introduced to by a cousin of mine. We met on appointment only in the evenings after he had been at work during the day. Meeting with the Swiss people was an absolute delight as they assimilated well with us during the day when we were on our own. In the evenings, we were in the company of my cousin, who was known to many Restauranteurs in the town of Zurich, being in the hospitality circle himself.

Our next move was to Paris to take in tours of Paris and its environs in the four days we allotted ourselves here as our last stop before flying into Heathrow Airport to visit the British family, friends, and acquaintances we met in the four weeks we were there in March 1979. In Paris, we thoroughly enjoyed our numerous tours of the Palace of Napolean, The Louvre Palace, the World's most visited Art Museum, The Gothic Cathedral of Notré Dame de Paris, the Champs-Elysées at The Avenue des Champs-Elysées and of course we spent half a day at the Eiffel Tower.

Our experience at the Eiffel Tower was unique as it had just been re-opened after a huge refurbishment of the highest section of the Tower. Our group of visitors were told that we were the first group to go up to the top level that afternoon after the Café was fully enclosed. The reason being that it was a common place for many a suicide. Likewise, in Paris, we met with some unfriendly Parisians who persisted in not wishing to help us as we spoke in English and not in French. This turned out to be what was an annoying part of our Parisian sojourn. The Parisian scene was very varied, and we noticed many African Americans residing in the city. In fact, our roommaid at our Parisian Hotel was an African American who turned out to be one of the most helpful people at the time. Yes, she was expecting a handsome tip at the end of our four-day stay in Paris.

Wherever we visited and whatever tourist activity we settled on, Ian and I enjoyed the multicultural people we met daily. We had absolutely no problem with this and felt very comfortable that we, too, were treated with great respect and interest as to our background cultures and the country we were new citizens of in Australia, the land "Down Under", as it was very affectionately termed and known as to people in other countries worldwide.

In England, we had our own hire car. We covered some extensive mileage touring from Abingdon, near Oxford, to Devon, Cornwall and Wales, and further ventures to the northernmost areas of Scotland, where we met delightful characters along the way. Travelling and touring certainly enriched our minds as we exchanged many anecdotes with people. We met in the pubs, which we frequented to get ourselves a good meal at the end of a tiring day of driving, touring, and sightseeing. Touring Scotland, we left for the end of our time in England, and we came back for a few days into Abingdon to say our goodbyes to family and friends.

Leaving Heathrow, we flew into Colombo in Sri Lanka to meet with family members and numerous friends of mine who were eagerly awaiting Ian's arrival in the country of Sri Lanka for the first time.

*

Having savoured a very multicultural first holiday together of eight weeks in 1979, four years since our marriage in 1975, we were very enthusiastically met by countless family friends of my parents too, who were eager to meet with Ian, the foreigner to the country of my birth.

Ian had the pleasure of meeting with all the older generation people I had referred to for years as "Uncles and Aunties." In fact, when we were engaged, he quipped one day when I spoke of a few people and referred to them as "Uncles and aunts," as he had asked me, "How many uncles and aunts I had living in Sri Lanka?" This became a standing joke ever since as I explained to him that it was a "cultural" form of respect to refer to one's elders as "Uncles and Aunties."

When we were in Sri Lanka, we took some short sightseeing trips with a few friends to show Ian the beauty of the resplendent Island of Sri Lanka, always known as "Ceylon" to me and "Serendib" in the earlier centuries. Ceylon/Sri Lanka was also known as "The Pearl of the Indian Ocean," and it was here that Ian embraced the multicultural society in which he was engulfed by family and friends.

We gathered the many resources handed to us on platters by the local people who were overwhelmed so that I could converse in the Sinhala language fluently. However, I had been away around eight years or so at the time. The colloquial language of Sinhala is different from the written language, and this was evident when we studied the language as a subject for our senior college examinations.

Our sojourn in the country of my birth and the country I will always call my "Motherland" ended very sadly as I knew that many elderly people I had visited with Ian I would never meet again for obvious reasons. These senior family friends and family members wished us well with our plans to come back to Australia and hopefully become parents, having fulfilled our initial plans to visit the "Countries of our Births" and introduce each other to the family and friends we had known individually.

We visited together and achieved many places of interest that had many imprinted memories in our minds to take back to Australia and share with others. These "memories" can never be erased in a lifetime.

*

On returning home, my Mum and Dad had done a sterling job minding our home and looking after our loveable pet dog "Benji." We were grateful to them for this as they had mowed the lawns, dusted, and vacuumed our home and visited our home with Benji so he could smell his own smells around "his own home" and take him back to their home for the extra tender, love and nurturing they showered on him.

We had many stories to share with our families on both sides, including our multicultural neighbours and their families. It was a very close-knit type of atmosphere that prevailed in our four-house Court.

A few months later, we had news from neighbours that neighbours situated at No. 4 were expecting their second child and neighbours at No. 2 were also expecting their second child. This gave us a buzz as we were still the "Seniors" of the four-house Court.

The excitement of more young ones playing in the very safe Court gave us a thrill, and each neighbour appreciated and realised the love that we had to share around for the excitement of other individuals' joy. We were at the time told that it was visible in our own actions and temperament that we were kind and sharing neighbours.

The next few months of early 1979 slipped by after we had returned from our eight-week holiday, and we had some exciting news to share with our families, friends, and neighbours in the Court. Ian and I were expecting a baby that was due to be born at the end of January 1980. The due date given was 27th January 1980, and we were thrilled as that was the birthdate of

Ian's good friend in the UK. We were delighted with our news and shared it with those we moved around with socially, too, who were all new and young parents themselves. We were almost the last "stragglers" in the group to be parents as we were keen to establish and achieve some of the "goals" we had set ourselves to achieve.

My pregnancy went well up to the fourteenth week when I sadly miscarried. It was a "trauma" that was made even more "traumatic" by the medical authorities that I had as my mentors and guide. Although we requested to know the "gender" of the foetus, that was not told to us. After my clean-up, I was "plunged" into the "Birthing Ward", where I heard the cry of babies all night and here was I, a young woman who had just lost her "foetus" at fourteen weeks. It was not a fair decision that was made by the Hospital authorities and has amazingly become a "memory" in my mind that I find difficult to erase.

Fortunately, I was blessed with a strong mind and character. I took this loss in my stride as I later told my General Practitioner at the time that "The bad apples fall off the tree, and the good ones stay on." That gave me the solace that there was a reason for this unfortunate mishap and that I should "turn the page and soldier on," and I did this with prayer and positivity of mind.

The year 1980 slipped by, and 1981 dawned. Yes, Ian and I were greeted with great news: that we were to be parents and that the due date of the birth of our baby would be around September 4th. I was under the care of another Gynaecologist and went through this pregnancy without any complications. A daughter was born to us on August 30th, and we named her Karen Lisa. She was everything we all wanted, my parents and my mum-in-law, who had specially made it out to Melbourne from the UK to be here for the births of 2 babies – her first great-granddaughter and Karen, who was her last grandchild.

Our neighbours were absolutely over the moon for us and showered us with the neighbourly love they could give us in their own way. We realised the love that shrouded us from all angles. Ian and I received great love from our work associates, who were all from mixed blends of multicultural backgrounds. All new migrants came to Australia at some time in their lives, and they had migrated from many Western and Eastern cultures to the "greener pastures of Australia."

The years trickled by, and I became a full-time stay-at-home Mum when Karen was two and a half years old. However, until then, my dear parents took on a role that they both specifically retired to accomplish as brand-new grandparents. A kindly deed that Ian and I were always indebted to them for their own sacrifice

In the Court, our children all grew up into lovely young single, figured individuals and were very well-blended young people of a multi-national group of neighbours who had mixed and diverse backgrounds. The children all attended the various schools in the area. They now only met on weekends in the Court on their bicycles to exchange the neighbourly "meet and greet" that prevailed.

One day, we were told that our neighbours were going to move house, as the neighbours of No. 4 in the court decided that they would try new pastures in Rosebud. The father of the two kids was a "bricklayer", and he told us that new estates were being built in the Rosebud, Rye, and Dromana areas as then he would get more work to take on and that he could build up his finances. It was good for them to seek a new life, and the children were growing. The mum was working part-time at Kmart, and she told us that she could transfer her position to Rosebud Kmart successfully and work part-time hours from 9 - 3.

The other couple, situated at No. 2 in the Court, decided to move out to Warrnambool to start afresh and build themselves a mansion home, which they did successfully, but sadly, it also cost them their marriage in the process. Ian and I got to have the pleasure of visiting the 'single' Mum in her beautiful mansion house in Warrnambool that was beautifully architectured to have double turrets and just looked spectacular.

*

The years slipped by, and the new buyers of the houses in our court decided to give two houses in the court for "rental," and this brought in varied tenants. This turned out to be an even bigger turning point for us as the most "Senior Citizens" of the four-house Court. We had tenants from varied backgrounds on either side of us, and they brought in loads of multicultural changes. We saw a family with young sons move to No. 2, and they were originally from South America. No disrespect to the country, but they were opinionated. Literally, they drove us to extremes, virtually insisting that they could turn on their music loud in their home and front garden till late at night. It was daunting to have them as neighbours as with two young sons, the peace and quiet of the neighbourhood was shattered, and we had boisterous ball games being played in a small and short Court. Our cars were in jeopardy as these young kids had no respect for the property of their neighbours.

Having these neighbours changed the scene of our Court from what was a quiet Court from the inception of its start in 1976 to a completely changed ambience of even a rowdy father of two sons often joining his two sons in the kicking of a 'footy' in the Court. There were numerous kindly requests made to the parents to take the boys to the reserve behind our homes to play, but this was deliberately ignored.

We realised that this change of attitude of tenants existed as they were in 'rental' properties, and the mutual respect and care for property meant nothing to the parents in order that they could instil into their children the respect and care needed for the properties of others.

We survived this brief period of mixed feelings in the court. However, we extended the "olive branch" to the South American family in numerous ways. It was like talking to deaf ears as it was violated even more as retaliation when we approached them to quieten down and respect the 'peace and tranquillity' of the four-house Court on Saturday and Sunday as well.

During the year 2010, we were also preparing for our only daughter's wedding, and this was an exciting time for us as our daughter and future son-in-law had chosen their wedding day to be the 10th of October 2010. Looking at these figures as 10-10-10, we were told that within the Chinese community, it was a very lucky day.

This was confirmed to us by a classmate of mine who lived in Sydney after Karen's Wedding Day. She was up in Sydney with guests she had. She had never seen so many "Chinese and Asian" brides as she had ever seen around the Harbour area having their photos taken with the Harbour Bridge, Sydney Opera House and 'The Rocks" as their background themes for their wedding photos.

Time slipped by, and we decided to 'ride the wave' and not move home just because some ill-bred neighbours had moved into No. 2 in the Court. It turned out to be a successful swing in our favour when we saw that the actual owner of the home, who had never resided in it, had purchased it for a 'negative gearing' purpose at the time, and he was now selling the house. This was realised in 2012, and we then hoped for potentially respectable neighbours.

Yes, our wishes were granted when we saw the "SOLD" sticker on the board with the 'Sale of the House' details. This gave us yet another anxious period of thought as to who our neighbours would turn out to be and whether they would be better or worse than the previous tenants.

Well, 2012 was the turning point year for us when a delightful Indonesian young couple purchased the house next door to us at No. 22. We felt that life in the Court had drastically changed for the better in more ways than one. This young couple was so eager to be guided by us, who they referred to as their "like a Mum and Dad" new parents in their lives as new migrants and as newlyweds too.

We did not do too much as we allowed the young Indonesian couple to settle in, but we told them that we were there for them if they needed to ask for any guidance as they set themselves up. We were there for them when they asked about the local doctors, pharmacists, and other medical sources in the area. They also turned to us for the names and phone numbers of plumbers, electricians and general 'handymen" who could be called for incidental jobs around the home. Yes, we did have those services ready to help as we also had a 'flip' book with numerous business cards of 'tradies and handymen' that we would use from time to time when the need cropped up.

Our friendship developed as next-door neighbours to the extent that we would exchange dishes and various tasty nibbles. Some of the food that was traded was food brought into the country by their parents, who would visit the young couple periodically. This would happen, and we would enjoy the treats we were showered with from Indonesia - a Country we were about to see ourselves. We were planning a holiday in Bali, and this excited our friendly neighbours living in No. 2 in our little friendly Court. We had the pleasure of meeting with both sets of parents each time they visited, and we were made to feel very special by our neighbours at No. 2.

*

Many sad and happy occasions took place in our lives, and we had family bereavements, and our neighbours wrapped their arms around us. The various multi-cultures of the residents of the Court understood death in their own ways of culture. Grieving with us when I lost my own Mum in 2014 took its toll with all the close-knit family of neighbours we were surrounded with amongst the other homes in No.1, No.2 and No.4. We cannot forget the kind acts that we were engulfed with according to their cultures.

Early in 2015, we had the satisfying news from our daughter and son-in-law that we would become 'Grandparents' in November of that year. We were absolutely over the moon when we received this news and shared it with our neighbours, who were themselves thrilled ecstatically for us. It was the kind of news we had been eagerly waiting for a few years.

During the same year, 2015, our Indonesian neighbours also shared with us the news that they, too, would be first-time parents early in 2016. We were delighted with their "baby" news, and we had two occasions to have countdowns. This became a source of fun and frivolity as we joked about the 'countdown' that we would encounter first as our first grandchild was expected in November 2015.

Our day dawned on November 4th, and this was a turning point in our lives. A moment of truth that we would never forget when we were informed by our son-in-law that we had become Grandparents in the morning. This news embraced our entire mindfulness of what a change in status was all about. We got ourselves organized to visit the Hospital and hold our delightful bundle of joy in our arms. We were at our daughter's bedside in the afternoon with gifts to shower her and our first-born granddaughter.

On returning home, our neighbours waited anxiously to come over to inquire how the birthing process had gone and to see photos of our little infant granddaughter. The joy that they had for us was phenomenal and warming. It was a multicultural scene to see them all gathered to express their happiness for us over the birth of our first and only granddaughter as it has panned out to be in true life.

We could only reciprocate likewise when our Indonesian neighbours welcomed their daughter on a very significant day of her birthdate - 29th February 2016 - a leap year baby she was, and significantly, she enjoys the fuss, fun and frolic she is showered with on every year and more so on the 29th February every four years. It was a lovely event in the Court, and we were certainly looked up to and respected for the tender love and care that we extended to this couple and their newborn little girl.

It was a roller-coaster year in 2016, as our neighbours living in No. 4 decided to sell their home and move to Devon Meadows. This resulted in another home going up for sale in the Court. We saw each day out with bated breath, wondering who the new buyers would be and how the neighbourly atmosphere would prevail with the newcomers due to move in shortly.

We were the more anxious neighbours about the newcomers being received into the Court. We waited to meet with the young family after a few weeks of their settling into their new surroundings. It worked out so well as we introduced ourselves and found out that they were new migrants from the Middle East. They were Muslims and were a little bit apprehensive about meeting with us until we explained that we were the "Senior Citizens" of the Court from its inception and that we were "welcoming" them into the close-knit family that we were in the Court. It was the best thing that we had done as the husband explained to us that he was Iranian and that his wife was a Muslim Indonesian. He also told us that she was not well conversed in the English Language and that it was her drawback. He told us that they had three children aged 3, 6 and 10 and that their fourth child was due in six months.

We congratulated them on this news and told them that we lived next door at No.3 and that we were there for them if they needed any advice on the "facts and figures" of the area. They were delighted to meet us and bowed down to us in sincere gratitude for our initiative in coming over to meet them and just say "Hello to our small and friendly Court residents." We did pass on the news to them that our neighbours at No. 2 were from Indonesia and that they could help them with the diversity of any language barriers that they could encounter. This was in the year 2016, and we were glad to see the young couple from No. 4 interact well with the neighbours of No. 2.

We have experienced a fair bit of gift exchanging as our neighbours had their new additions to the individual families that resided in the Court. We, too, have had numerous gifts given to us as we were the "Senior Citizens" of the small Court where only four houses and four families existed.

Our Indonesian neighbours requested of us, as their daughter grew up from a baby into a toddler, what they should tell her to call us. We vehemently mentioned that we would not be comfortable with a young child calling us by our first names, so a compromise term of endearment had to be investigated. There were many suggestions bantered with, and after many weeks of careful consideration, our own daughter Karen came up with a brilliant suggestion, which we and our neighbours graciously accepted.

The terminology used by a young child to call us what we were seeking for too had to be a congenial name of respect, endearment, and acceptability by both parties concerned, that is, ourselves as well as our neighbours who had to instruct their daughter to use the new word to refer to us and to call us in person.

Our daughter suggested many names that could have been used, but the best word amongst the many suggestions she came up with was the word - "Kpa & Kma." The "K" stands for the first letter of our surname, followed by the "pa" and "ma" to the prefix letter "K." This was a perfect word and very apt to be used by a third generation of young ones to be living in our Court.

We were so impressed that the little daughter of the young Indonesian Couple living at No. 2 adapted very well to calling us affectionately "Kpa" and "Kma" whenever she saw us out in our front garden. This turned out to be a fun way for us to connect as well with our neighbours' parents, who would visit the young couple regularly from Indonesia. It was so evident that the parents of both the young couple would visit periodically and bring us gifts from their Country.

*

In 2018, our neighbour from No. 1 in the court decided to move down to Drouin as that was her hometown, and she wished to go back down there to be closer to some of her siblings. She, too, felt that they needed to get back to family and reap the closeness and togetherness of watching each other's families grow. We saw a "For Sale" board up in the Court, which drew interest and very heavy 'weekend' traffic to walk through the home as it would be open for inspection.

It was advertised for 'Auction' and, on the day of the auction, was sold to a young Vietnamese couple who were buying the home as their first home in Australia. We attended the 'Auction" for many reasons, mainly to witness the 'sale price' of the house as well as to meet with our new neighbours, which turned out to be a very successful 'meet and greet' event on the date that the young Vietnamese couple were to be 'Congratulated' by the Auctioneer as successful owners of their first home in Australia.

Our approach to new neighbours in the Court was warming and very well received by the young Vietnamese couple. They turned to us for kindly advice on Doctors, Pharmacies, Shopping Centres, and general other help, even for phone numbers of a Plumber and an Electrician not long after they had moved into their home in the Court. Their first big expense was a big split-system air conditioner, which they were keen to install.

We allowed them to work their way through and learn the basics of adapting to the new lifestyle of living in Australia. The young couple were from Ho Chi Minh City (the old City of Saigon). The young man was attached to Monash University to complete his PhD, which he was taking in his stride. The young lass was an Accountant with qualifications from their Country of birth. These new neighbours who hailed from Vietnam were younger than our Indonesian neighbours and were missing their own families from their 'homeland.'

A couple of years slipped by after our neighbours at No. 2, the Indonesian couple who had their daughter in February 2016, informed us that they were expecting their second child, who was due at the end of June 2019. The joy we had for this young couple was overflowing, and they shared and took us with them throughout her pregnancy as they prepared for their second child, who turned out to be a son, born on June 30th, 2019.

Again, we were the "temporary" Grandparents for this couple as we stepped in to help them feel that "adopted" older neighbours were like their own family to them at this joyous time as they battled through handling the two children and going back into a working routine like most young couples' juggle with in life.

With all the excitement of our neighbours at No. 2 having their second child, we had the glorious offer to take in a Mekong River Cruise, which we were very excited to do mainly because we had new neighbours living in No.1 of the Court who hailed from Vietnam. This holiday was scheduled to take place in September 2019. In the meantime, we also noticed that our Vietnamese neighbours were getting on with their lives and were very active with renovations in their homes. On Saturday, they came over to our front gate to inform us that she had just passed three months of pregnancy and that they were expecting a little son to be born in November of 2019. We were ecstatic that this news meant that we would be back from their homeland to be in the Court to greet their firstborn.

As coincidence and luck would have it, the little boy came into the world on November 4th, the same day as our little Granddaughter's birthday. That was a fluke of luck, too, and we were all rejoicing in the Court about the birth of this little boy and son to a delightful young Vietnamese couple living at No. 1 in our Court.

With the 'multicultural' mixtures in our Court of Vietnamese in No.1, Indonesian in No. 2, British and Sri Lankan mixtures in No. 3 and Middle Eastern and Indonesian Muslim in No. 4, we did enjoy the mixed cultures and various foods we exchanged and shared amongst ourselves.

Multiculturalism is a widely used word in Australia. Still, where we originate from, our backgrounds go back to our 'Motherlands' where we were born into individual countries that were a part of a multiculturalism status. My classmates were Indian, Chinese, Muslim, Malay, British and Middle Eastern. Ian was always in mixed classes in school, and his best friend throughout his school days was a guy from a family where his father was African and his mother was British. This itself denotes that we have always blended into these mixed cultural backgrounds.

We have learned that communication across cultures, languages and generations comes with a great responsibility. We have grown up realising that with respect and compassion, regardless of our backgrounds, we have lived experiences, communication preferences and accessibility needs throughout the diverse communities that prevail in Australia.

As responsible citizens of Australia, to sustain social awareness amongst our fellow citizens, we are toned to identify ourselves with various targets in our multicultural audiences. We need to prioritise the close-knit communities and extend and reach out to them all. Also, I realise that within the cultural norms of our diversified Australian society, we live in and travel through the decades of new migrants that flood this country called Australia, and this is now the new home for us alike.

ANNABELLE AND THE OLDE LOST VILLAGE LIBRARY

BY BRONWYN VAUGHAN

The steam locomotive had pulled in for a brief stopover in the quintessential town of Berwick outside Melbourne, one of the most charming, heritage-European-inspired villages in Victoria. Cobblestone streets, countless alleyways, 19th-century architecture and old-world buildings based on the town of Berwick-on-Tweed in Northumberland, England that, would inspire any artist

Annabelle loved this township and its farmland precincts, so on the spur of the moment, she decided to transport herself and a carry-on suitcase to visit her heritage over the summer vacation. She had given herself six days to immerse into the culture of the village with a short stay-over in the postmaster's cottage. Annabelle had always dreamed of this moment, surrounded by kinship and her love of the country. It was here that she rediscovered her love of literature and history.

"If only I had more time", she thought to herself as she stepped off the train onto the station platform and rounded the corner of the clock tower.

The station itself was a quaint, weatherboard building with the ticket master's office to the right just in sight. It was only a short walk through the gate and past the low-lying bridge that she had just crossed over by train with the local creek and tree fern gully ahead. Traversing the undulating landscape, she then followed the gravel path to the main road. It would only be a perchance discovery that she would find what she was looking for.

Annabelle made her way to the village, noticing all the sounds of her childhood she remembered, the flutter of tiny wings in the long grasses, the trickle of the creek as it meandered through the village and the smell of freshly baked bread at the baker's shop. But it was the clock tower which would eventually lead her to a lost part of the village, the old-world library, now a bookshop.

For now, Anabelle had only enough time to frequent the bakery for a bread loaf so she could make the postmaster's cottage on the hill before sundown. She had packed in her carry-on a picnic hamper full of gourmet foods and delicacies. That would have to suffice until she arrived at the cottage and slept a few hours.

The house itself was a two-bedroom, finely built for the Victorian Era, circa 1884, with lemon-myrtle, coloured timbers, an external verandah which wrapped itself around the building, olive green trims on the posts, window frames and door and a solid tin roof. On entry, a sitting room to the right held a large, open fireplace leading to the generous-sized dining room, and to the left, the bedrooms and central kitchen at the rear of the house. The outside porch contained the recently renovated bathroom, originally the wash utility room. The gardens were expansive, with fruit trees dotted on the left boundary, a vegetable patch close by and a dainty cottage garden towards the front tree-lined property.

Annabelle noticed that nothing much had changed since 1884, and it was now 2024, one hundred and forty years since it was constructed. She trundled her carry-on into the original main bedroom to find the most exquisite pearl-white fireplace and comfortable furnishings to match the era.

The postmaster's cottage has been converted into a local bed and breakfast in recent days, acquired by a renowned family within the area, who had retained all of its original charm and character.

"Oh," Annabelle exclaimed as she walked quickly through the cottage, opening every door to see what was behind. "They've even left a basket of local produce from the village shops for me to enjoy."

With that, she entered the kitchen, made a long, brewed pot of coffee, and organised supper from the bakery, which was the food she had just purchased. Tomorrow was planned to be a very exciting day of discovery.

Annabelle dressed early the next morning, and as she gazed through the rear windows of the house, she noticed the sun rising in the east through the evergreen trees in the distance, creating a mystical sun dance through the leaves. She knew this place was magical, but the sight of it made her stop and reflect on what she might find.

What seemed to be hours but was actually only minutes later, Annabelle quickly grabbed her rucksack and headed out the front door, which was large and wooden with an antique door handle that needed some adjustment, she noticed, closing it loudly behind her.

Annabelle decided to walk the distance again rather than grab one of the bicycles provided in the shed so that she could take in the history. It was only a short, descending stretch down High Street, and she would be at the first corner café. The clock tower was located just north of the train station, in the centre of the village. It always drew Annabelle's attention as a child, and today, it was no different.

It was perfectly positioned from most of the heritage-listed buildings she wanted to visit, the old post office, courthouse, hotel inn and, of course, the old, lost library. Few in the city or even the village knew of the existence of this library. Certainly, none had the knowledge of its treasures that Annabelle had been told of as a child. Most would walk past the little weatherboard building, not realising the history it held. It, too, had a tin roof with a small pergola roofline that welcomed inquisitive visitors through its large midnight blue doors.

To her right and left, village shops descended the High Street. "Which one should I enter first?" she thought to herself.

One in particular drew her attention. It was the old-world library, now a bookshop, that held the most interest. Annabelle pushed open the double doors, which led into a small atrium. She stepped over the threshold and was greeted by the attendant on duty for the day, small in stature, with long brunette hair neatly tied in a chignon, striking emerald eyes and a curved mouth.

As Annabelle looked around, she noticed the collection of old books it housed, leading from a spiral staircase to the ornate rort, iron balcony.

"Is there anything in particular you are looking for?" asked the bookshop attendant.

"Yes", Annabelle replied. "A 19th-century German folklore poetry book written by my great-grandfather. It contains unique details of stories and places he visited as a young adult growing up in this village and bringing up his family."

"I'll be right back", said the bookshop attendant as she darted from behind the counter and through a curtained opening. Time seemed like it stood still at that moment.

"Could it be possible that the bookshop attendant knew of the book she spoke about?" Annabelle asked herself.

As she waited, she sat down on the stool and flicked through the pages of a novel left on the countertop. It was then that she became mesmerised by the chatter of the villagers browsing and the countless new books perfectly positioned on the bookshelves in the shop. Still, it was the old parchment books that drew her attention. Annabelle noticed an old gazette newspaper from the late 1880s, perfectly kept behind a perspex box with each page protected by a clear, sheer film. She carefully removed the newspaper from the box and started to read the history between the pages.

Annabelle smiled to herself as she placed the old newspaper back into the glass box, "I can just imagine such an evening", she thought. "Each villager gazing up to the rort iron balcony led from the spiral staircase as each local actor and theatre attendee watched the evening recital and theatrical performances, what an incredible gift", Annabelle exclaimed.

"I hope the bookshop attendant won't be too much longer", she murmured to herself quietly. At that moment, the curtain opened, and the bookshop attendant returned with a large wooden box wrapped in brown paper and held together by string.

"This is what you are looking for", she said. "We have kept it safe for the traveller who requested it. Tell me a little more about your family and heritage, and you can take it, but you must place it in your rucksack, keeping it with you at all times," she spoke softly as her eyes began to smile. "My great-grandfather's name was Wilhelm, born of Lutheran, German descent, and he was a few years older than my great-grandmother, Jane, the only child of an English couple who also immigrated to Victoria. They lived in this village upon marrying", Annabelle explained.

Something in particular intrigued Annabelle about this place. It wasn't just the opportunity to purchase a new book or even find an old book read little. It was the sight of all those manuscripts encased behind glass cabinets. She could feel the history of the town, the conversation of the now infrequent village guests and the treasures each shelf still held.

By this stage, it was nearing midday, and Annabelle hastily walked back up High Street about two hundred and fifty yards to the 1891 Taphouse Restaurant situated at the top of town. Originally, she had been told that it was the corner grocery store, and historical pictures from the State Library indicated such. It was now fully restored with distinctive Selkirk bricks, all produced by hand in response to the building boom created by the gold rush.

As she entered the reception area, she noticed the tall ceilings, roof trusses, original beams, and posts made of cedar.

"It is just like stepping back in time", she thought to herself. She decided to ask for a table by the window so she could watch the passers-by in the lunchtime rush.

Just then, she looked up and noticed the waiter had arrived with the menu and was recommending a local house cider with her meal. Considering her options, she selected a starter of gourmet cheeses and a plate of barramundi and salad, all prepared from the finest local Gippsland produce.

Annabelle made her way the last eight hundred yards to the local Bed and Breakfast Postmaster's cottage, where she was staying for the next few days, very excited. Still in her possession was the old wooden box carefully stored in her rucksack at her feet. She couldn't wait to open it and discover the contents. On reaching the cottage, she knelt down in the garden to collect a few of the lisianthus planted in a row along the verandah path. These were some of her favourite summer cottage garden flowers, admired by many not only for their colour and beauty but also for their ease of growing in a cottage garden.

Annabelle turned the old iron doorknob of the front entrance to be greeted again by the welcoming ambience of the Victorian-era cottage. Quietly, she sat at the dining table closest to the antique bookshelf as the coffee pot brewed and retrieved the brown packaged box from her rucksack. As she began to untie the string and unwrap the brown paper, she noticed a pile of books neatly stacked on the antique writing desk next to her and the bottom drawer slightly ajar.

"The wooden box will have to wait", she announced to nobody except herself. The writing desk was strategically located next to the matching bookshelf, and she wondered why these books, in particular, were left on the desk.

"Perhaps I will find time to read a few before my village vacation has ended," Annabelle remarked. The antique desk retained a scent of the old wood stain, oak in colour, rustic with gold brass knobs on each of the drawers and lined with green felt. With her inquisitiveness sparked, she reached into the bottom drawer of the desk, which was still ajar. To Annabelle's amazement, she discovered a box that looked similar to the one she was given at the village library but was smaller. She couldn't help but notice that they had been carved by the same hand.

"Could it be possible that these two boxes belonged to the same person," she exclaimed.

"Oh, my!" she gasped as she opened the smaller of the boxes first. It was lined with a fine silk padded cushion at the base of the box, azure in colour and in it was an envelope addressed to someone called Jane, dated 1906.

As Annabelle began to scan the script, she read of the days nearing Jane's own wedding, penned in the hand of her dear mother. Tears began to roll down Annabelle's eyes as she suddenly realised that she was reading a letter from her great-grandfather's mother-in-law. Annabelle had heard stories of her great-grandfather and even his mother and father. Still, she knew little about Jane's mother and father.

Annabelle continued reading, and as she did, she pulled out of the box a small bag of gold coins, all marked in the year of the marriage. Annabelle wondered to herself why the gold coins were left in the box and not spent.

"Could it have been a dowry or inheritance from Jane's late father?" she wondered.

Her attention turned to the larger wooden box, still partially unwrapped. As she opened the lid of the box, to her amazement, she found two gold coins, one dated 1886, the year Annabelle's great-grandfather was born, the other 1906 and a collection of other important historical pieces, together with a very old parchment book of German folklore poetry, penned in what appeared to be a fountain quill.

As she continued researching the items discovered in the larger wooden box, she asked herself, "Was this the actual cottage my great-grandfather grew up in as a child?" As Annabelle reached further into the box, she pulled out a birth certificate, a land title and house deed, a school report and an antique key which appeared to resemble the one she had in her possession to open the front door of the Postmaster's Cottage.

Excitedly, she leapt to her feet and quickly ran down the cottage hallway towards the front door. She placed the key into the lock, and to her amazement, it not only fitted but turned the key mechanism perfectly. She was now even more intrigued by her findings and couldn't wait to see what other mysteries she might unearth in the next few days.

She returned to the dining room only to find that the coffee she had brewed was now cold. "Oh, well!" she exclaimed to herself. "I will have to make another."

Annabelle spent the new few hours between sunset and midnight reading each of the poems in her grandfather's parchment etched by hand. She now knew where her love of history and literature stemmed from. This book of poetry her great-grandfather had written must have been frequently recited in the village library all those years ago.

The remaining two coins in the larger box intrigued her, and so, too, did the collection of historical documents. Annabelle understood that they had been kept safe for all these years, "But why were they still in the old, lost village library?" she asked herself.

Not only did she now have in her possession many interesting historical items relevant to her family, but the village itself still posed an intriguing mystery.

"There was more to explore, I know it", Annabelle announced proudly to no one in particular. "I've yet to visit the school my great-grandfather attended, the old village post office he was postmaster of, the courthouse and the original Berwick Inn. And I'm certain that when I return to the old village library, I'll be able to discover more."

With that, she finished her coffee, safely placed the larger box back in her rucksack and retired for the evening.

Tomorrow and the days following were planned to be very interesting indeed.

"One hundred and forty years on and still today, the Postmaster's Cottage with its ornate, decorative verandah fixtures and gardens has remained intact", she thought to herself, "and stories of old to tell for those with an ear to listen."

SMELSTORIUS

BY MADISEN WHITE

Austere—
But never in the way of love and affection.
On the contrary,
She would throw herself onto sharp rocks.
before letting her grandchild come to harm,
Always ready at a moment's notice.

Raising five children on a research scientist's wage in the 1970s,
Her love stretched wide—
Embracing both the human and the animal.
Hand-weaving, spinning, stitching clothes from angora goats,
despite her teenage daughter's protests,
Never quite catching the trends on time.

Roadkill was assessed with precision.
Fresh enough? Take it home. Clean it.
How will we cook it tonight?
But never hungry—not in Australia.
Žagarėliai, or 'fatty cookies,'
black pudding, smoked herring, sour cherries—
Dark, bitter, and sweet.
Ivan Rebroff and Luciano Pavarotti on the record player,
children in bed by 7 p.m.,
Even when they were old enough to fight it,
Ready for when her husband arrived home.

Blunt, but never unkind.
Dry humour but never cruel.
An earnest, gentle voice thick with a European accent.

"Huh! No kidding."
"Gee, that woman is quite fat."
"Eh, what do the doctors know?"

Cataract surgery, knobbled, bulbous hands,
arthritis and high blood pressure,
Decades of hard work etched into her bones.
Chainsawing gum trees, digging driveways and dams,
Cutting the heads off chickens—though beloved.
Why? Because that's just what you had to do.

A far cry from how they grew up.
Nazi-occupied Lithuania,
fleeing to a displaced persons camp,

a teenager held at gunpoint
for stealing a chicken to feed his family—
Spared by the farmer he had stolen from.

Their past feels like a world away.[1]

---

1   Smelstorius is the maiden name of my mother. Lithuanian in origin, and the source of many "smelly" schoolyard jokes in Australia. The language is considered one of the oldest languages in modern usage. Preserving its Indo-European roots, it still contains archaic features similar to Vedic Sanskrit and Ancient Greek. Lithuanian is a gendered language, and surnames often differ slightly between men and women. They consist of the same stem or root (Smelstor), but use various suffixes depending upon gender and marital status for women (Smelstorienė and Smelstoriutė). These variations were often shed through immigration, adopting the same surname as husbands and fathers upon arrival to a new country.

THE FISHERMAN

BY STEPH WEBB

Fishing rods clasped firmly in one hand, the fisherman took long, even strides from his car towards the river. The morning air lingered with the traces of last night's dew, causing him to inhale the crispness of the new day appreciatively. He stepped onto the pathway leading into the densely forested bushland. Over his shoulder hung a battered canvas rucksack, rhythmically bouncing against his back as he navigated the beaten track.

His boots were scuffed, cracked, and weather-worn, crunched over dry, loose pebbles and a well-trod, uneven sand track. A slouch hat, battered and stained from years of use, shading his eyes from the brilliant morning sun's rays. A wooden tackle box swung from his right hand, rattling with meticulously handcrafted lead sinkers, fishing lures, and fishing flies. Though alone, he felt the presence of the bush, alive with the rustling of unseen creatures. The incessant *'chet-chet'* calls of the weaver birds from their upside-down nests along the riverbank and the occasional cry of *'piet-my-vrou'* from the re-chested cuckoo bird

rang out about the forest canopy above him.

The coolness of the early morning was already yielding to the promise of another scorching day. Tall rustling river reeds, clumped together as a lush dark green screen, obscured his view of the river. To his left lay the African bushland, dense with Buffalo thorn, Marola, Sour Plum trees, and small thorny thickets. Towering fever trees with vibrant yellow trunks, arched elongated thorny limbs skyward, like guardians of an ancient empire. He let his fingertips brush against the rough bark of trees, testing the long, sharp thorns on various *shrubveld* bushes, grounding himself in the moment, and feeling the pulse of the wilderness around him.

The mighty Crocodile River, reduced to half its usual size by the drought, no longer lapped at the river's edge next to the bull rushes and river reeds along the track. In its place were exposed stretches of riverbed, wide sandy banks, and a trickling stream leading to deeper water pools. Here, life continued as hippos wallowed, yawned, and grunted in lazy abandonment. Crocodiles lay silently and unmoving in the shallows or sunbathed on sandy banks, their golden prehistoric eyes unblinking. The air vibrated with the humming of cicadas, their ceaseless song mingling with the occasional splash of a fish leaping in the water.

A deep, guttural roar echoed across the bush- a lion, its voice carrying across the vast expanse. The fisherman paused momentarily, head tilted, listening. The sound stirred no fear, only familiarity. He continued his journey, confident that the lion was far away. He knew the bush well, its sounds, shadows, and secrets. He always claimed, 'knowing the bush as well as he knows the back of his hand'. Today, he welcomed its solitude. The river was his sanctuary, a place to unravel tangled thoughts, put aside disturbing memories, and where the weight of family could be set aside for a while.

The sudden flurry of wings broke through his reverie. A Southern Yellow-billed Hornbill alighting on the path ahead, its banana-shaped beak snapping up an unsuspecting insect. The bird barely acknowledged him before taking flight in one flowing movement. Black and white feathered wings carried it into the foliage. Tracking the bird's flight drew his attention to a long, dark shape, sinuous and silent, undulating across the path.

A black mamba.

The sight of it sent a memory crashing over him. The baby's pram bounced gently, tiny feet kicking. His daughter, only three months old, giggling in the shade of a picnic tree. A casual stroll to peek inside the pram. And there, draped across the pale-yellow knitted blanket, the ominous coil of another black mamba.

One fluid movement, and he gripped the snake's tail and yanked as hard as he could, flinging it up and into thorny undergrowth. Adrenalin pumping, heart thundering in his chest, as he lifted the covers. Rough, calloused hands ran over the baby's body. The pent-up emotions whooshed out between his ghost-white lips as relief washed over him. She was unharmed. Picnics under the shade of trees near the river were far more closely monitored after that. Images of sheer terror and fear dissolved into misty memory, and the black mamba on the path ahead slithered into the vegetation.

Sweat dripped from his nose. Salty droplets seeped from his brow. Peering through the pouring sweat, he pursed his lips and blew away at the bothersome flies that hovered around him. He tugged out his handkerchief and mopped his darkly tanned face, his pale blue eyes shaded under the hat brim. His cotton shirt, damp and clinging, darkening in patches, clung to his slender frame. The temperature in the bush, bordering South Africa and Mozambique, climbs towards the high forty degrees.

The water's edge beckoned with the promise of comfort and coolness. As he neared the water's edge, gaps in the tall reeds offered glimpses of the slow-moving river, where yellowfish and tigerfish leapt in brief flashes of silver, sending ripples across the surface. Above, the majestic shape of an African Fish Eagle cut through the pale blue sky as it cast its eyes over the waters before it swooped. The fish eagle sailed on wings carried by the wind under its feathers, legs reaching into the water and scooping up a large glistening catfish. It soared over the trees, festooned with colonies of weaver bird's nests. Finding the tallest tree, it landed and proceeded to tear its beak into the tough leather-like skin and flesh of the catfish.

His journey was almost complete, and he decided to stop his dilly-dallying. Up ahead, the track forked, one path leading to his favourite fishing spot. As he took the familiar turn, it was only a few steps before he reached the steep boulder that sloped down to the dry riverbed below. Eyes cast down, and looking at his feet, he carefully stepped onto the dark grey rock. The fisherman adjusted his grip on the fishing rods and tackle box. An elbow pushed at the canvas bag, positioning it comfortably for his descent. Lowering himself into a seated position, he slid down, his boots skidding on the smooth, sun-warmed stone until they sank into the soft, dry sand at the bottom.

But something was different.

Two massive boulders, unfamiliar and out of place, loomed in the riverbed a pace from where his feet had landed. He frowned. And then, slowly, very slowly, his gaze travelled upward. A towering shape swayed, blocking out the sun's rays. Huge ears flapped lazily, and a trunk lifted, tasting the air. An elephant. No, two. Their immense bodies, covered in dust and wrinkled like ancient parchment, stood directly in his path. The first one shifted slightly, its huge head turning and revealing a dark blinking eye fixing on him. The second elephant swayed slowly like a silent shadow behind its companion.

Adrenaline coiled in his stomach as bile raced to his oesophagus, almost causing him to gag. There was no way forward. Only the rock behind him. Slowly, cautiously, he placed one foot back, then another, his body crouched low as he inched back up the boulder. His eyes never left the elephants, watching for any sign of aggression. The wind, mercifully, was in his favour. They had not yet caught his scent. Still, they knew he was there. Their ears twitched, their trunks swayed.

Heart thrumming, he reached the top of the boulder and turned, walking briskly back the way he had come. His breath was steady, but his pulse raced. Only when he reached his car- a little black Prefect- did he allow himself to exhale fully.

Back at his car, he lingered for a moment, looking back at the river, the bush, the place that had become a second home to him. He smiled, knowing he would return, drawn once again by the call of the wild and the quiet solace it offered. With one last glance, he turned the key in the ignition and drove off. Leaving only the fading sound of his engine in the vast, endless bushland.

That evening, as he recounted his adventure to his wife and his best friend, his words were met with sceptical amusement…

"I don't know about this elephant encounter of yours," his friend chuckled. "How big was it between the eyes?"

Grinning, the fisherman spread his hands wide. His friend mirrored the gesture, widening the gap further with exaggerated disbelief. Laughter erupted between them, the camaraderie of old friends seasoning the tale with familiar jest.

But early the next morning, they returned to the river together, determined to settle the matter. The rising sun painted the fever trees gold. The call of the fish eagle, *the voice of Africa*, punctuated the hush of dawn. And there—below the steep boulder imprinted deep in the sand, were the unmistakable, mammoth footprints of elephants.

The fisherman's friend ran a hand through his hair, whistling low. "Well," he conceded, shaking his head, "I suppose it wasn't just another fishing story after all."

The fisherman merely smiled, his pale blue eyes twinkling beneath the brim of his hat. Some stores, after all, were better lived than told.

ROCK BOTTOM

BY NORMA SAVIGE

Mary hauled up the last sheet, struggled to shove it into the clothes dryer above her head, and slammed the door shut. She leaned against the sink momentarily, then wandered over to the laundry door with a sigh. Standing in a small shaft of sunlight, Mary closed her eyes and blocked out the view before her. She hated the motel and all it represented in her life and imagined she could see her old backyard or, even better, her mother's garden for just a moment.

'Morning, love. Why don't you come over and take a load off for a while?'

She looked over to see a woman with a colourful scarf tucked around a head full of rollers pointing to a seat next to her at a picnic bench near the communal clothesline.

'You sit down, and I'll just nick inside and get you a quick cuppa – what do you like: tea or coffee?' the woman smiled as she moved along the seat, 'Come on. I won't be a second.'

Mary found her voice and murmured, 'I'd love a strong white tea, please.'

She was still leaning in the doorway, watching a small swarm of wasps as they came and went to their nest above the laundry window. A pretty cup and saucer were soon placed on the table next to a matching plate holding a piece of fruitcake.

'I've been dying to meet you, love. My name is Ronnie, Veronica really, but I prefer Ronnie. As you saw, I live in that cabin with roses painted on the door. My husband, Nigel, is away a fair bit - he's a pilot for Qantas Airways and has covered the New Zealand routes since Vietnam.' Without seeming to draw breath, she continued, 'I was going to introduce myself to you yesterday, but you fell asleep in the laundry, and I didn't have the heart to wake you. You've only been here a week or so, but I have noticed you come down with a load of laundry almost every day.'

Mary looked down and was embarrassed to realise she was still wearing her nightie with an unbuttoned woollen coat over it. 'I'm Mary. I'm sorry I'm not dressed properly.' She tried to tuck her feet under the bench. Short black gumboots were her best defence against the puddles along the path from her cabin to anywhere else in the park. 'I must look a sight. Sorry.'

'Don't worry about it; just sit here, drink your tea, and please eat some cake. You do look like you could use some fattening up - and maybe about two days of sleep, I might add.'

'Mm. I can't remember when I last had a good night's sleep. You see, my husband ….'

What to say? It was all too hard to tell, too miserable and too despairing. It was awful. She had been brought up to keep her business to herself; what's private is private. And, anyway, talking wouldn't change anything. It would just make her even more miserable and exhausted. Nothing would change.

She realised she had closed her eyes again. When she opened them, Veronica was studying her closely. 'Your husband ….?'

'I don't know what to say.'

'Darl, we've noticed some commotions coming from your cabin at night and heard him yelling. Some of us are a bit worried about you. Are you OK? Do you need some help?'

Mary stood in horror. 'People are gossiping about us? How dare you all? You were looking for bruises, weren't you? You know nothing. You shouldn't...'

Veronica reached out and encouraged her to sit down again. 'I'm sorry. That was clumsy of me.' She smiled apologetically. 'You are right. We don't know anything about your life, but we do care about you and whether we can do anything to help.'

'I'm too tired. Couldn't I just sit and relax over this cuppa and not think about things for a while?'

'Of course, you can. I'm sorry. I've got a big mouth, but I can keep it shut when I'm told to.'

Veronica sat quietly, opened a paper scroll, and took up a pen. She wrote a couple of words and smiled.

Curiosity got the better of Mary. 'What's that?'

'It's my gratitude scroll.' Veronica held up a rough scroll made of cardboard rolls and lined paper. 'I made this in high school while studying the Egyptians.' The ends of the top and bottom rolls were made from cotton reels and decorated with carvings. 'These are hieroglyphics I invented,' She laughed, 'They probably say something rude, but I told everyone they said Love, Happiness, Friendship and Family. I found it in a drawer when we packed up and moved here last year and started writing in it again. I love it.'

She looked at Mary and gently suggested, 'You look like you could use one too.'

Mary sneered. 'A gratitude scroll? Are you kidding me? What's to be grateful for?' She swept her arm around as she spoke, 'Look at all this; I can't believe I live in a dump like this and look at me. I'm a wreck. I'm just a drudge. I've got nothing and will never have anything. My life will never change until my husband ....'

Oh, my God. She covered her face with her hands. *What is wrong with me? Was I really thinking that?*

She stood abruptly and placed the unfinished cake back on the plate. 'Thank you for your hospitality, but I must go,' she said. She stumbled towards her cabin and was surprised by three motorbikes slowly rumbling along the road beside her path. The riders all waved, but she turned away in disgust. *I can't believe I live in a motel park with these thugs. Rock bottom!*

*

Mary listened at the cabin door, and all was silent. Instead of going in, she sat on the porch outside and quietly wept. Now that Pandora's box had been opened, she couldn't stop her thoughts. She had managed to suppress them for so long, but they all bubbled up like a volcano. All the negatives began to appear. The result was an overwhelming sense of self-pity and exhaustion. Eventually, she fell into a fitful slumber in the weak sunlight filtering through the tall gum trees on the park's edge.

She dreamt of a Sunday afternoon spent on the beach in St Kilda with her older brother. It was to be their last time together for who knew how long. He was leaving the next day to join the Australian Armed Forces Transport Division in World War Two. She was sixteen and self-centred, complaining as they feasted on their usual double ice cream cones – one chocolate and one strawberry for each of them.

Mary sighed. 'You're so lucky going off on your big adventure. I'll be so bored at home; no one will bring me here and spoil me like you do.'

'Don't be silly. I won't be gone long – this will be over before you know it, and we'll be back here yacking away together as if I'd never been gone.'

'Promise?'

'Promise. Just don't you go off getting married before I get back.'

'Look at me. Who'll ever marry me?'

He turned to her and repeated what he had told her many times. 'You are beautiful, and you will be married to a wonderful man one day. He'll be a doctor or lawyer, buy you a beautiful house, and give you two children.'

'A boy and a girl,' she interrupted.

'Yes, one of each, and they'll be clever and beautiful. You will all live happily ever after in your beautiful house. You will never want for anything.'

She put an arm through the crook of his elbow and smiled up at him. 'I think I'll have a doctor, please; he will know how to look after the children. And he will be tall and handsome with a little grey at his temples and lovely hands.'

A chill interrupted her dream as a cloud moved over the sun. 'What happened to me? What happened to my dream life?' she said aloud.

Before her brother returned four years later, she met a soldier named Frank, who had swept her off her feet. She married him and had a daughter. There were no more afternoon strolls with her brother or talk of her dream future. After the war, she moved to the country to the dairy farm of Frank's family and a roughly built, bark-clad hut.

From then on, her life was more challenging. Her returned soldier had been afflicted by malaria and night terrors. He had a permanent nervous tic and drank excessively. Despite these war-related issues, their relationship was loving and sympathetic, and soon, a second baby was welcomed. She was tender and understanding, supporting him in his effort to return to his old self rather than the war-ravaged man whose suffering she shared. Now and then, she had glimpses of the young man he was before he was sent to New Guinea and the Kokoda Trail. He was a fun-filled larrikin who adored her, and they trusted that if they had each other, they would work their way through their trials together – just as thousands of other couples were forced to do.

They moved into a housing commission home up the hill from the town and enjoyed the privacy away from his parents and seven younger siblings. Although sometimes unwell, he worked hard felling trees, and she enjoyed being a housewife, wife, and mother. 'I know it's sometimes hard at the moment, Mary, but I will get better, and we will have a wonderful life together.' They snuggled on the couch, watching the children play nearby, and smiled at the thought.

He was offered the family farm by his father, who wanted to retire but rejected the offer. 'No thanks,' he told Mary. 'Life's too short to be tied to milking cows every morning and every night.' He shuddered. 'I've seen how Mum slaved away on the farm, and I don't want that life for my darling Mary.' He held her and kissed her gently on the forehead. 'I know the old man wants to retire to an easier life, and he deserves it, but it's not my responsibility to take that life on. I'd be crazy. He will have to sell the farm to get rid of it.'

*

Over the next thirty years, their life together developed a pattern. They moved into the town centre for a couple of years, then even further up the hill until, eventually, buying a home of their own using a returned serviceman's home loan. Money became tighter and tighter. His drinking became even heavier, and his mood swings worsened.

Mary boiled the washing in a huge copper over a wood-burning firebox in the outside washhouse beside the toilet. Clothes were dragged out of the copper into cement troughs, rinsed and wrung by hand – rain, hail, or shine every week. She roasted in summer and got chilblains on her hands and feet in winter. She cooked for them over an old wood stove, which was fine in winter but hell in summer.

His malaria flared up every now and then with a raging fever, sweats, hallucinations, violent shaking of the bed, sometimes waking the children. He found steady work in a government-owned corporation, which favoured ex-servicemen. His pay was low despite undertaking shift work for the penalty rates, and there was never enough money to go around. They lived from pay to pay, scraping to make ends meet.

He told her he loved her and apologised repeatedly – for the poverty, moodiness, drinking, and hard life. He complained that no matter what he tried, Frank couldn't find his feet – but that *one day*, he would get better, and life would be better. However, there came a time when the house, garden, and nursing all became too much for her and a month ago, she reluctantly agreed to sell up, pay off what was owed, and move into a small cabin in an old motel. She was devastated. Life had reached rock bottom, but she was too tired to resist. Her one compensation was knowing her children were now healthy adults with their own lives, both overseas and small families. She always assured them she was fine and did not need any help from them.

She blushed if he asked why she stayed putting up with it all and replied, 'Because I love you.'

Gazing around this new, run-down neighbourhood and listening to the rumble of motorbikes nearby, she wondered whether she loved or hated him. She was horrified to find herself thinking that if he hadn't returned from the war, she might have had that fantastic dream future conjured up for her by her brother.

He stepped out onto the porch. 'Is everything all right, love? I heard you talking out here, and you sounded a bit angry?'

'Yes, I'm fine, Frank; I didn't want to wake you, so I've been out here talking to the magpies in the trees. Let's go in, and I'll make us a snack.'

*

For the third night in a row, Frank dropped off to a fitful sleep interrupted by a fever and night terrors. She fled the bed as he thrashed about, screaming,' I'll kill you, you bastard,' over and over again. She knew better than to try to wake him but to wait until the nightmare finished and she could change his soaked bedding as he settled back to sleep.

The cabin door burst open, and a man stepped in, surveyed the room, and ushered in two men dressed in biker gear – a man-mountain and his slightly built, almost dainty companion. Mary screamed involuntarily and backed away into a corner of the cabin. The intruders scanned the cabin and quickly took in what was happening. They hesitated for a moment, nodded to each other, and approached the bed. Frank was crouched against the bedhead, his voice trembling as he pointed, unseeing, into the distance.

'Look behind you. They're behind you. Look out.' He scrambled to the other side of the bed, terrified.

Suddenly, a voice boomed through the cabin. 'Stand down, soldier! Stand down!' the smallest man ordered. 'All clear.' His voice softened. 'Stand at ease, Digger. It's over.'

Frank seemed to awaken, saluted shakily, and spoke more calmly. 'Yes, Sir, thank you, Sir,' he said. He looked around, 'All over?'

Veronica entered the cabin and crossed over to comfort Mary. 'I'm sorry, love. We misunderstood what was happening. We thought you were... We were wrong.' She found Mary's dressing gown and wrapped it around her shoulders.

Mary stood bewildered. She struggled to understand what was happening around her as Veronica led her towards the couch. 'This is my husband, Nigel,' Mary indicated the first intruder. 'The guys call him Wings,' she smiled.

'Missus, do you have dry pyjamas and sheets for him?' Mary pointed to the linen cupboard and watched the man-mountain start to strip the bed while his mate gently changed Frank, speaking quietly as he did so. Together, they bundled up the wet linen and handed it to Veronica.

'Ronnie will take this over and run it through the wash.' Veronica took the load and left the cabin with a smile for Mary.

'You just curl up on the couch and have a snooze,' said the man-mountain, 'and we'll sit with him tonight. He's already drifting off, and he'll be disoriented when he wakes up tomorrow, so we should be here to explain to him.'

Mary hadn't spoken a word since the door opened and remained silent. Numb, she obediently lay on the couch and soon drifted off to sleep.

*

'Wakey, wakey, sleepyhead,' Frank smiled at her. 'Mouse is making us breakfast – pancakes, would you believe?' He indicated the man-mountain, who turned to her, displaying her best apron covering part of his torso.

'Mouse?'

'Morning, Mary.' He bowed, 'My mate Thor here has set up the table on the porch in the sun. It's a lovely morning out there, so let's go out and enjoy it.'

Mary found herself laughing for the first time in months. 'Mouse and Thor? I'm sorry. It's rude of me, but your names are well ….'

'Reversed. Yes, ridiculous, we know, but Thor has a voice like thunder. As you can hear, I squeak like a mouse, so we're stuck with them, and that's that.' He grinned and opened the door to lead the way. 'Let's eat; I'm starving.'

Frank stepped out through the door into the sun to sit at the table for the first time since arriving in the park. He patted the seat next to him, inviting her to join him.

Ronnie clomped up the steps, arms full of warm, dry linen, with Nigel following close behind. 'Yum. Mouse's pancakes, I presume? Enough for two more?' Mouse nodded and handed her a plate with a broad grin.

'OK. Where are they?' called two bearded bikers who came around the corner of the cabin next door. 'We can smell pancakes. Are there strawberries? Good. Breakfast, compliments of Mouse. Our favourite.'

Soon, both were seated on the steps with plates on their laps, and Nigel introduced them, 'Mary and Frank, these are Bones and Bluey.' He winked at Mary, 'I'm sure you can work out who is who.'

She laughed as she looked across at the chubby man and his red-headed friend. 'Glad you two came,' smiled Mouse, 'We needed someone to do the dishes.'

'We don't mind,' Bluey laughed and turned to Frank, 'Actually, Sir, we came over to thank you for your service to our country and to offer any help we can give you both.'

Mary saw Frank's eyes glisten as he tried to speak. He gave up and just nodded gratefully. Her own eyes prickled as she reached for his hand.

As Mary watched the small crowd enjoying their breakfast, she turned to Nigel. 'The nicknames of the others are opposites, but yours isn't – you *are* a pilot?'

Mouse spoke up with a mouthful of pancake, 'Well, he'll tell you he got it because he was a pilot in 'Nam, but it's not.' He crossed to gently put a hand on Wing's shoulder.

'We call him Wings because he has gathered us bunch of misfits around him and has taken us all under his wings like an old mother hen. We were all struggling Vietnam veterans, and most of us probably wouldn't still be alive if it weren't for old Wings here.' He smiled and ducked as Nigel threw a tea towel at him.

Mary smiled at Frank and stroked his cheek. 'You are older than these guys, but I can still see you with a motorbike,' she held his hand, 'or perhaps a scooter to start with?'

KALEIDOSCOPIC DREAMSCAPES

BY HECTOR DAVID SOSA

Cohesive transcendental transformation,
Kaleidoscopic dreamscapes of all that exists,
Moving from a time beyond time,
Billions of stars scattered in the grand galaxy,
With their luminosity sparking out to the distance of space,
The Solar System proceeds through its normal activity.
On Earth, as the rocky planet turns upon its axis,
Living things of all species breathe in the elements,
All hearts are beating steadily,
Every sense is working thoroughly,
Neurons and nervous systems responding accordingly,

As consciousness manifests individually.

But it isn't all peaceful, gentle, or pleasant.

Daily stress consumes energy efficiently,

With work requirements draining all,

Society's systems interacting in consistent blends,

As people endure the ins, outs, ups, and downs of it.

But there's a ray of sunshine in existence,

A hope of an everlasting love that permeates in all dimensions,

A deep, emotional, and transcendental connection to the purity of living,

A guarantee that all will be fine.

This ray of sunshine is the enigmatic driver for many,

Those who always look forward to the future,

For it will bring joy, happiness, and peace of mind,

And all problems will be solved.

A momentary pause for absorption,

And without any precaution,

We escape the atmosphere of the planet,

And see the Solar System,

And the billions of stars in the Milky Way.

In a time beyond time,

We see kaleidoscopic visions of eternity,

And we instantly return to nothingness.

A COLLECTION

BY DIANE BROWN

THE OCEAN

Broken buildings, walls collapsing, running from gunshots. Fleeing to the jetty, reaching towards outstretched arms that pull me aboard. I stared at the burning coastline, chugging out to sea, realizing that I would never see my seaside home again.

The journey, so long, so hard. Coastguards, paperwork, Christmas Island, prison. Two years, searching eyes through wire fences, smelling the sea but unable to see it. Fear, uncertainty, loneliness, unwanted.

Open gates, freedom, Sydney, and, at last, the ocean. Soft water cooling, caressing, healing my spirit, flooding my memories of my homeland. Calmness, peace, acceptance, a new home.

*

HOME

Red dust covered him, he could taste it, his eyes gritty and sore.
His bones ached; two months of mustering had taken their toll.
At last homeward bound, his faithful mare needing no direction.
The corrugated iron house coming into view, smoke rising from the chimney.
His woman running towards him, holding her close, a red dust embrace.
A cold beer waiting, lamb stew simmering on the stove,
Together on the creaky verandah, her old dog snoring.
The frog chorus from the creek, a dingo howls.
No bellowing cattle, no saddle soreness, no loneliness,
For now, he was home.

SPRING

I'm four and I'm riding my bike
There are big cracks in the dirt
That swallow my wheels.
Daddy says it's the drought.
Red dust blows in my eyes. It hurts.
The sky looks funny; it's dark purple, and it's moving.
I have never seen it like that before.
A splash of water hits my face,
Then another, then lots more.
I am frightened. I call out to Mummy.
"What is it, Mummy, this water from the sky?
Mummy hugs me. "After three long years, she says
It's the Spring rain."

HERITAGE AND HEARTACHE

A STORY FROM A FRACTURED LAND

BY RODERIC GRIGSON

The ceiling fan whirred lazily in the sitting room of the Greig household in Colombo, its rhythmic hum punctuated by the occasional clink of teacups. Life in post-colonial Ceylon was an intricate dance for the Burgher community, navigating the shifting tides of a nation striving to define itself after independence in 1948.

For Helena, the matriarch of the family, this dance required poise, strength, and a deep love for her family and their way of life. Helena, whose Scottish father worked in an important position for the British Colonial Administration on the island, had married an English Tea Planters daughter. Helena had a privileged life, given her father's ancestral roots and standing on the island. Born on the island, she was one of the first women of her background and generation to go to secretarial school, passing out with flying colours. She had worked most of her adult life in senior office administrative positions at British companies based in Ceylon.

Helena's husband, Edward, had a fascinating history that shaped his outlook on life. Edward, the son of a British Tea Planter from Lancashire who married a local Sinhalese woman when Ceylon was a Crown colony of Britain, served in the Royal Ceylon Navy during World War II, an experience that exposed him to the complexities of global conflict and the value of camaraderie across cultural lines. Stationed at the port of Trincomalee on the east coast, he witnessed the naval base's strategic importance. Edward worked alongside British and Allied officers, controlling the movement of maritime traffic in the southeastern theatre of operations. The discipline and structure of military life left a lasting impression on Edward, instilling in him a deep sense of duty.

After the war ended, Edward transitioned to civilian life, finding work with a British-owned shipping company in Colombo. His time in the Navy made him an asset in the maritime industry, where his knowledge of logistics and his ability to navigate the intricacies of international trade proved invaluable.

Edward's tales of his naval days—from watching grand warships dock at Trincomalee to the long nights spent working underground in the freezing cold of air-conditioned operations rooms, communicating in secret cyphers with warships and troop transports at sea—fascinated his children Christopher and Elizabeth.

"You know," Edward would say with a wry smile, "the sea teaches you patience. It's vast and unpredictable, but if you learn to respect it, it'll guide you safely home."

Helena often listened with a mix of pride and affection, appreciating the strength and wisdom her husband brought to their family.

"You know, Helena," Edward said one evening over a cup of tea, "there was a time when being a Eurasian meant something special. We weren't just clerks or railway engineers; we were the bridge between worlds."

Helena smiled, stirring sugar into her own tea. "And we still are, Edward. But the world is changing, and we have to find our place in it. And remember, we are no longer classed as Eurasians! We are now considered Burghers."

Edward sighed, leaning back in his chair. "Yes, I know. I just hope Christopher and Elizabeth will have the opportunities we had. This Sinhala Only Act the opposition party is talking about ... it's going to make everything so much harder."

"They're resilient," Helena replied firmly. "And so are we."

The Burghers, descendants of Dutch, Portuguese, and other European settlers who had intermarried with locals, had once enjoyed a privileged position in Ceylonese society. But independence brought uncertainty, as the new government prioritized Sinhala and Tamil identities in its quest for national unity.

In 1956, when Christopher was six, the political landscape shifted dramatically with the election of S.W.R.D. Bandaranaike and the introduction of the Sinhala Only Act. The Parliamentary Act replaced English with Sinhala as the sole official language of Ceylon, with Tamil excluded from the act.

The Greig household buzzed with concern. Edward and Helena discussed the implications over dinner, their voices hushed so as not to alarm the children.

"This is going to be a big problem,' Edward said, shaking his head. "Not just for us Burghers, but also for the Tamils."

Helena nodded. "It seems a very short-sighted policy. I think the future looks very uncertain, but we must learn to adapt."

Peaceful protests against the Act by the Tamil community, who constituted 25% of the population and faced disadvantages in government jobs, education, and public services, were met with police and mob violence, further alienating them.

For Christopher, the changes were first felt at school. The Burgher boys, once fluent in English and confident in their European heritage, now found themselves caught between worlds. Christopher began learning Sinhala, but his accent and unfamiliarity with the language marked him as different. To improve his diction, Helena sent him to the Buddhist temple down the road, where a Buddhist priest schooled him in the language.

Despite these challenges, Helena was determined to preserve their family's unique identity. She taught her children to bake festive breudhers and Christmas cakes, cook lamprais and love baila music while ensuring they respected the Sinhala and Tamil cultures around them.

"We are part of this country," she often told them. "Our roots run deep here, just as theirs do."

Christopher, who was born in 1950, grew up in this period of transition. He attended the esteemed St. Thomas's College in Mount Lavinia, where his father and uncles had also schooled. The sprawling grounds, colonial architecture, and towering banyan trees evoked a sense of tradition and discipline. The prestigious college was a melting pot of Burgher, Sinhala, Tamil and Muslim students from wealthy families, and it instilled in Christopher a strong foundation in Western education and Christian values.

Mornings at the college began with chapel services, where hymns filled the air, and students recited prayers that echoed through the halls. Christopher excelled in literature and history, developing a love for Shakespeare and a fascination with the stories of the British Empire. His afternoons were spent on the cricket field, where he honed his skills as an all-rounder, earning the admiration of his peers and coaches alike.

"You've got quite the arm, Greig," his cricket coach said after Christopher bowled out the captain of a rival team. "Keep at it, and you'll lead this team one day."

The college also encouraged debates and discussions, where Christopher often found himself defending the legacy and identity of the Burgher community in a changing Ceylon.

"We're not just relics of colonial rule," Christopher argued during a student debate. "We've contributed to this country in countless ways, from the railways to law and education. Our place here is as valid as anyone else's."

Sunday mornings were spent at the Anglican church, followed by cricket matches on the sandy grounds near the beach. His evenings, however, were steeped in the sounds and smells of Ceylon: the rhythmic drumming of temple ceremonies, the aroma of curries wafting through the streets, and the chatter of Tamil vendors at the market.

By the 1960s, Christopher had grown into a curious and sensitive teenager. He often confided in his mother, sharing his thoughts about their family's place in a rapidly changing Ceylon.

"Do you think we'll always belong here?" Christopher asked one evening as they sat on the verandah, watching the sunset paint the sky in shades of orange and purple.

Helena tilted her head thoughtfully. "Of course, we belong here. This is our home."

"But so many are leaving," Christopher said, his voice tinged with worry. "Uncle Ashton wrote from Australia last week. He says there's more opportunity there, less… less judgment."

His mother reached for his hand. "Maybe. But leaving isn't easy either. Think about all we'd leave behind—the people, the culture, everything that makes us who we are."

"I guess you're right," Christopher said with a small smile. "But sometimes, I wonder what it would be like to start afresh."

"You can start by not forgetting where you come from," Helena replied softly.

While some spoke of leaving, Christopher's heart clung to the island—its turquoise seas, swaying coconut palms, and the mosaic of cultures that had shaped his life.

A few of his friends decided to go upcountry during the Esala Perahera in Kandy. This grand procession, dedicated to the Sacred Tooth Relic of the Buddha, was a spectacle unlike any other. Elephants adorned with lavish gold and silver caparisons paraded majestically through the streets, their rhythmic steps keeping time with the beating of geta bera drums. Dancers in vibrant costumes spun and leapt with unmatched grace, their anklets jingling in harmony with the music. Fire dancers twirled flaming torches, creating patterns of light against the dark sky, while whip-crackers announced the procession's arrival with sharp, resonant cracks that sent shivers of awe through the crowd. The Perahera was not just a religious event but a celebration of heritage that united people from across the country, showcasing the island's diversity and shared reverence for its history and traditions.

Christopher stood amidst the throng of spectators, his senses overwhelmed by the grandeur unfolding before him. The air was thick with the mingling scents of burning oil lamps and fresh jasmine garlands. The pulsating rhythms of the drums resonated deep within him, stirring something primal and ancient. As the massive tusker carrying the golden casket of the Sacred Tooth Relic passed by, he felt an inexplicable reverence wash over him. There was something mesmerizing about the unbroken continuity of tradition, a bridge between the past and the present that made him feel deeply connected to his homeland.

It was during this time that Christopher met Juliana, a colleague at the engineering firm where he worked. Juliana came from a prominent Dutch Burgher family in Colombo, whose roots traced back to the Dutch colonial period of Ceylon. Her family had built a reputation for excellence in architecture, with her grandfather designing several well-known colonial-era buildings in Colombo. Their paths crossed in the bustling streets of Kandy, the echoes of the Perahera still lingering in the air. Amid the flickering torchlight and the hypnotic sounds of the procession, Christopher found himself drawn to Juliana's quiet yet perceptive presence. It was as if the magic of the Perahera had woven its spell beyond the spectacle itself, forging new connections in its wake.

Their first real conversation took place during a meeting about a joint project.

"I've seen your designs," Juliana said, pointing to Christopher's blueprints. "You have a talent for blending practicality with elegance."

Christopher smiled, a little surprised by the compliment. "Coming from you, that means a lot. Your work on the new courthouse was brilliant."

Over time, their professional relationship blossomed into friendship and, eventually, love. They often stayed late at the office, discussing not just engineering but also their shared experiences growing up as Burghers in a changing Ceylon. Juliana's upbringing, steeped in traditions like Dutch-inspired baking and celebrating St. Nicholas Day, complemented Christopher's more hybrid blend of Sri Lankan and Western customs.

"Do you ever think about leaving?" Juliana asked one evening, her voice contemplative. "With so many of our friends moving to Australia or Canada, it feels like we're holding on to something that's slipping away."

Christopher nodded. "I think about it all the time. But leaving isn't just about moving; it's about letting go of a part of yourself. I'm not sure I'm ready for that."

Juliana often spoke of her family's history, recounting tales of her ancestors who had sailed from the Netherlands to Ceylon in the 17th century.

"My great-grandfather used to say," she once told Christopher. "We brought tulips and windmills in our hearts, but Ceylon gave us cinnamon and warmth."' Her pride in her heritage was evident, but so was her adaptability to the changing world around her.

Their shared heritage and values deepened their bond, but their relationship wasn't without challenges. Juliana's family, while supportive, worried about the uncertainty of life in Ceylon and encouraged the couple to consider migration. Christopher's parents, Edward and Helena, welcomed Juliana warmly, seeing her as a reflection of the Burgher traditions they cherished.

In 1975, Christopher and Juliana married in a grand Anglican ceremony at St. Paul's Church in Colombo. The wedding brought together Colombo's Burgher community, with guests celebrating the union with Portuguese-inspired baila music, traditional dishes, and heartfelt toasts. Their marriage symbolised hope for a community striving to preserve its identity amidst the tides of change.

Tensions simmered outside their home. Ethnic violence was becoming more frequent, and whispers of division filled the air. They welcomed their first child, Maya, during this time; however, the escalating ethnic violence and economic hardships pushed the Greig family to make the difficult decision to migrate. Christopher, Juliana, and the rest of the family packed their lives into a few suitcases and boarded a flight to Melbourne, Australia. The departure was bittersweet. As the plane took off, Helena clutched Edward's hand, tears streaming down her face as she whispered a quiet goodbye to the land they had called home.

Life in Melbourne was a fresh start. The family settled in the modest suburb of Noble Park, surrounded by other migrants from Ceylon and beyond. Edward found work as a bookkeeper while Christopher joined an engineering firm. Juliana, ever resilient, worked for a construction company and became involved in community work, helping newly arrived migrants navigate their new lives. Helena, with her warmth and culinary skills, turned their house into a home where the smell of rice and curry mingled with the crisp Australian air.

For Christopher and Juliana, life in Melbourne was a blend of challenges and opportunities. Ralph and Lilani were born at this time, and they raised their children with stories of Ceylon—of the vibrant streets of Colombo, the golden beaches, and the cultural mosaic that had shaped them. Yet, they also embraced their new identity as Australians, building a life that honoured both their past and their present.

As the years went by, the Sri Lankan Civil War erupted in 1983, and its impact reverberated through the diaspora. The conflict weighed heavily on Christopher and Juliana as they watched their homeland descend into chaos. Letters and phone calls from relatives described harrowing tales of displacement and violence, making them feel both connected to and distant from the struggles back home. Juliana, deeply affected by the suffering of her friends in the Tamil community, organized fundraisers within the Sri Lankan diaspora in Melbourne, advocating for peace and aid for those caught in the conflict.

Life in Melbourne continued to evolve for the Greig family, and with time, they began to distance themselves from their Sri Lankan roots, embracing Australian culture with enthusiasm. Yet, Christopher maintained a connection to his past through the Old Boys' Association of St Thomas's College in Mount Lavinia.

Through letters, annual newsletters, and occasional reunions, Christopher stayed in touch with his former classmates. The association, consisting of alumni scattered across the globe, was a lifeline to the memories of their youth in Ceylon.

"Did you hear from Richard?" Juliana asked one evening as Christopher scanned a freshly delivered newsletter.

"Yes," Christopher replied, smiling. "He's organizing a gathering in Sydney next year. It'll be good to catch up with everyone and share how far we've come."

The Old Boys' Association was more than just a social network; it was a way to give back. Christopher often contributed to the association's efforts to fund scholarships for students still studying at the college in Sri Lanka. "It's our way of ensuring that the traditions and values we cherished continue," he told Maya, his eldest daughter, one evening. "Even if we're far away, we can still make a difference."

These connections allowed Christopher to balance his Australian identity with his enduring love for the place he once called home, ensuring that the spirit of his alma mater and the community it fostered lived on in his heart.

Maya excelled in academics and became deeply involved in local Australian activities. She joined school sports teams, participated in cultural festivals, and spoke with a broad Australian accent that blended seamlessly with her peers.

"Dad, can we have a barbecue this weekend? Everyone at school loves it," Maya suggested one afternoon. Christopher chuckled but obliged, realizing that their family's future lay in creating new traditions.

Ralph, their middle child, quickly embraced Australian life as well, developing a passion for Australian Rules Football and taking pride in his local team's victories.

"One day, I'll play for the AFL," he declared, his excitement infectious as he practised kicking the ball in their backyard.

Even Lilani, the youngest, adopted a distinctly Australian perspective in her art, painting kangaroos and eucalyptus trees alongside the peacocks and coconut palms inspired by her parents' stories of Sri Lanka. Their home began to reflect this shift; the walls that once displayed traditional Sri Lankan tapestries now featured framed landscapes of the Australian Outback.

Christopher and Juliana adapted as well, finding joy in Australian traditions like outdoor barbecues, ANZAC Day parades, and even learning to enjoy Vegemite. Juliana started incorporating Australian flavours into their meals, blending her signature curries with locally sourced ingredients.

"You know," she joked one evening, "if Ceylon had this much lamb, I might have never left!" Christopher laughed, toasting her creativity with a glass of Australian Shiraz.

Over time, the Greigs' connection to Sri Lanka became more symbolic than practical. Their conversations about the island shifted from daily struggles and memories to broader reflections on heritage. The children's occasional questions about their roots were met with stories of cultural pride but without the urgency of reclaiming their Sri Lankan identity.

By the late 1990s, the Greigs were firmly rooted in Australian society. They celebrated Australia Day with as much vigour as they once did the many festivals in Ceylon, and their children identified more strongly as Australians of Sri Lankan descent than as Sri Lankans living abroad. Christopher and Juliana took pride in the life they had built, knowing they had successfully blended their past with their present, ensuring a future where their family thrived as Australians. The Greigs remained steadfast in their efforts to bridge cultural divides, hosting gatherings that brought together Sinhala, Tamil, and Burgher families in Melbourne.

Though the Civil War raged on for decades, the Greig family's commitment to their roots and their new life in Australia became a beacon of hope. They continued to honour Sri Lanka's rich heritage while advocating for reconciliation and unity. For Christopher, the war underscored the fragility of the island he loved, but it also deepened his resolve to instil in his children a sense of compassion, strength, and the enduring belief in the power of diversity to overcome division.

As the years went by, the Greig family flourished. They remained connected to other families from Ceylon who had made Australia their home, keeping some of the old traditions of food and celebration. Christopher often reflected on their journey—from the bustling streets of Colombo to the wide avenues of Melbourne. While they had left Ceylon behind, the island remained alive in their hearts, a testament to the strength of their roots and the enduring hope for a brighter future.

Years after their life in Australia had blossomed, Christopher, Helena, and their family embarked on a memorable two-week journey to explore Sri Lanka, eager to immerse themselves in the vibrant culture and heritage of the island that had deeply touched their hearts. Upon arriving, the warm, humid air, scented with jasmine and sea salt, welcomed them to an exotic and inviting land.

Their days were filled with adventures through bustling markets that dazzled with vibrant colours, enticing textures, and captivating sounds. Bright stalls overflowed with aromatic spices artfully arranged, baskets brimming with fresh mangoes, papayas, and bananas, and street vendors enthusiastically promoting fragrant local delicacies. The children tasted sweet coconut cakes and crispy, savoury snacks with delight, their excitement mixing harmoniously with the lively chatter of local merchants and shoppers.

Exploring further, they visited ancient temples adorned with exquisite carvings, serene Buddha statues, and gardens lush with tropical flowers. At historical sites, they wandered among ruins steeped in history, marvelling at stories of ancient kings and legends. The children's curiosity led to endless questions as they connected deeply with their family's heritage.

One afternoon, as they strolled through lush tea plantations in the hill country, their son Ralph asked, "Dad, did you ever see places like this when you lived here?"

Christopher smiled thoughtfully. "Yes, we visited these tea plantations often. This beautiful land was a big part of our childhood memories. We loved the peacefulness and the fresh air."

Their daughter, Lilani, hugged Helena's arm. "And what about you, Mum? What's your best memory of Sri Lanka?"

Helena smiled gently. "The warmth of the people, sweetheart. No matter where we went, everyone treated us like family. It's something I'll always carry with me."

Their evenings were spent by the sea, dining under breathtaking sunsets painted with fiery oranges, pinks, and purples. They savoured dishes of coconut milk curries, freshly grilled seafood, zesty chutneys, and spicy sambols, each meal a sensory celebration of their heritage.

After two weeks of exploring the beauty and cultural richness of Sri Lanka, Christopher and Helena felt profoundly connected to their roots. The trip not only rekindled cherished memories but also created vibrant new experiences, deepening their love for a country whose warmth and spirit had become an essential part of their family's story.

For the Greig family, however, Sri Lanka was not the name they used in their reflections. Even decades after the country's official renaming in 1972, the Greigs and many other migrant Burghers continued to refer to their homeland as Ceylon.

"The name Sri Lanka feels foreign to me," Edward said one evening after they arrived back in Melbourne. "It's not just about the name; it's about what it stood for. Ceylon was where we grew up and built memories. Sri Lanka feels like someone else's story."

Helena, now in her 80s, nodded in agreement. "Ceylon is the land of the tea plantations, the cinnamon fields, the churches and the baila music. That's what we carry in our hearts. Ceylon… it's distant now."

Their children occasionally teased them for their insistence on using the old name. "Dad, you know it's Sri Lanka now," Maya said with a playful smile.

"Yes, yes," Edward replied, waving his hand dismissively. "But to me, it will always be Ceylon. And don't forget it, young lady!"

The use of "Ceylon" became a way for the Greig family to preserve their identity and honour the memories of the land they had left behind. In their gatherings with other Burgher families in Melbourne, the name Ceylon was spoken with affection, evoking images of warm beaches, bustling markets, misty green hills covered in tea bushes and a way of life that now only lived in their stories and traditions.

WRITERS' PROFILES

DIANE BROWN

Diane was born in Kogarah Bay, a suburb of Sydney, in 1944. She completed her high school education as a boarder at St Catherine's Ladies College, Waverley, NSW.

Diane moved to Wodonga in 1986 with her husband and young family. In 1990, she joined a prominent Albury law firm, working up to a senior para-legal position, where she remained for 16 years. After re-marrying in 1990, Diane and her husband moved to Melbourne in 2001, where she continued to work for the Albury law firm from her home office until she retired in 2006.

Diane served on the Board of the Mental Illness Fellowship Victoria for 14 years, was elected Vice-President in 2008 and also served on the Research and Ethics Committee of Melbourne Health for two years.

Diane is the author of a memoir, *The White Cockatoo*, which was published in 2012 and an autobiography, *Echoes of Life*, published in 2023. Diane has been a member of The Scribe Tribe for over 6 years.

NORMA SAVIGE

Norma is a retired educator, counsellor, and bureaucrat. She is a member of a large family, and the story is important. Since her retirement, Norma has indulged a long-held passion by undertaking creative writing classes and joining two writing groups. She has had a particular interest in the short-story form and contributed to the Scribe Tribe Vol I Anthology, published in 2019 and Vol II, published in 2021.

Her past careers have fostered a genuine curiosity and appreciation for the vagaries of human behaviour. Norma published her own book, *The Tangled Web*, which explores this further. She lives in Victoria, is married, and has two adult children.

Norma is a voracious reader who belongs to a book club and an online strength-building group. In her spare time, she studies the French language and is a member of a French Conversation group. You may discover any or all of these creeping into her writings.

ZOE SKJELLERUP

Hello, all readers. Thank you for choosing this book. My name is Zoe, and I live in Melbourne. I'm diagnosed with a rare genetic disorder, CDG syndrome type 1A. It affects my speech and causes loss of vision and balance. I also have a slight auditory processing delay. For these reasons, I prefer to communicate by writing. I'm very strong-willed and have been published in Anthology Vol One in 2019 and Vol Two in 2022.

HECTOR DAVID SOSA

Hector has been an active blogger for the past decade, sharing artistic, philosophical, and cultural insights through his writing. He began his journey with humorous short stories, which gradually evolved into existentially themed pieces and explorations of metaphysical concepts.

In 2005, Hector wrote the screenplay for *Episode X: The Halloween Special*, part of the Spanish and Latin-American community TV show *Fusion Latina*. The episode aired on Channel 31 in Melbourne in October of that year and went on to win the "Best Culturally and Linguistically Diverse Program" in 2006 at the Antenna Awards after showing footage of the Halloween Special episode.

His interests span art, philosophy, science, and science fiction. A fan of *The Matrix*, he speaks Spanish at home and is currently learning German. Recently, Hector joined the Scribe Tribe, bringing a fresh perspective to the group.

Follow Hector's latest work on his blog, *Constructed Chaos from the Aether*, at thesosastudio.substack.com.

STEPH WEBB

Steph Webb is a fiction and speculative fiction writer. She is a member of Scribe Tribe, Bunjil Writers, and Writers' Victoria. She writes short stories and is working on her first speculative fiction novel.

Steph was born in South Africa, spending her early childhood years living next to the Kruger National Park, enjoying the African bush and wildlife. She later moved to the coast, where she completed her schooling and enjoyed beach life.

Steph immigrated to Australia in 1999 with her husband and three children. Before retiring, Steph was an early childhood educator for over 30 years. She holds a bachelor's in early education. She is Nana to one precious grandson.

When Steph, is not writing, she enjoys nature walks, watercolour painting, gardening, cooking and reading.

Follow her on Instagram: *@writerladysteph*

MADISEN WHITE

Madisen is a disability support worker and educator based in Cardinia Shire. She accompanies her fellow contributor and long-serving Scribe Tribe member, Zoe Skjellerup. Madisen is rekindling her own love of the written word while she has the privilege of attending The Scribe Tribe. She feels fortunate to have been embraced by the group and included in Anthology Vol III. Madisen's contributions to this anthology honour the memories of her immigrant grandparents and the family stories, which so often take on a mythic quality each time they are retold and trickle down through generations. With no formal publishing history, Madisen is hesitant to call herself a 'writer', but she believes that every person has a culture and a story which deserves to be told.

JANE E WOOD

Jane is a retired teacher living in the outer suburbia of Melbourne. She has been a member of the Scribe Tribe for several years and was delighted to contribute several stories to this anthology. Jane's first novel, *The Legacy*, was published in January 2025. When not writing, Jane enjoys reading, gardening, playing with her dog and spending time with family.

CORINNE KING

Corinne is a passionate writer with a rich heritage and a life full of diverse experiences that shape her storytelling. Born in Matara, Ceylon (now Sri Lanka) and raised in Galle and Mount Lavinia, Corinne's early years were steeped in the legacy of education and academia.

Corinne migrated to Australia in 1972, where she began her professional career as a secretary at the Holden's Car Plant. It was there that she met her husband, Ian King, who had recently migrated from the UK. Over the years, Corinne built a dynamic career as an Executive Secretary and Personal Assistant, working across various industries, including automotive, pharmaceuticals, and mental health administration.

Beyond her career, Corinne's life has been an extraordinary journey of travel and adventure. Alongside Ian, she has explored destinations across the world, from the islands of the Pacific to Europe, Asia, North America, and beyond.

In addition to travel, Corinne is deeply committed to community engagement. Having faced significant health challenges in 2023, she has been a source of support and guidance for other women dealing with similar health issues, working closely with the Cancer Council of Victoria.

Corinne and Ian are also well-known radio presenters. They host the highly successful program "The King & I" on 97.7FM 3SER—The Sounds of the South East. Their Friday night show, running for over a decade, has attracted a global audience.

As a writer, Corinne's work is deeply influenced by her rich cultural background, global travels, and personal experiences. A long-time member of the Scribe Tribe, she contributed stories that were published in Scribe Tribe Anthologies Vols I and II. She brings warmth, insight, and a deep connection to history and community to her storytelling.

MARIANNE ACTON

Raised on fiction, Marianne now writes her own, where comfort is never a certainty.

MARYANN GRIGSON

Maryann hails from the beautiful island of Sri Lanka and is an ardent admirer of Mother Theresa. She is passionate about writing and has been a member of the Scribe Tribe writing group for many years. She has written and published her first book, *Links In A Memorable Chain*, a story of her life journey, and she enjoys reading, walking, and dancing.

Maryann migrated to Australia in 2007 and resides in Melbourne. She has three wonderful children, eight beloved grandchildren and a cute little great-grandson. She is a 'people person' and serves as a volunteer at the 'VINNIES' shop on Glenferrie Road.

ROBYN KING

Robyn is married with two grown boys. The drama in her writing comes from having a hairdressing salon for eleven years. There, she came across many fascinating stories from clients and their experiences. She exaggerates them when writing her tales.

Nothing surprises her. 'People are the best source of stories,' she says with a knowing grin. She notices the consequences and how people react to their grief or happiness when listening to their plight. It all makes for a good story.

Robyn then took the Creative Writing course at the Balla Balla CC to learn how to put it all into words. She was the joint winner of the Balla Balla Story Competition for her story *The Diary*, which was featured in the Scribe Tribe Anthology Vol Two.

LAUREN MCCARTHY

Lauren is an avid reader who loves family, walking and playing in the surf at Inverloch. When she began her role as Program Coordinator at Balla Balla

Community Centre, she was excited to learn that the centre has a flourishing writing group. Her first task was to read and enjoy the Scribe Tribe's first anthology. Lauren was delighted to be involved in proofreading the second anthology and has read and thoroughly enjoyed the novels published by five Scribe Tribe members. She is grateful to Rod Grigson for reigniting her passion for reading and his encouragement to contribute to this anthology.

Lauren grew up in the inner suburbs of Melbourne in the midst of a migrant community of Italians, Greeks and Macedonians during her Primary School years. According to her mother, she spoke fluent Italian phrases before she began school. Her playground was her street, the Edinburgh Gardens, and in summer, she lived at the Fitzroy Baths. *Aqua Profonda* was inspired by her love of swimming at the Baths and memories of the little girl next door.

BERNIE WEISS

Bernie's lifelong love affair used to be reading books written by others. On retiring from the workforce, she worked towards her childhood dream of attending university, finishing two degrees, and focusing on history. One in Australian History and Honours in World History, with her thesis on the missionaries working in New Guinea between 1902 and 1920.

The next challenge came in two community-centred Creative Writing Courses, the second being wholly online due to the personal contact limitations imposed on society by COVID-19. The two years of isolation were used to write a 95,000-word manuscript, expanding on the history thesis concept. The characterisation of the Europeans living and working in New Britain, the island north of New Guinea, was loosely based on the religious community diaries, internal magazines, and Australian newspaper reports. Unfortunately, the religious community withdrew its support for the project before the manuscript reached publishers.

Bernie's interest in writing had to take a backseat to life-changing events that uprooted her living place. After a sojourn of 18 months, she has returned to the writer's group with a view to having more of her short stories published.

BRONWYN VAUGHAN

Bronwyn is an Australian scientist and educator with specialisations in education intervention and case management. Her career of over 30 years has spanned teaching across the sciences, gifted education and special needs, researching State and Commonwealth medical projects and working in business. She is a trained soprano and a lover of poetry, and you'll often find her reading and volunteering her time in local politics.

Bronwyn spent a year in the office of the current deputy premier and education minister as a campaign assistant. Her love of learning is evident, and she is committed to keeping up with the latest in medical and educational research related to COVID-19 policies and applying her knowledge in business.

This short-story entry into the Scribe Tribe Anthology III is a historical fiction piece based on her own research, and it's dedicated to the local storytellers who have shared their own memories with her since childhood.

RODERIC GRIGSON

Rod is a published author whose works seamlessly blend adventure, history, and cultural exploration. Born in Ceylon (now Sri Lanka) with British heritage tracing back to the colonial administration, Rod's early years were marked by a deep curiosity for reading and travel. His journey has taken him across continents, from working at the United Nations in New York to peacekeeping missions in the Middle East, experiences that have profoundly shaped his narratives.

During his tenure at the UN, including two years with the Peacekeeping Forces in Egypt, Israel, and Lebanon—where he earned the prestigious UN Peace Medal—Rod witnessed the intricacies of global affairs firsthand. His return to New York in 1980 saw him pioneering foreign language development in computing at the UN Technology Innovations Programme, an early glimpse into his ability to translate complex solutions into engaging processes.

After migrating to Australia in 1986 and serving in senior executive roles across the Asia-Pacific, Rod eventually embraced his true passion—writing. His debut novel in 2013, *Sacred Tears*, a thrilling adventure spanning the war-torn city of Beirut to the jungles of Sri Lanka, set the tone for his literary journey. His subsequent works, including *After The Flames, The Sullen Hills* and, more recently, *The Governor's Lover*, reflect his deep-rooted love for history and intrigue, weaving gripping tales that transport readers across time and place.

Based in Melbourne, Rod continues to write while dedicating his time to mentoring aspiring authors through the *Scribe Tribe Writing Group*. He also teaches *Creative Writing Courses* at the Balla Balla Community Centre and empowers seniors and new migrants in the City of Casey with essential technology skills.

With four published books and a fifth in the works, Rod remains committed to storytelling, ensuring that every new chapter he writes captures the imagination and spirit of adventure that have defined his life.

Visit *www.rodericgrigson.com* to explore his books and latest projects.

MEANING OF "BALLA BALLA"

INDIGENOUS SIGNIFICANCE

The history of the name Balla Balla has links to the Indigenous community as part of their language. While there are no strict interpretations for the word 'Balla', taken in context has two meanings. In one Indigenous language, Balla means 'resting' which is also part of the word and suburb, Ballarat which means 'resting place'. In the second Indigenous language, Balla means 'mud', which is a very significant description of the particular area the facility is located in. Initially, at times throughout the year, this land sat at the 'bottom' of the swamp. This was a precious resource for the indigenous people and was seen as a 'seasonal supermarket'. In winter, they would come to the edge of the swamp to collect birds' eggs, eels, reeds and to harvest bark.

HISTORICAL SIGNIFICANCE

Interestingly, Balla Balla was also the name of one of the first homesteads to be established in the area and is the name of the council ward in which the centre is now situated. Balla Balla may have different meanings in other languages; however the intent in choosing this name was to reflect the history of the area, as well as the indigenous significance.

The Balla Balla Community Centre is part of the City of Casey's network of fourteen Neighbourhood Houses and Community Learning Centres' in the municipality.

www.ingramcontent.com/pod-product-compliance
Lightning Source LLC
Chambersburg PA
CBHW030850170426
43193CB00009BA/559